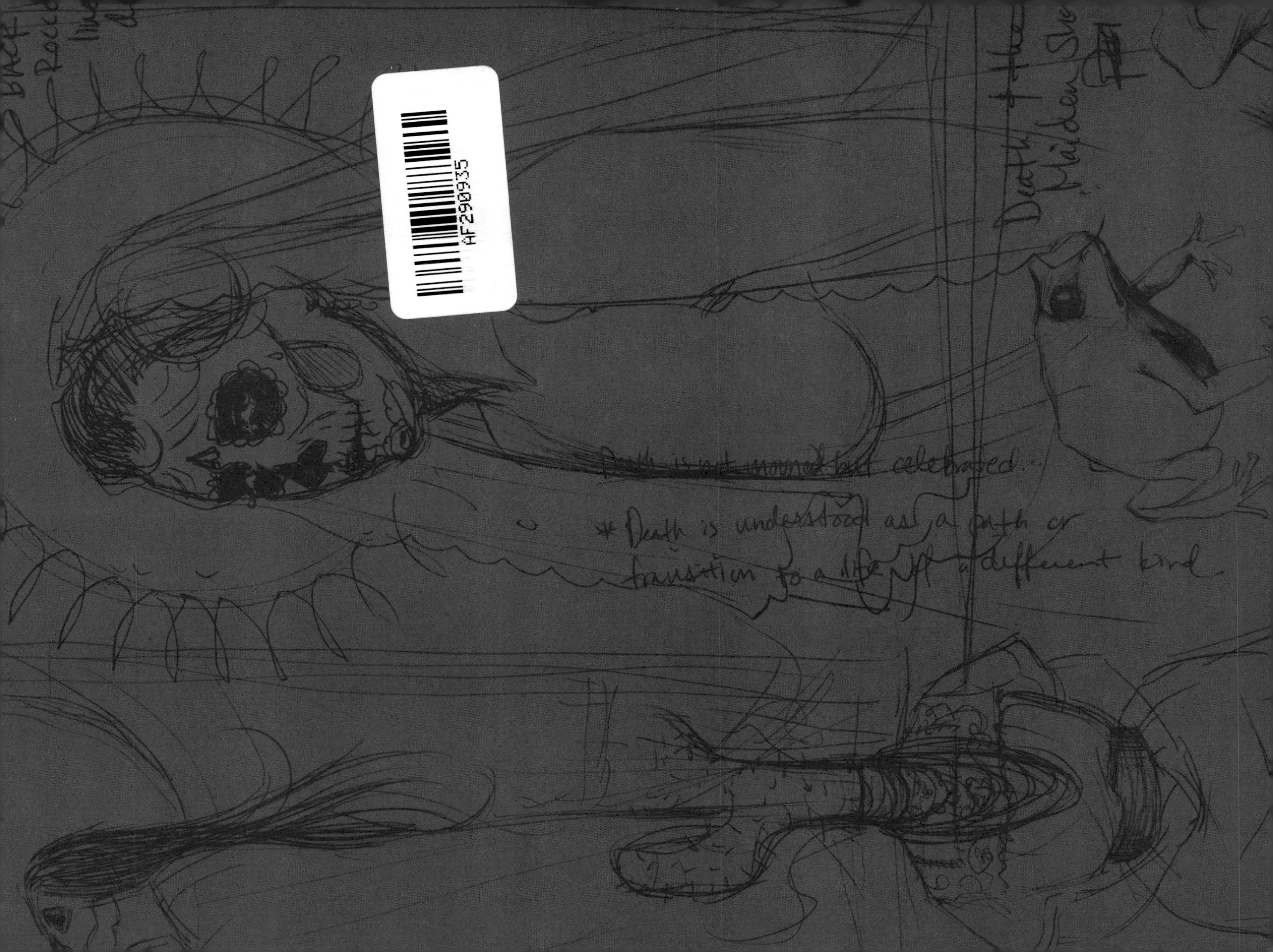

Death is not mourned but celebrated.
* Death is understood as a path or transition to a life of a different kind
Death + the Maiden She

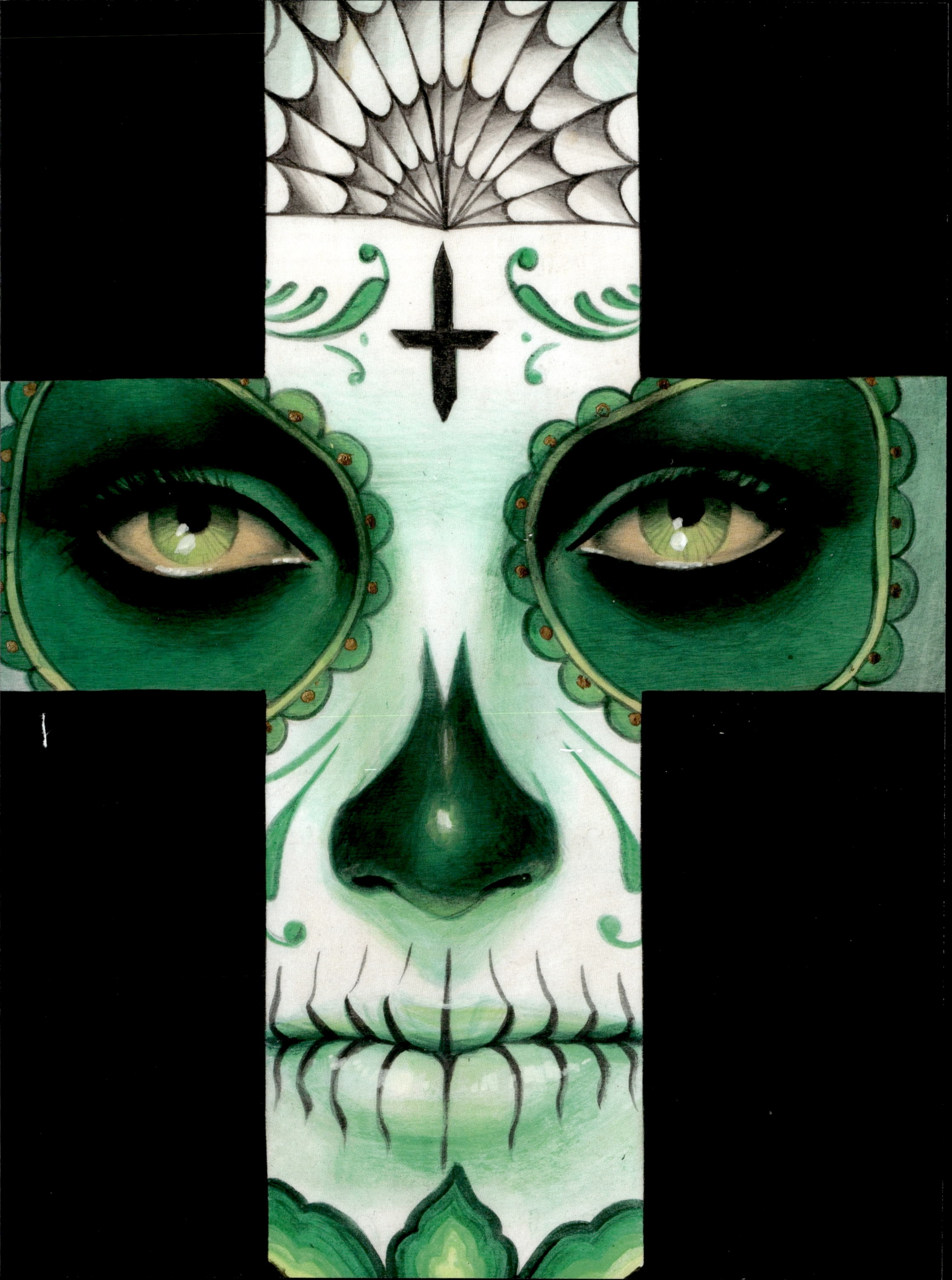

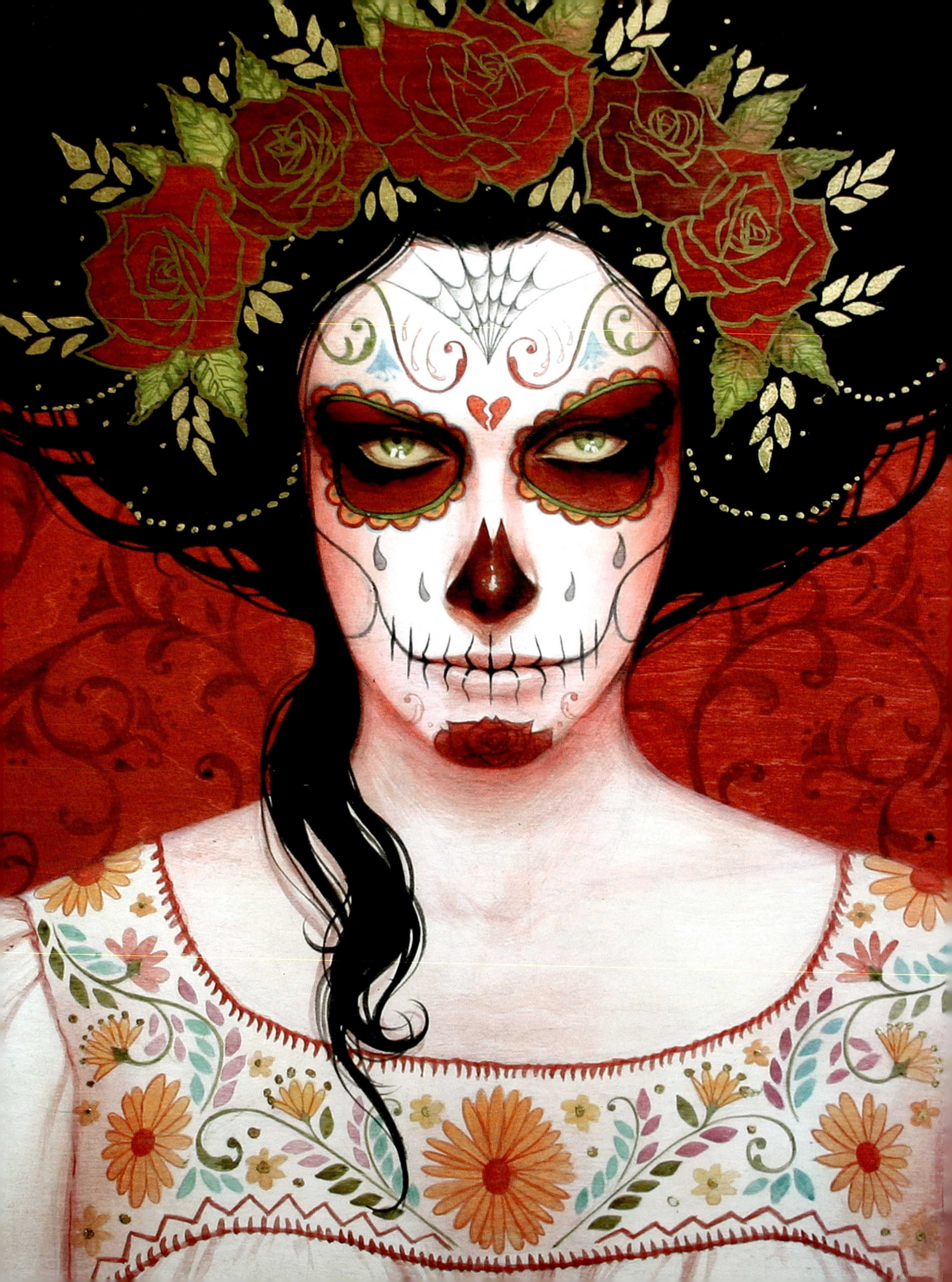

DAY OF THE DEAD

Dedicated to P.S & M.S, my two loves.

Korero Press Ltd,
157 Mornington Road,
London, E11 3DT, UK

www.koreropress.com

First published in 2014 © Korero Press Limited

Images © Sylvia Ji

ISBN-13: 9780993337413

A CIP catalogue record for this book is available
from the British Library

Previous pages: *Cruz Verde*; 8 x 10 inches; acrylic on wood panel
and *Maria*; 32 x 18 inches; acrylic/mixed media on wood panel

Right: and following page: *Calavera Left* and *Calavera Right*; 8 x 10 inches;
acrylic/copper leaf on wood panel

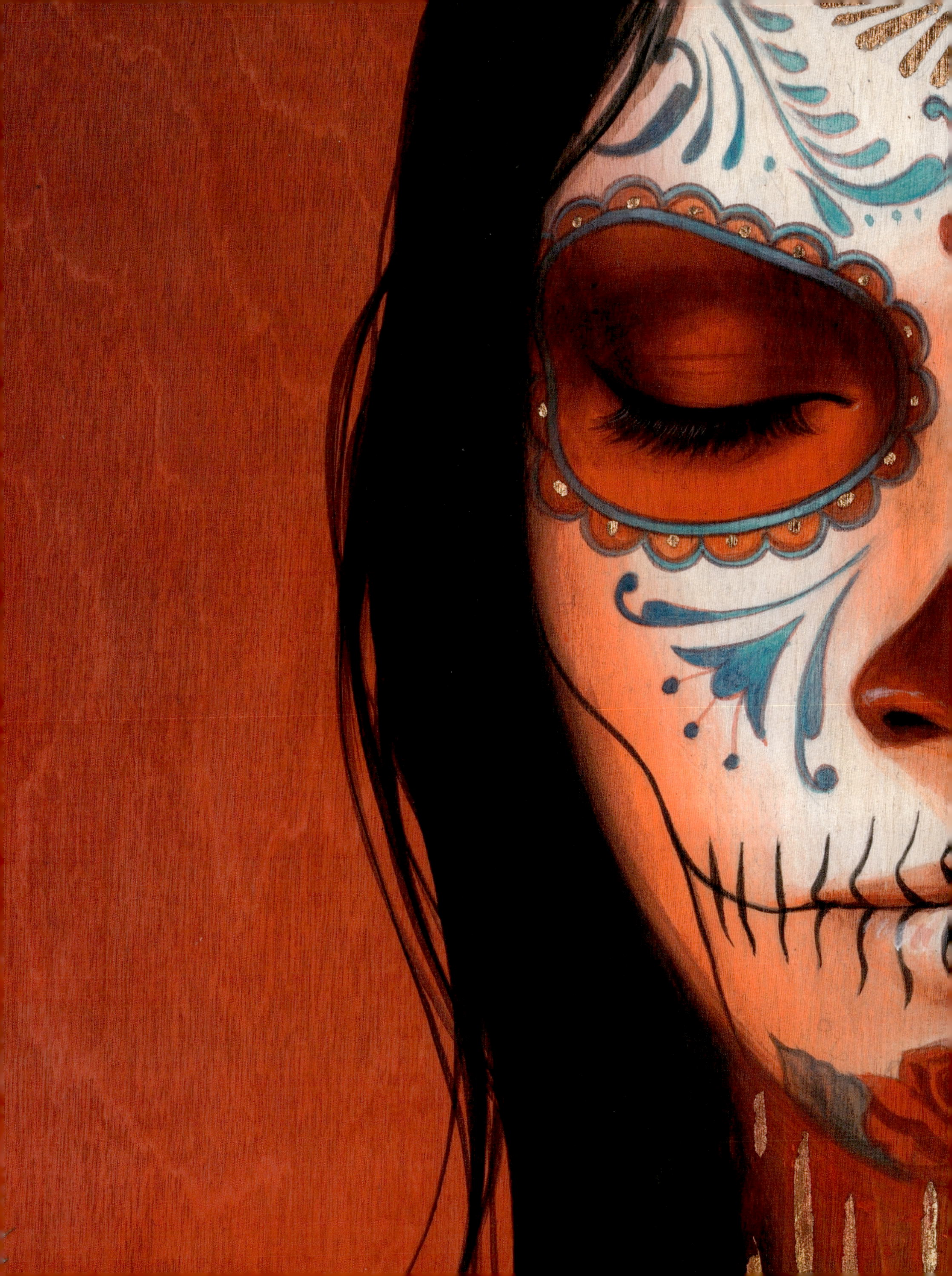

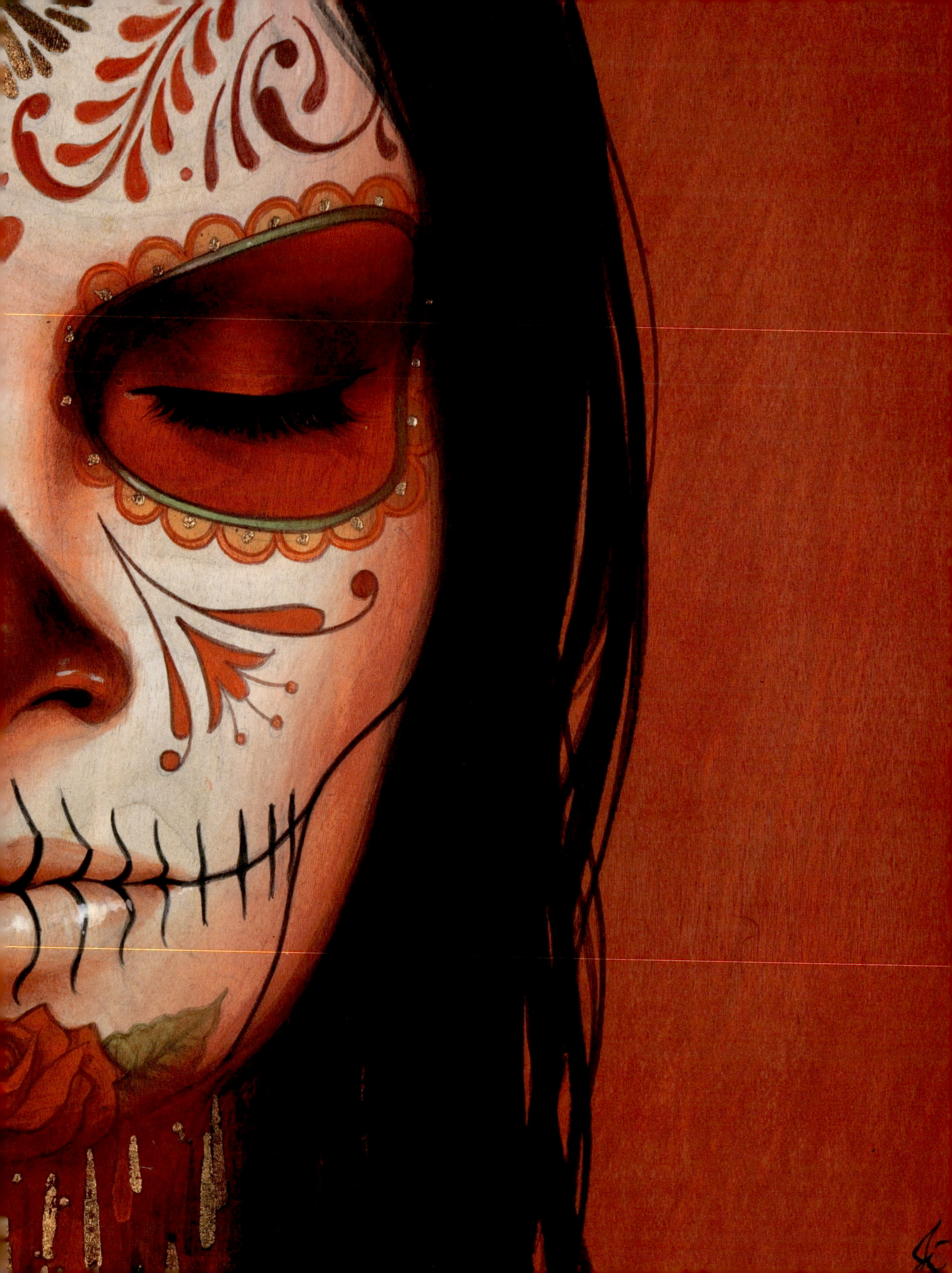

DAY OF THE DEAD

AND OTHER WORKS BY SYLVIA JI

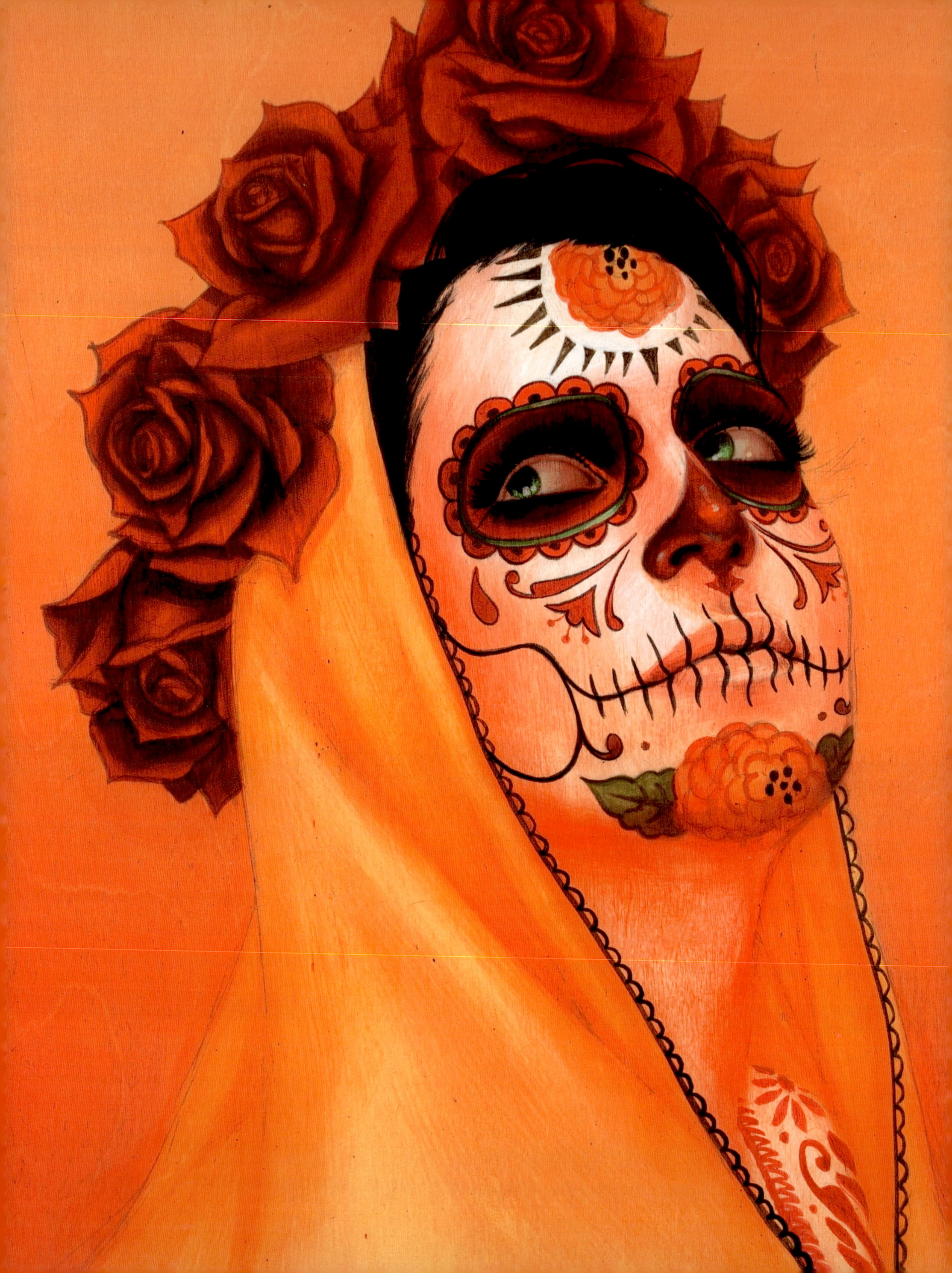

CONTENTS

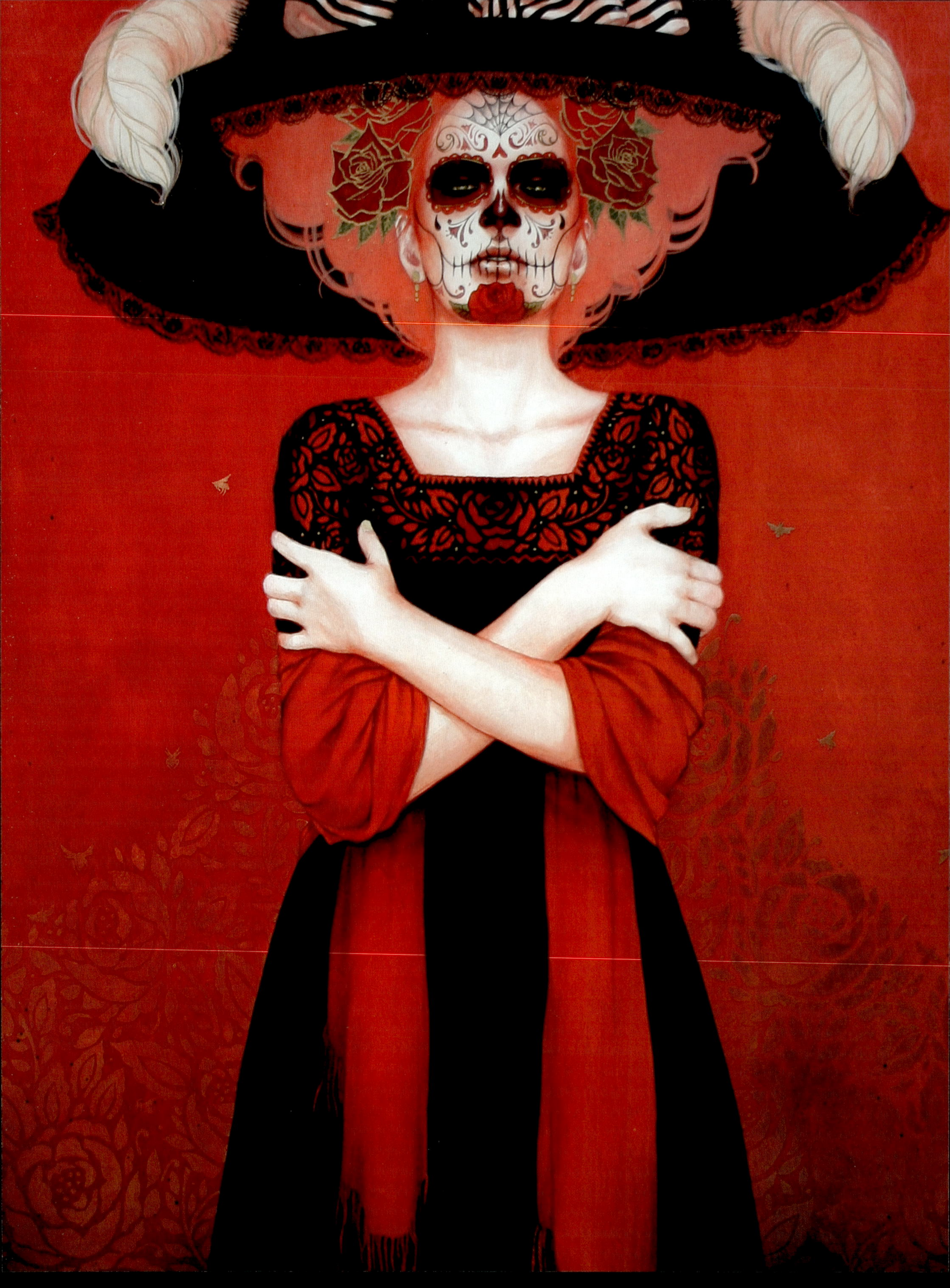

FOREWORD

Sylvia Ji is a remnant of the future. An old soul with the Baroque eye of a master and a fresh approach to the contemporary portrait. We fell in love with her earliest works – depicting impossibly beautiful women entering the state of death following their poisoning by equally beautiful venomous creatures – and watched her evolve into the icon of portraiture she is today. And we've been fortunate enough to have our galleries honored with her exhibitions since 2006: the first of which drew lines that wrapped around the block and gathered everyone from celebrities to cholas – all anxious to see Sylvia's newest ancient images.

In many cases, these people graced their skin with Sylvia's women in the same way her paintings graced our walls – her Day of the Dead faces have launched a thousand tattoos and created a new symbol of strength, mystery, and eternity on the arms, legs, and torsos of the bold new women and men of the millennium. We encourage you not just to enjoy this book of her sumptuous works, but to recognize the impact of its creator on the new voices still emerging and the evolution of the New Contemporary genre as it continues to grow throughout the world. Possibly best known for her seminal and eternally imitated Day of the Dead paintings, and her lush Victorian-garbed (and dis-garbed) women, Sylvia Ji is a wealth of the treasures of the past spilling all over the portraits of today.

Jan and Bruce Helford
Corey Helford Gallery

Previous page: *Catrina Sol Amarill*; 12 x 12 inches; acrylic on wood panel

Left: *La Madrina*; 48 x 36 inches; acrylic/mixed media on wood panel

2005–2006
DEATH AND THE MAIDEN

This early body of work was spawned from a dark place within my life. The paintings here feature elements and themes – venomous insects, poison dart frogs, coral snakes – that remind us of our own mortality, and finding the beauty in that.

During this period I was also inspired by Art Nouveau design, along with 18th- and 19th-century fashion; these are themes that can be seen throughout all of my later work, too.

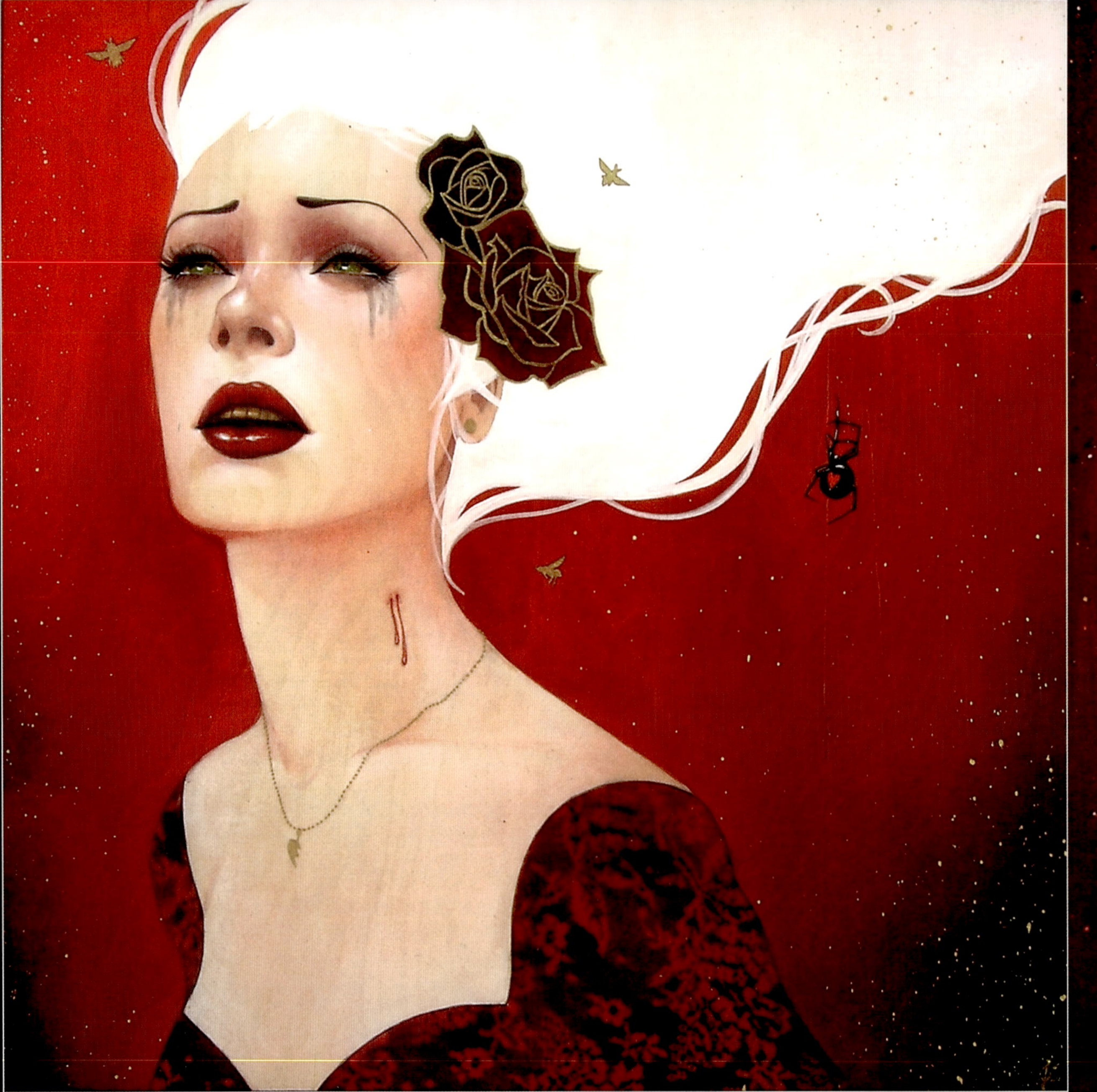

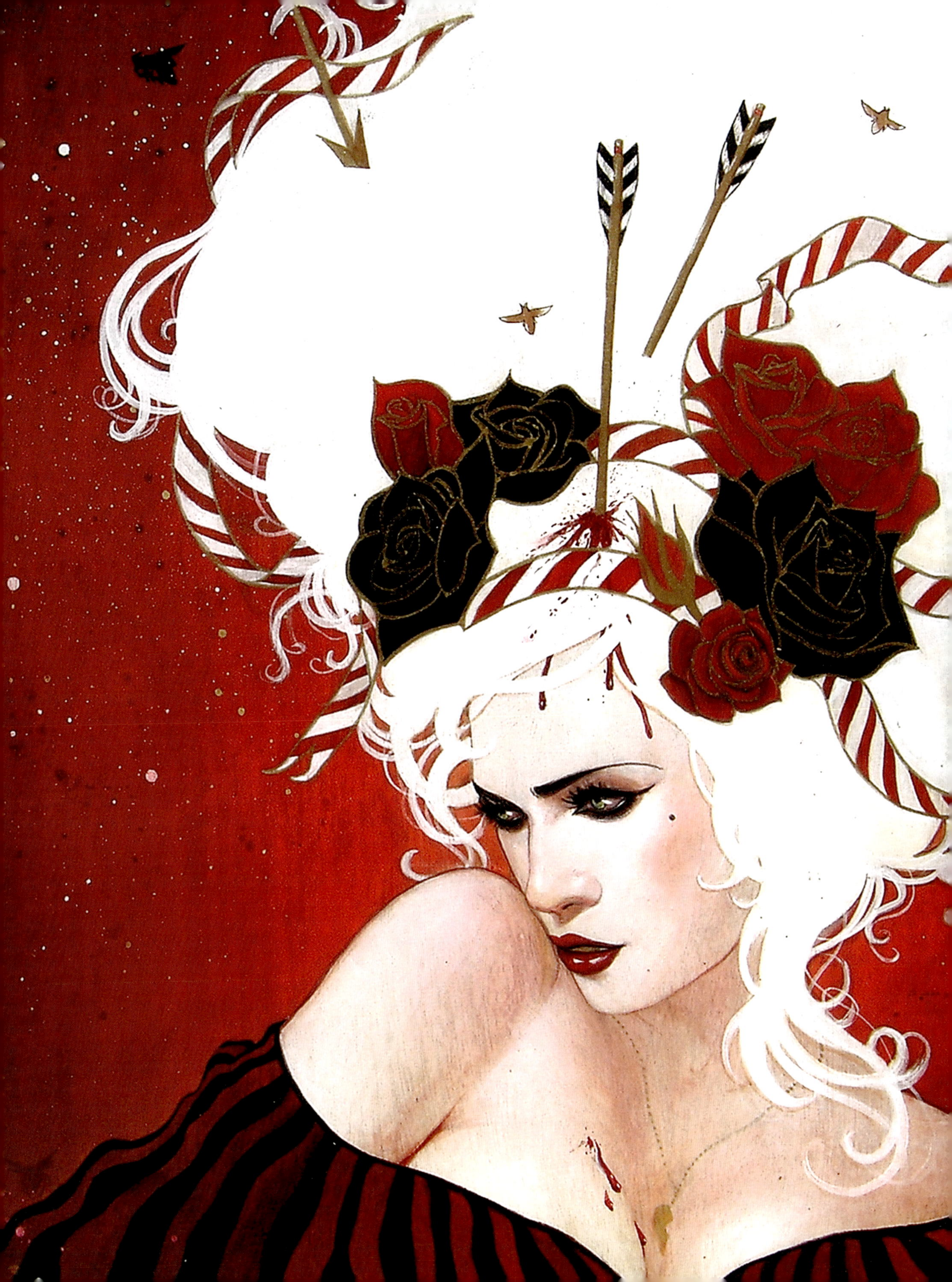

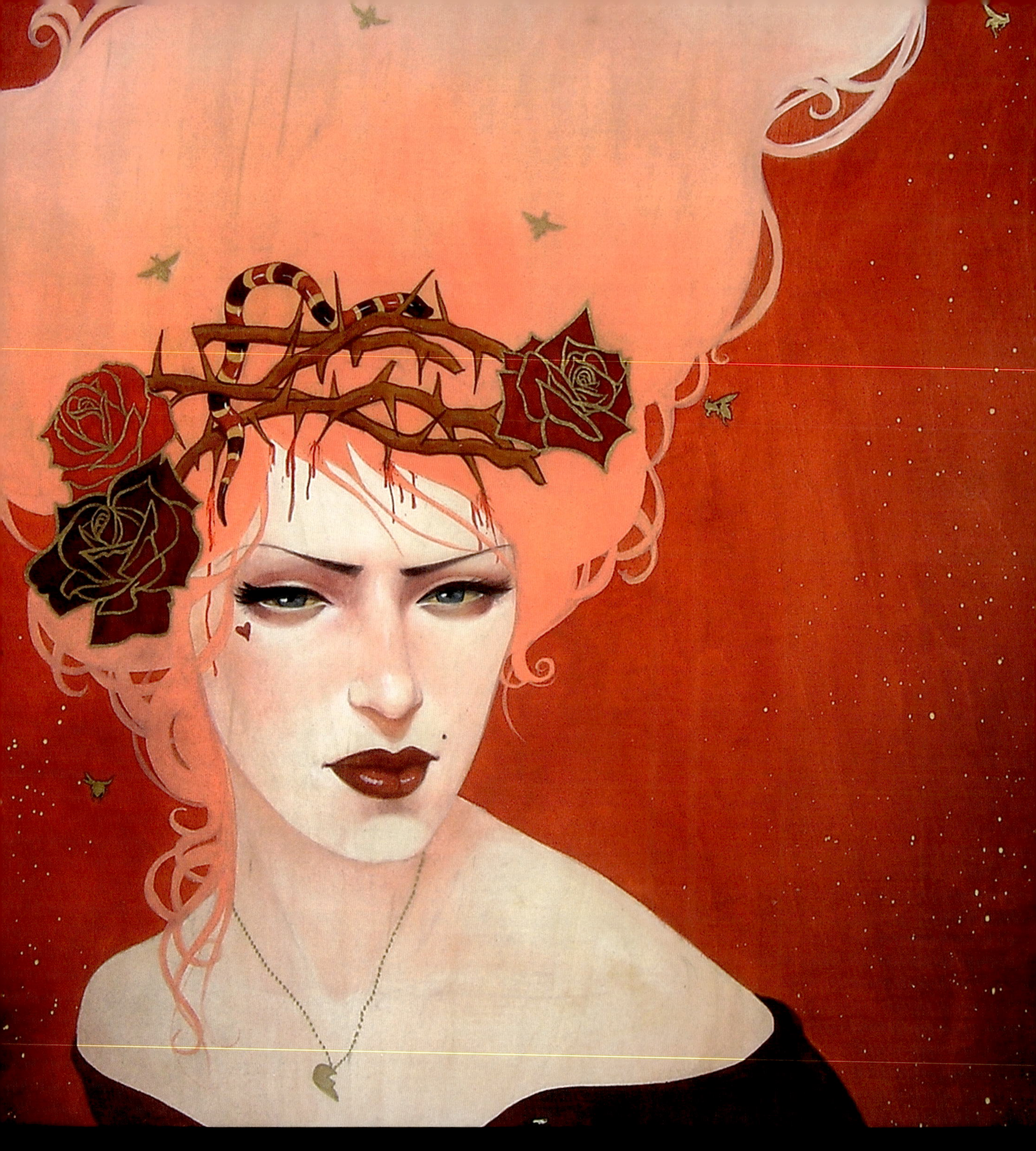

Hopeless Romantic; 24 x 24 inches; acrylic on wood panel

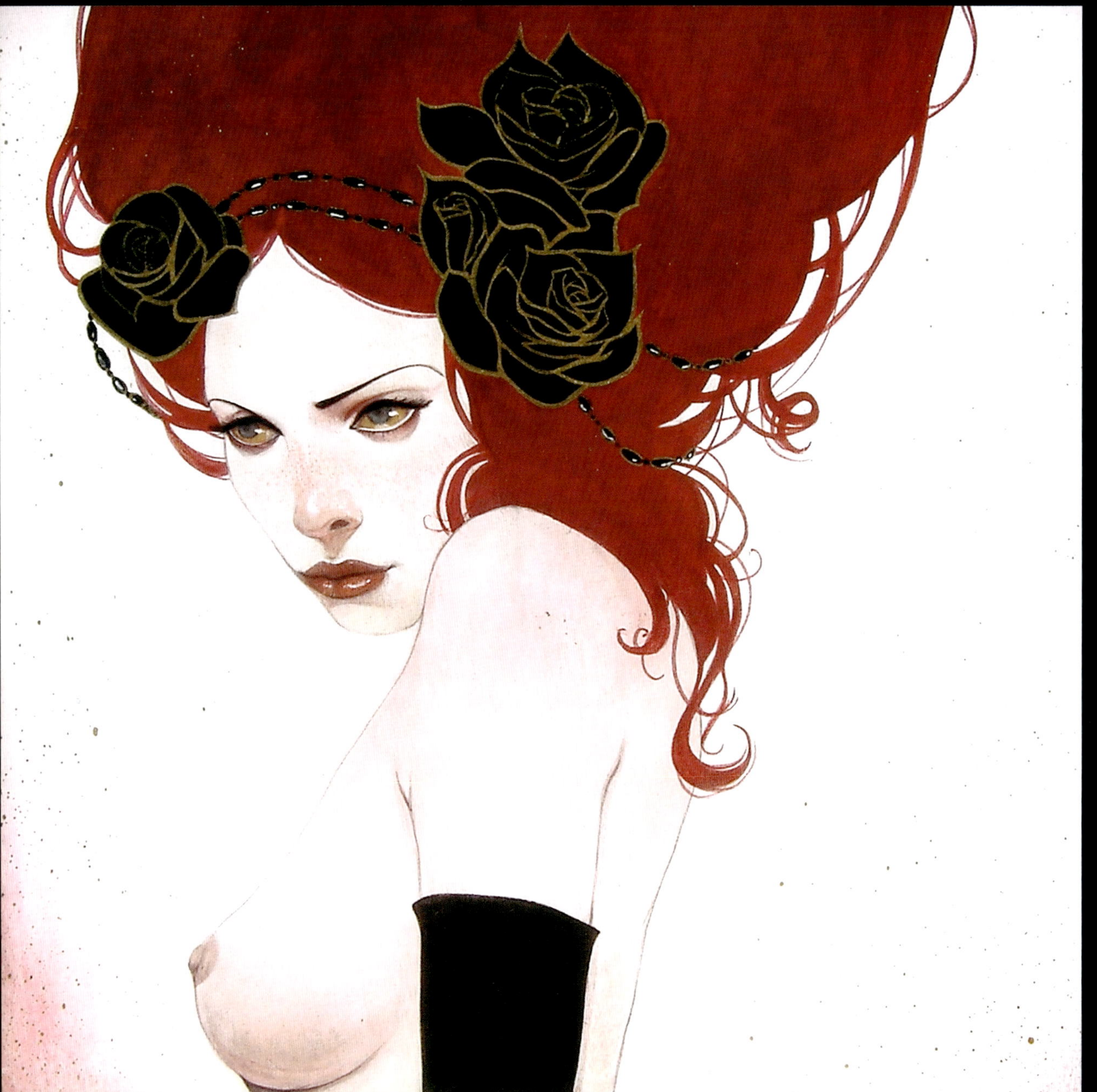

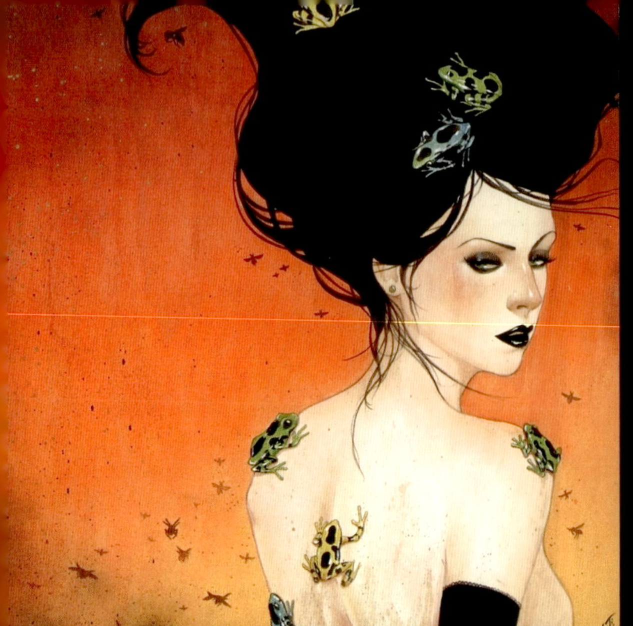

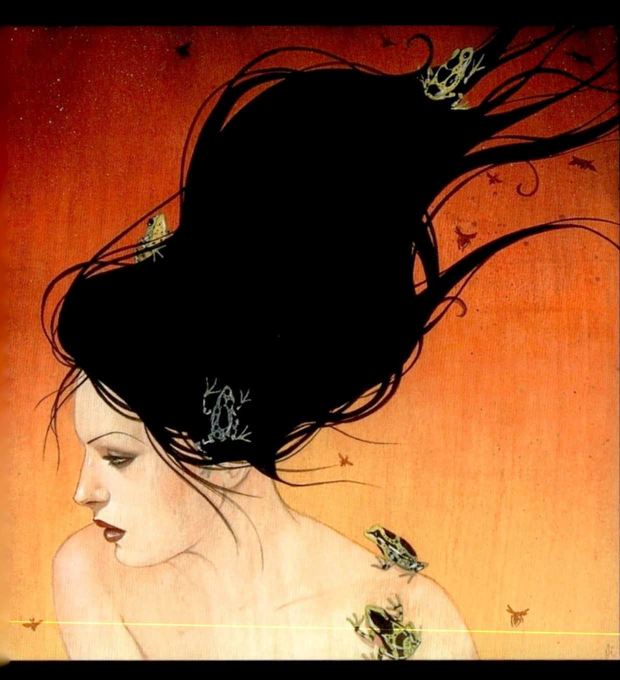

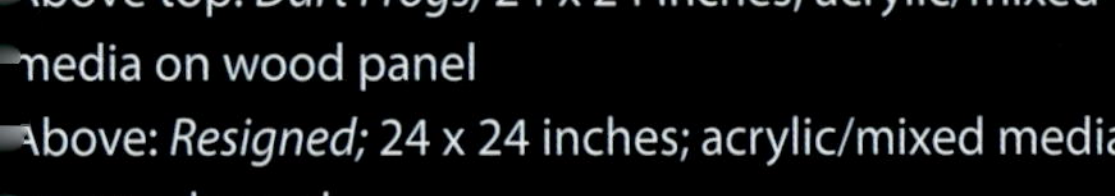

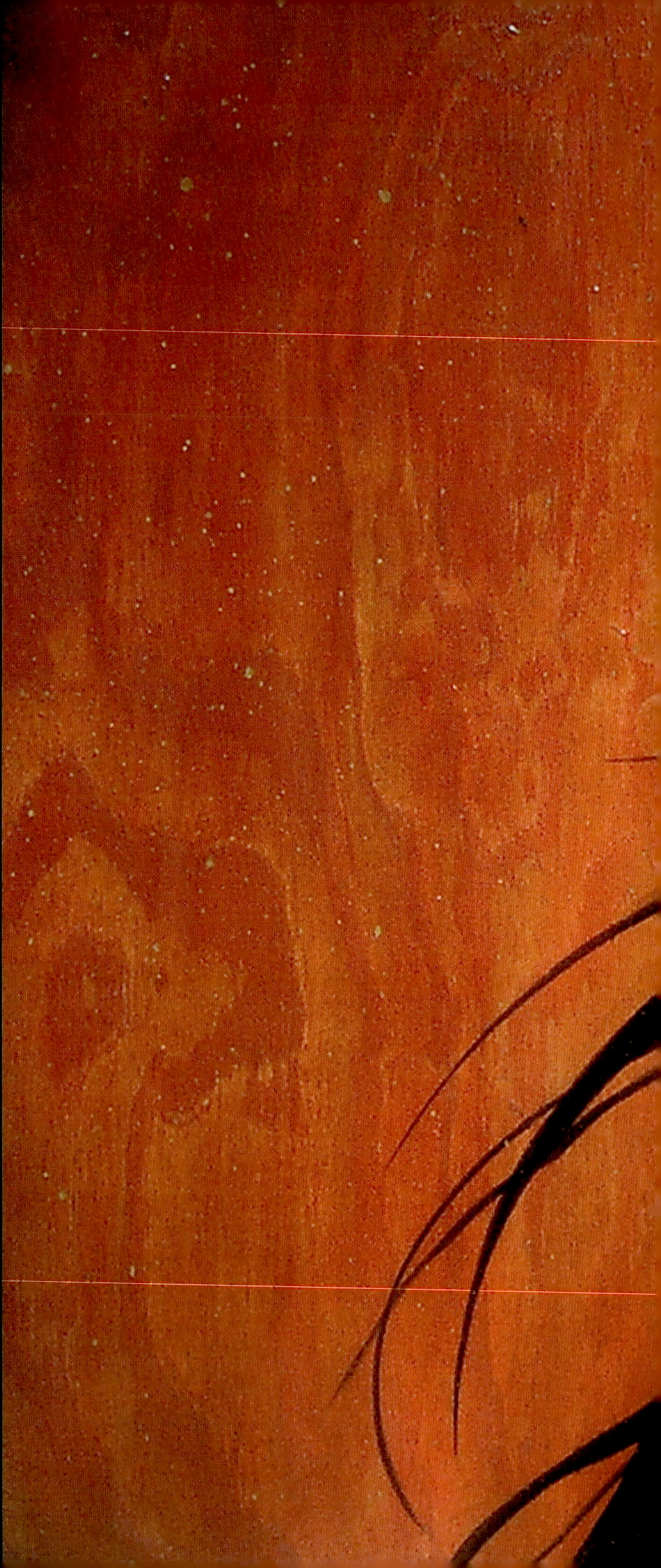

Above top: *Dart Frogs;* 24 x 24 inches; acrylic/mixed media on wood panel

Above: *Resigned;* 24 x 24 inches; acrylic/mixed media on wood panel

Right: *Fading;* 16 x 24 inches, acrylic/mixed media on wood panel

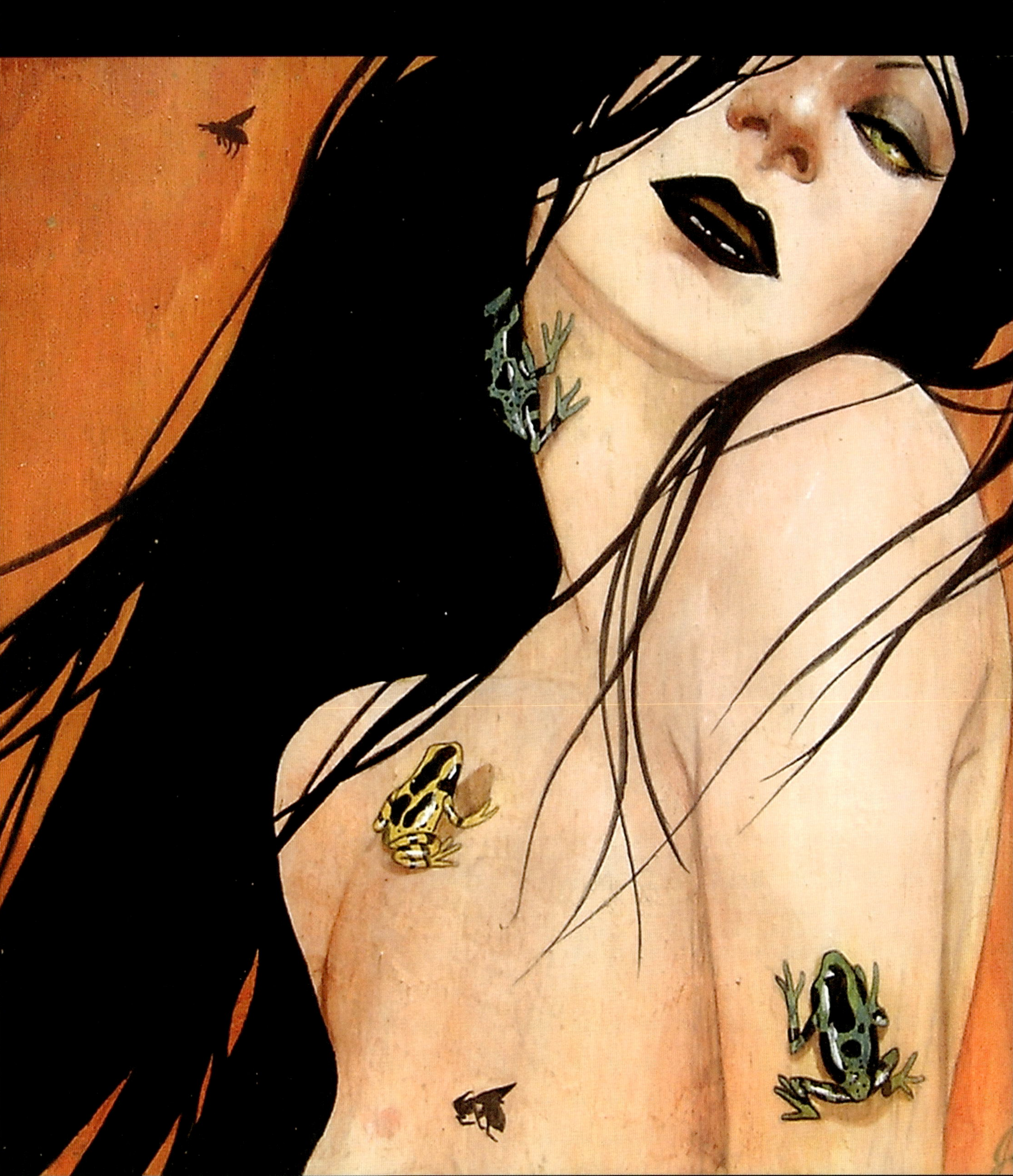

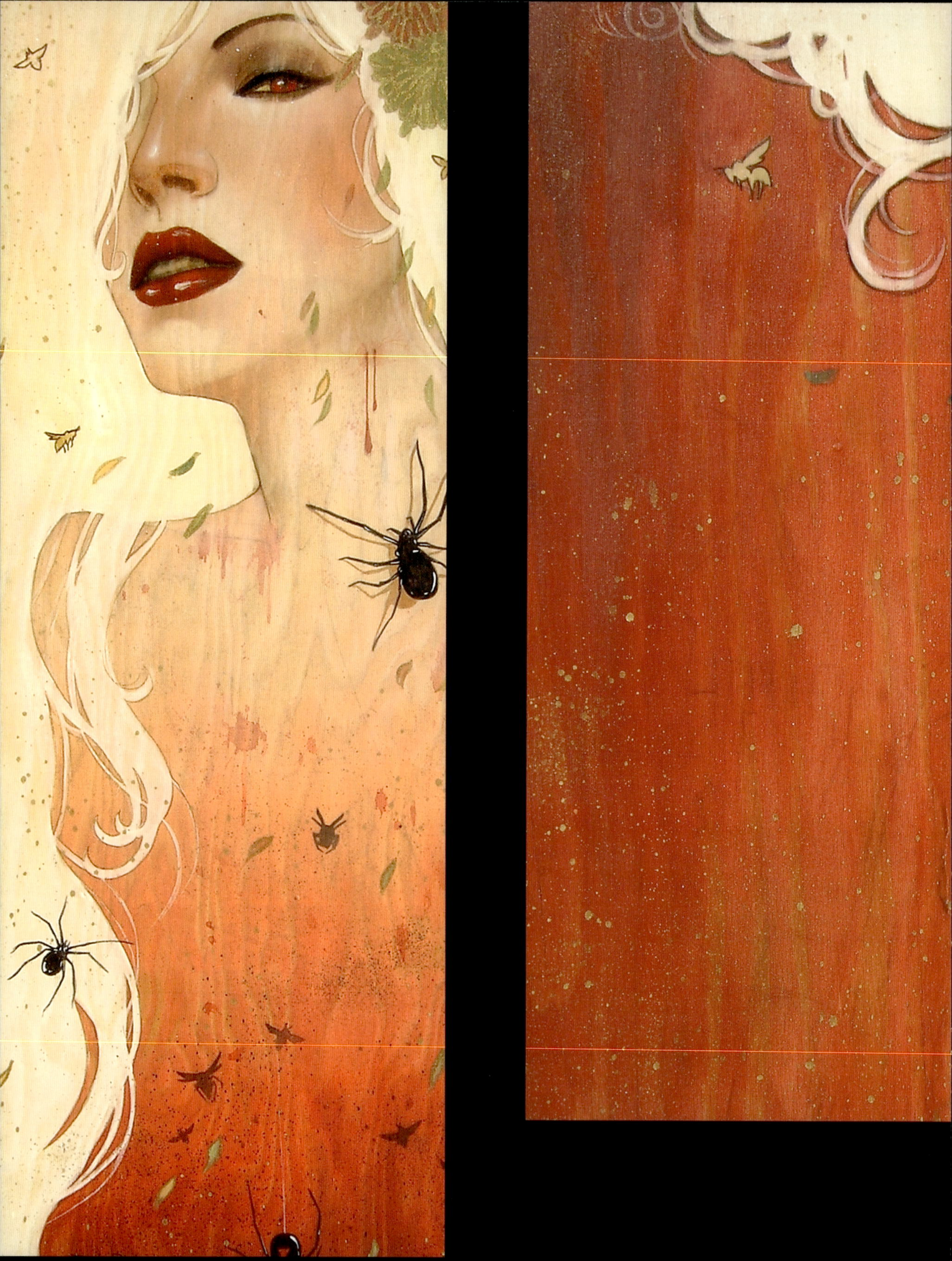

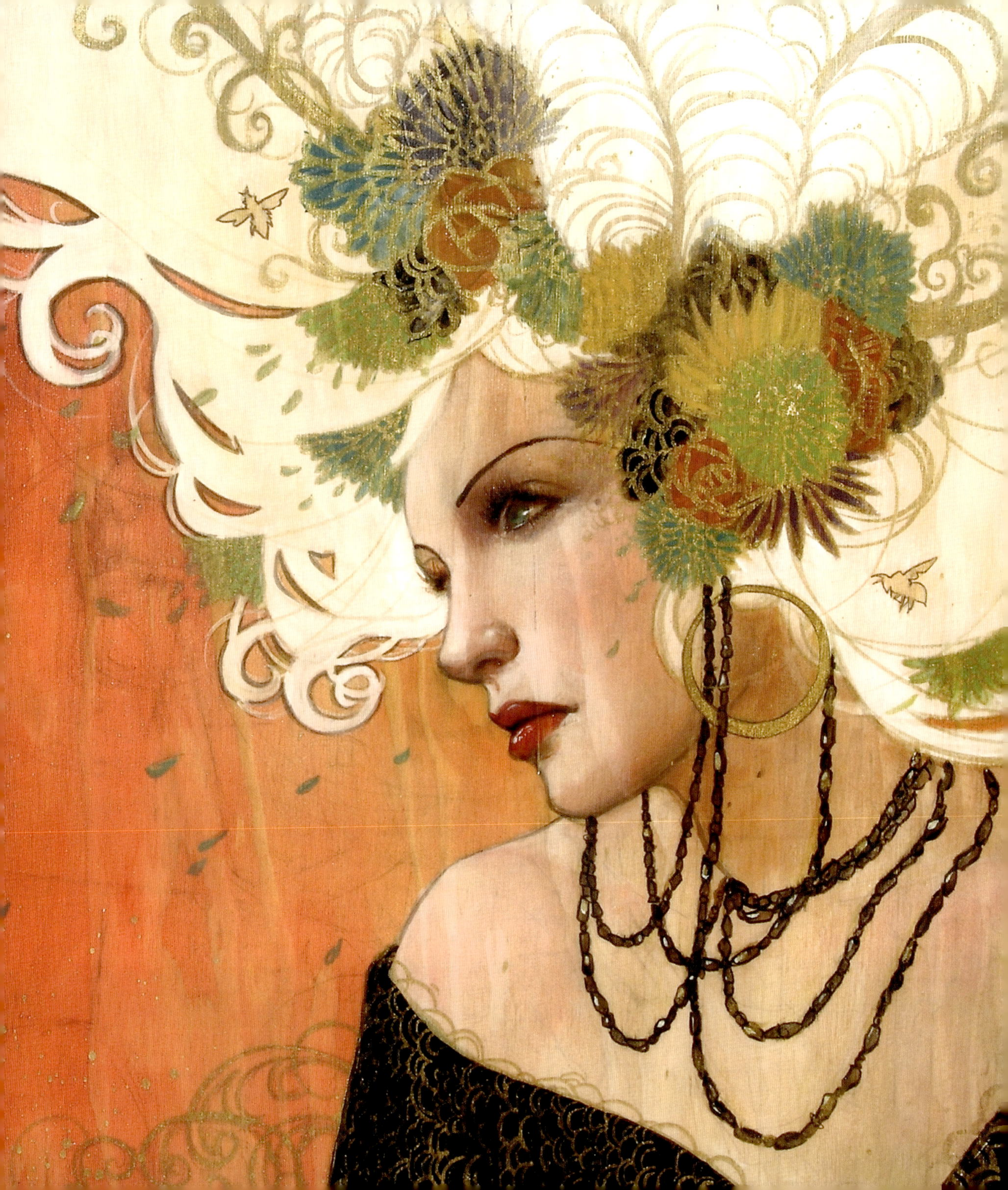

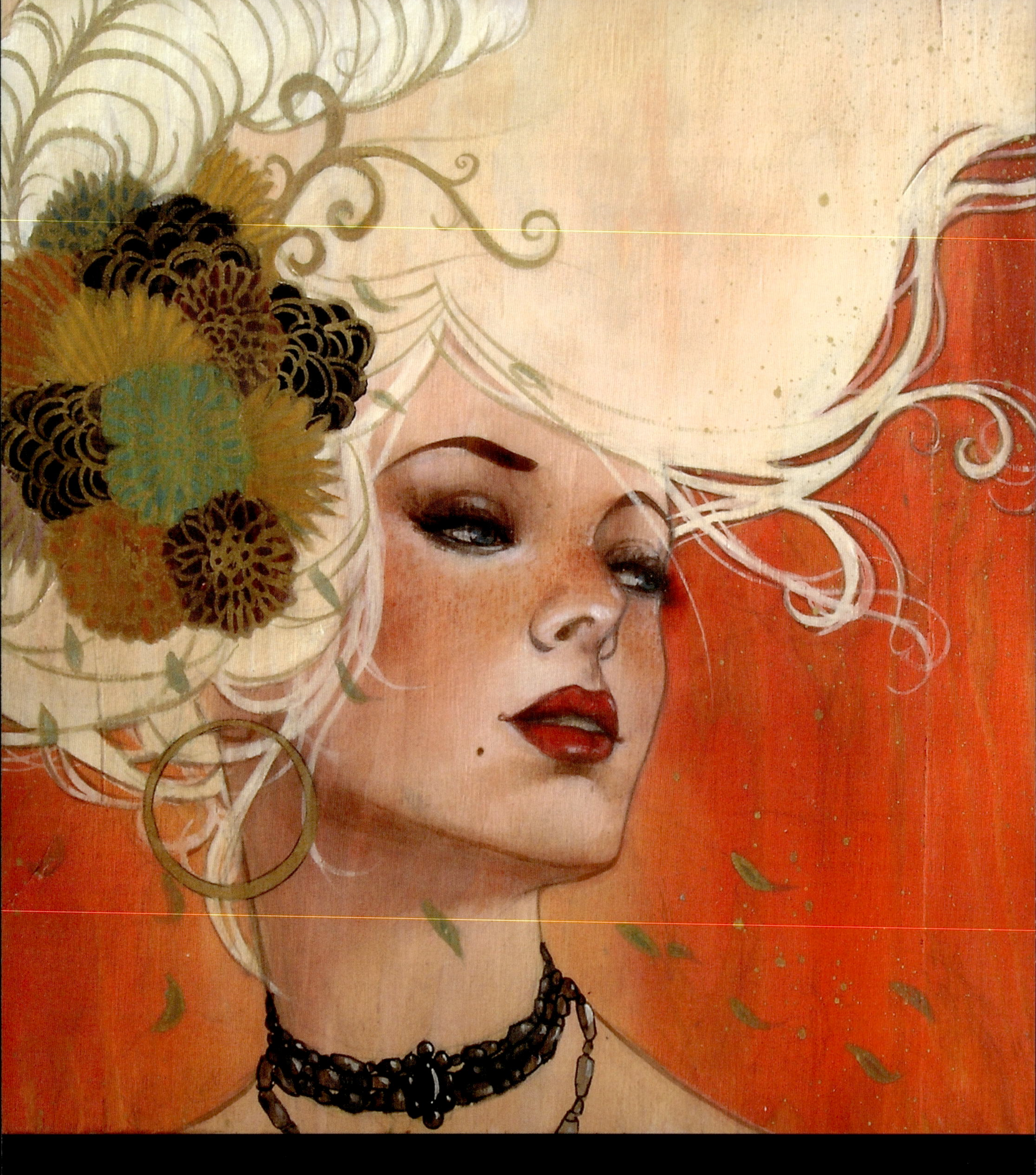

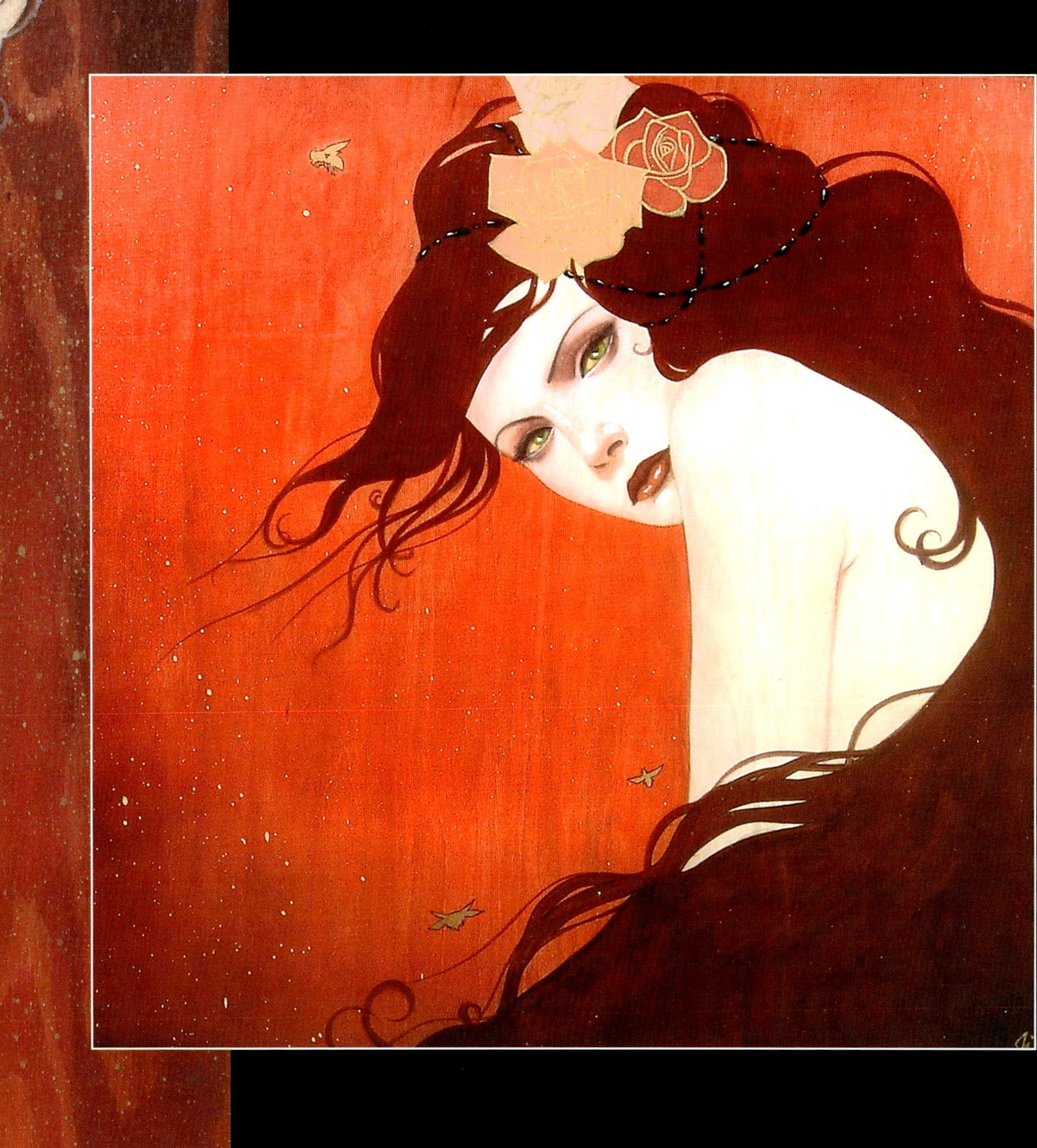

Left: *Mademoiselle*; 18 x 24 inches; acrylic on wood panel

Right: *Waiting*; 24 x 24 inches; acrylic/mixed media on wood panel

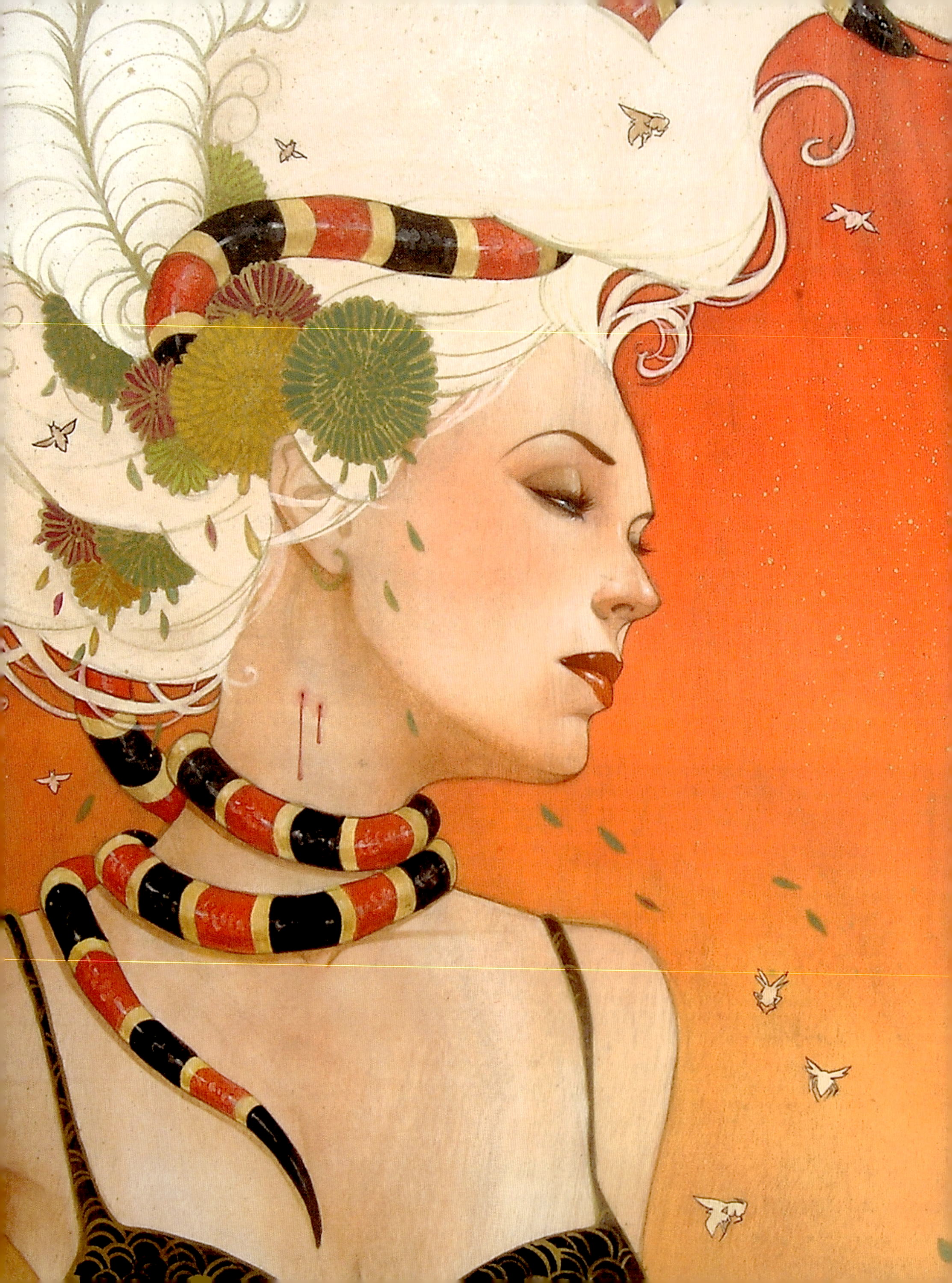

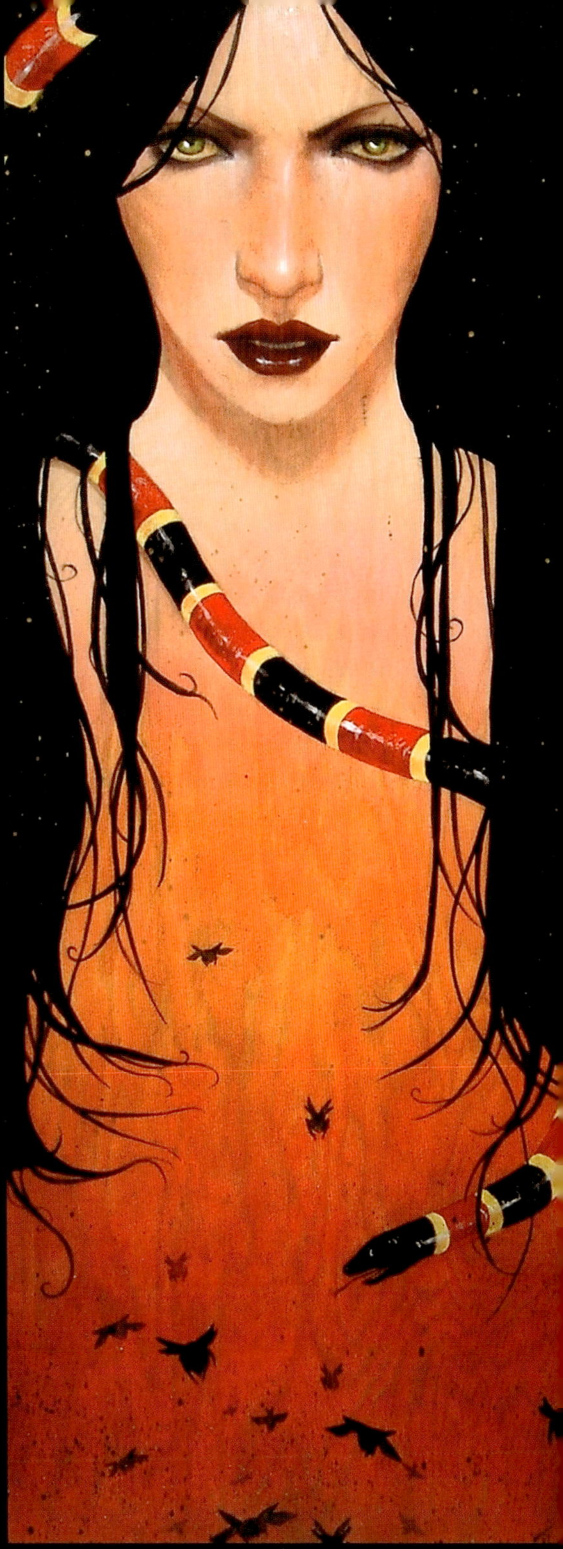

Left: *Coral Snake;* 24 x 24 inches; acrylic/mixed media on wood pane

Above: *Coral Snake 2:* 18 x 32 inches; acrylic on wood pane

Sylvia J

2007–2008
LA CATRINA

During this period, I was invariably pulled towards the macabre. One night while sketching – drawing faces on skulls – I suddenly recalled the Mexican artist José Guadalupe Posada's "La Calavera de la Catrina": the skeleton of a high-society lady wearing a large, fancy hat, which later became an icon of his country's Day of the Dead celebrations.

A lightbulb went off in my head. Immediately, I began drawing on a wood panel what was to become my own interpretation of "La Catrina". From this seed, grew my first Catrinas, blended with the Baroque, Victorian, and Gothic styling that characterized my earlier work.

Sylvia Ji

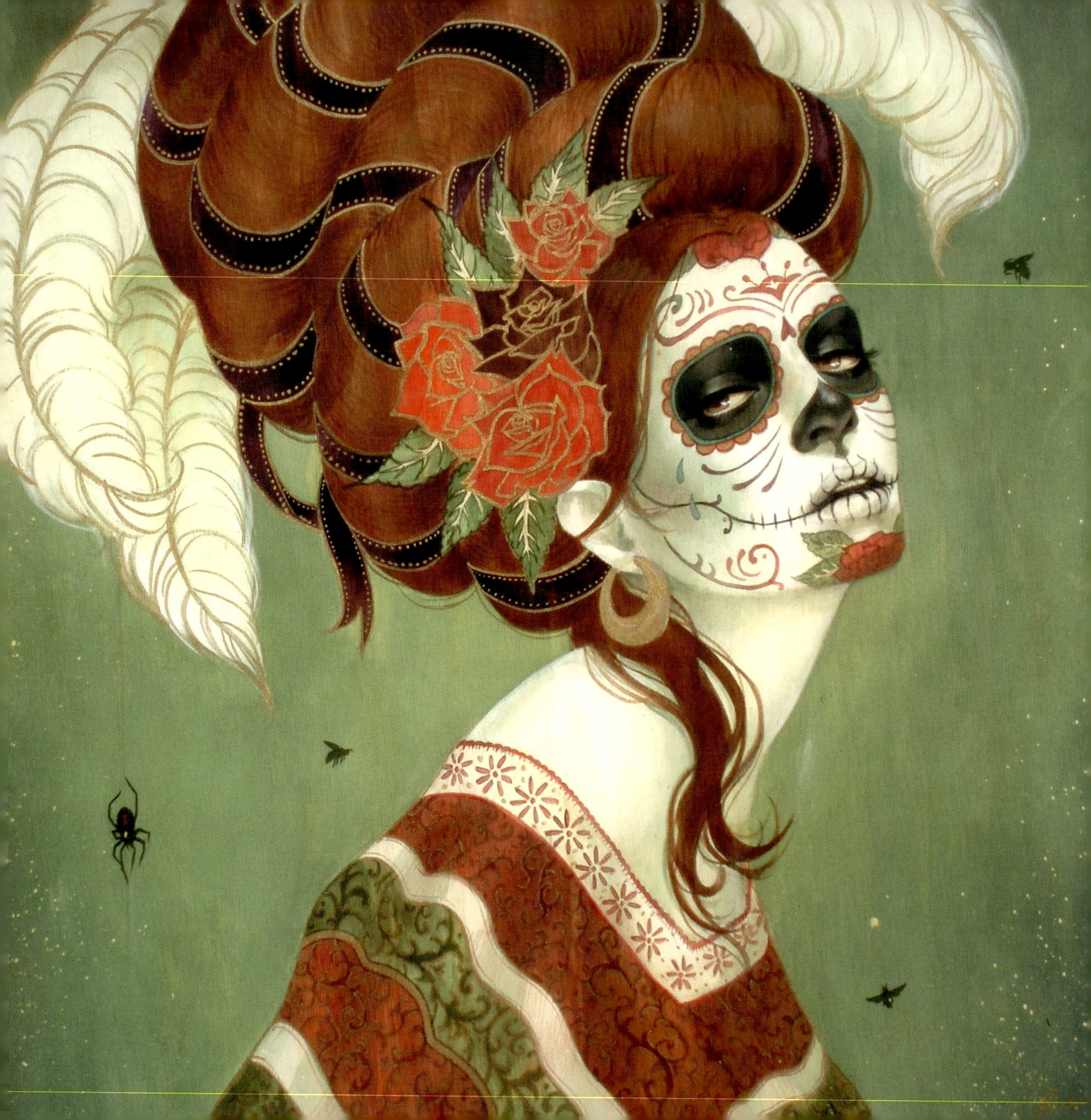

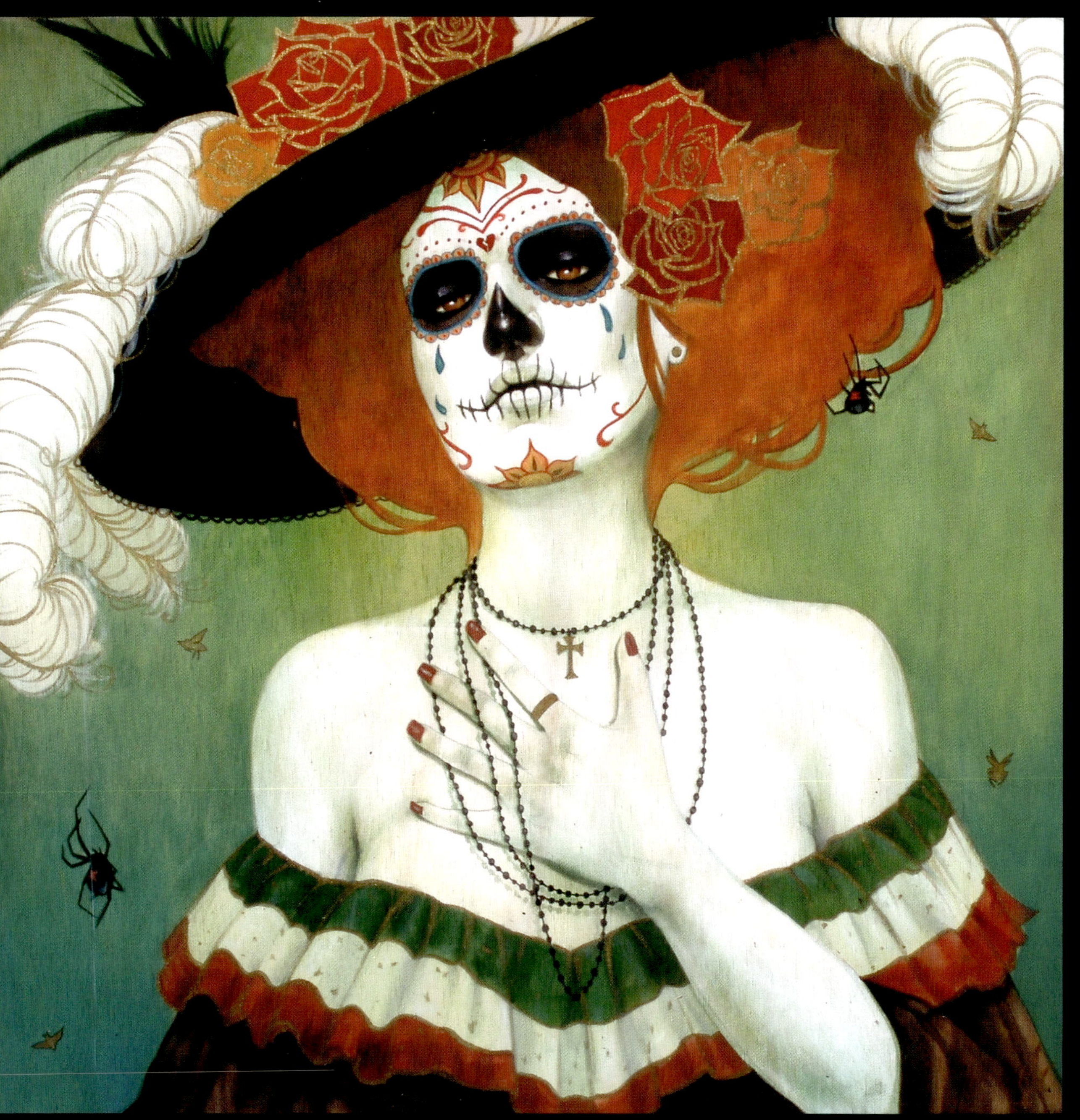

La Catrina; 24 x 24 inches; acrylic/mixed media on wood panel

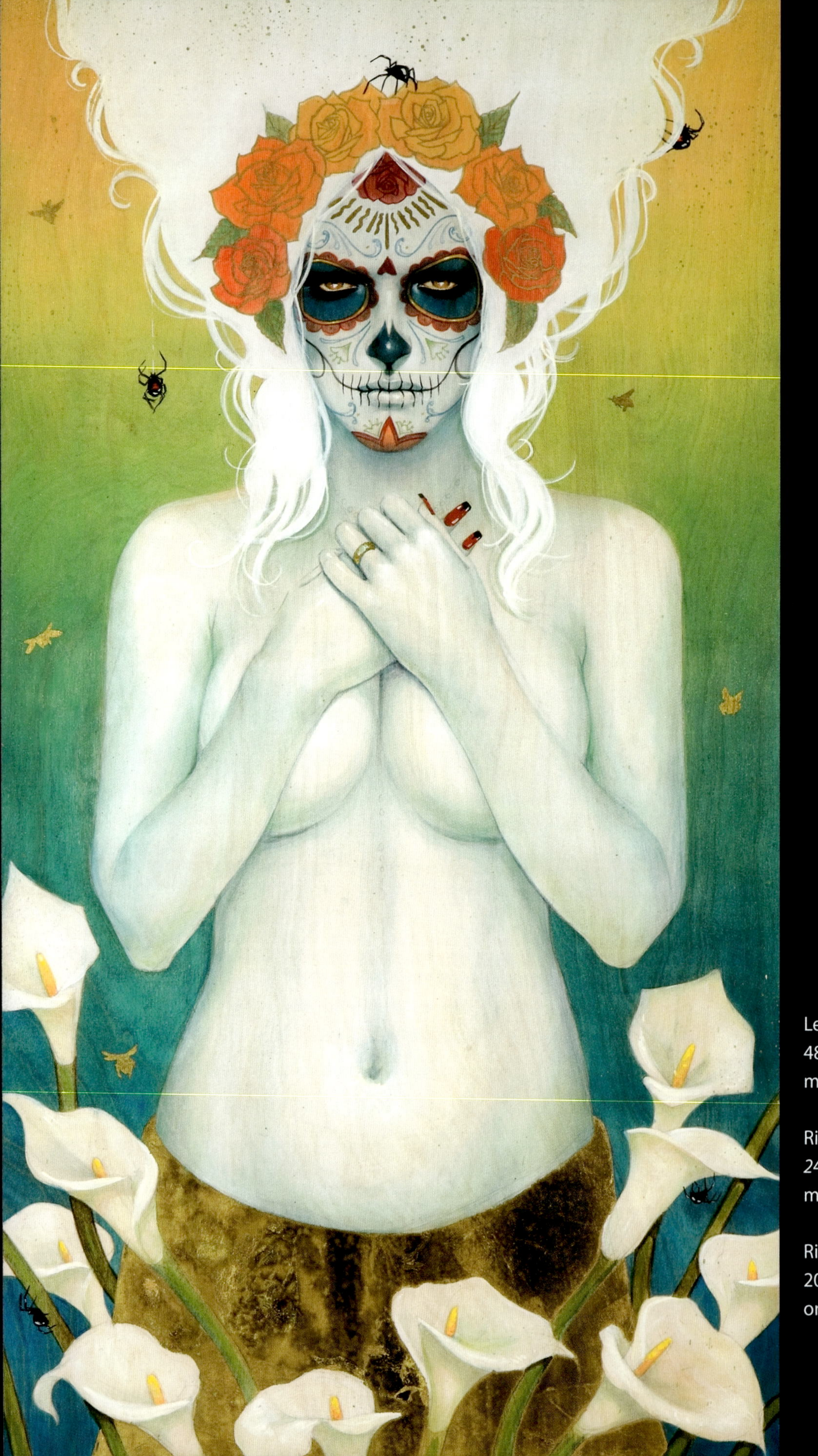

Left: *White Widow;*
48 x 24 inches; acrylic/mixed
media on wood panel

Right top: *Marigold;*
24 x 17 inches; acrylic/mixed
media on wood panel

Right below: *Blackout;*
20 x 15 inches; acrylic
on wood panel

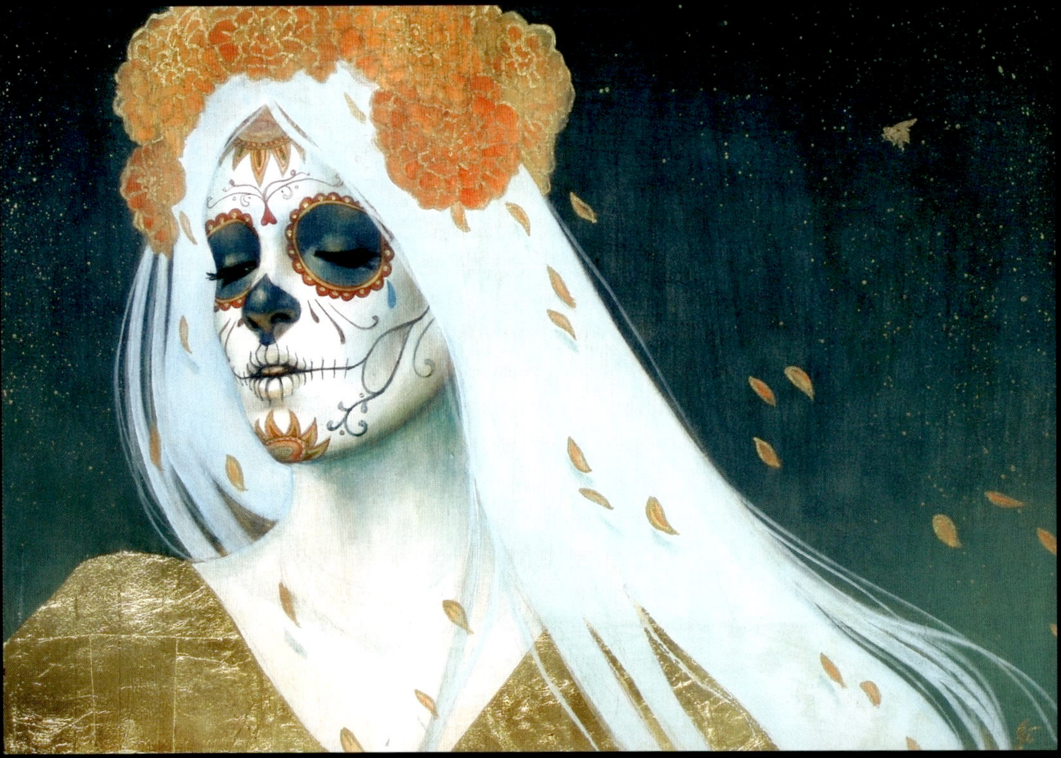

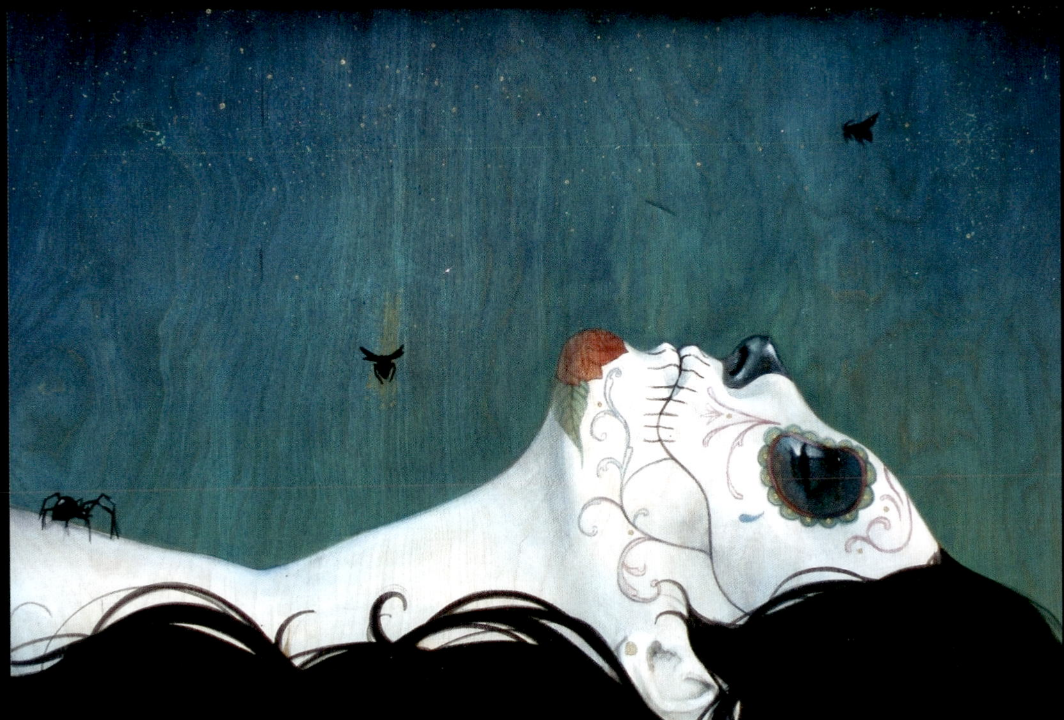

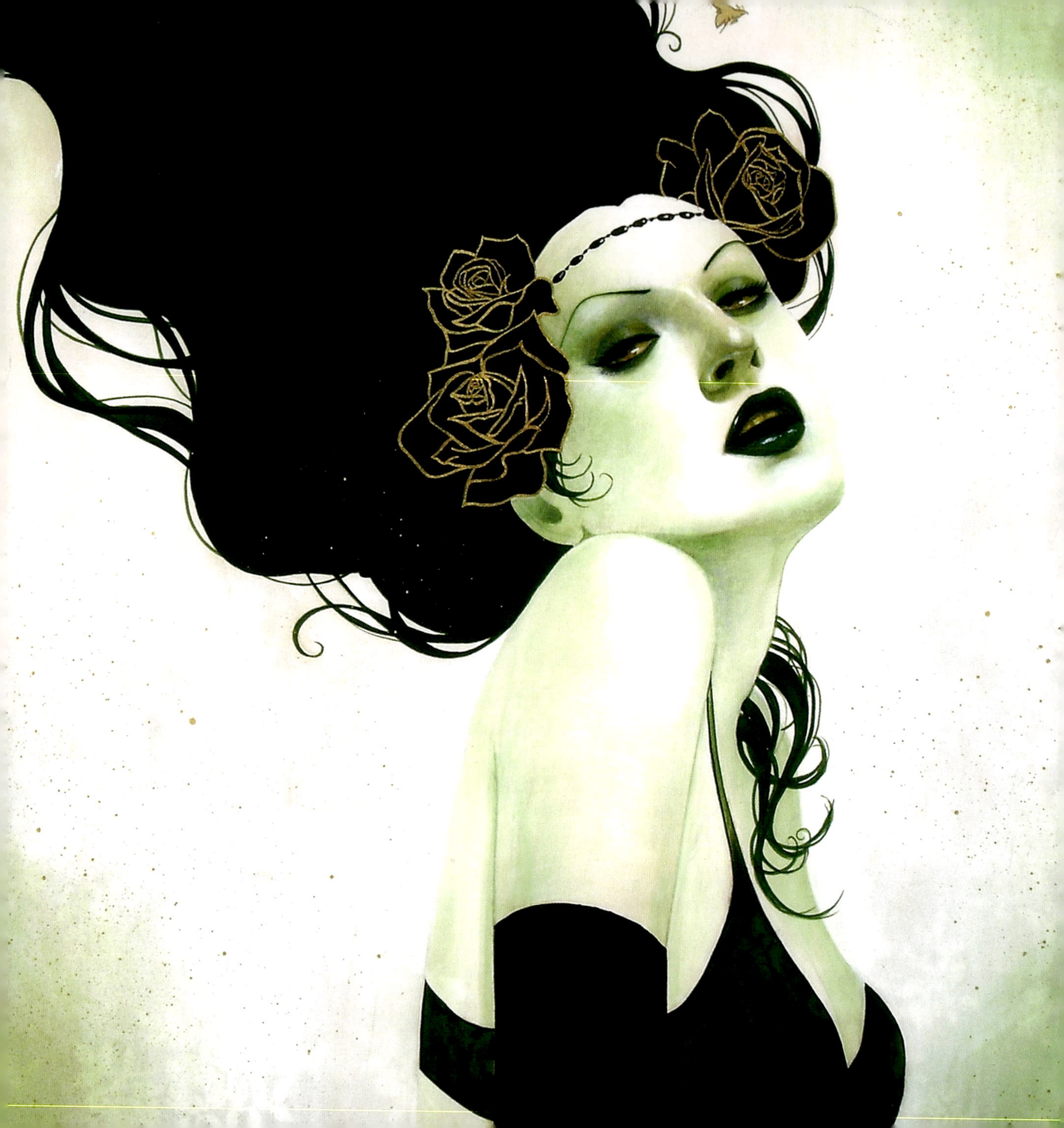

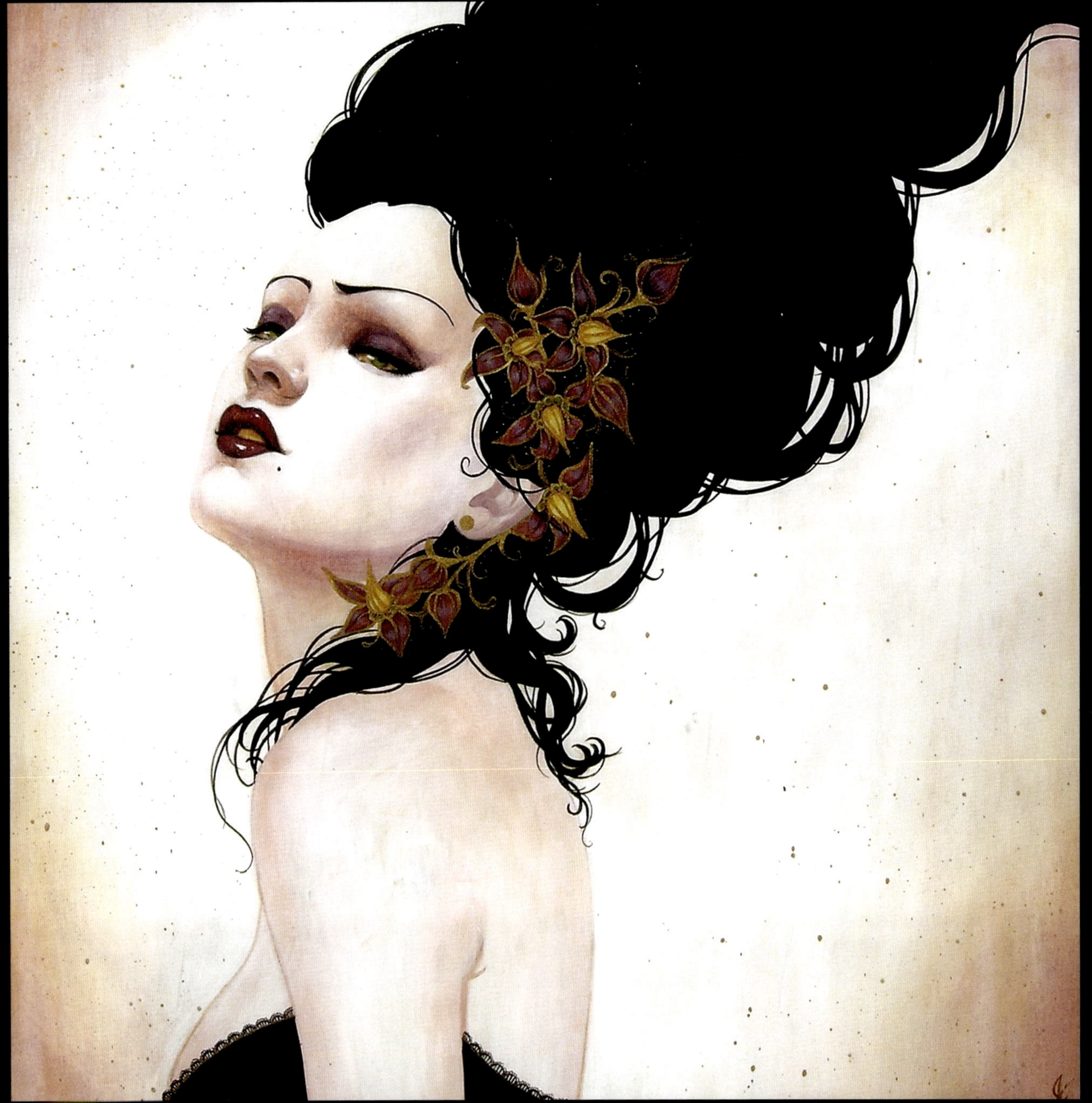

Nighshade; 24 x 24 inches; acrylic/mixed media on wood panel

  Sylvia Ji

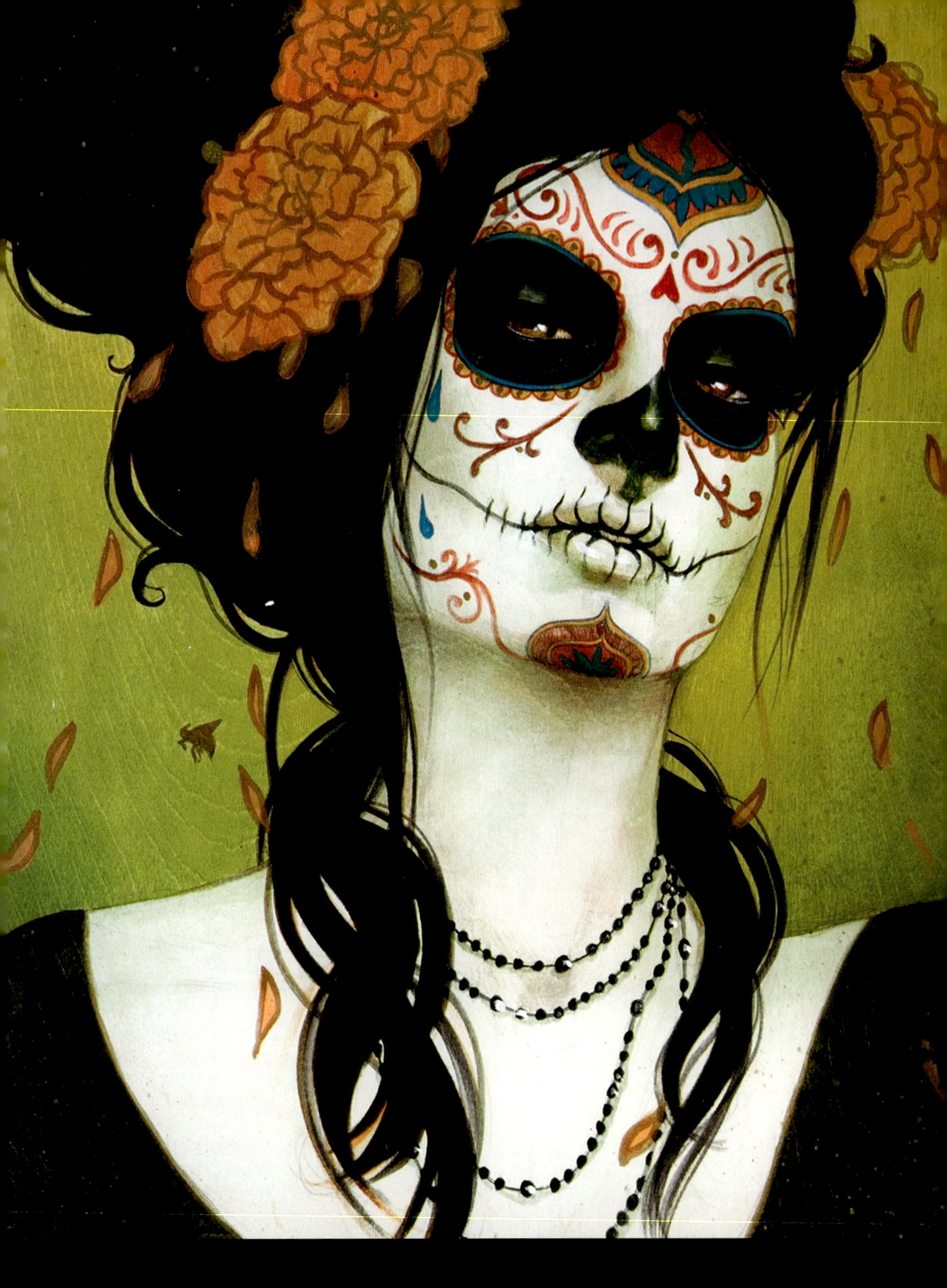

Above: *Green Catrina;* 8 x 10 inches; acrylic/mixed media on wood panel

Right: *Vow of Silence;* 18 x 16 inches; acrylic/mixed media on wood panel

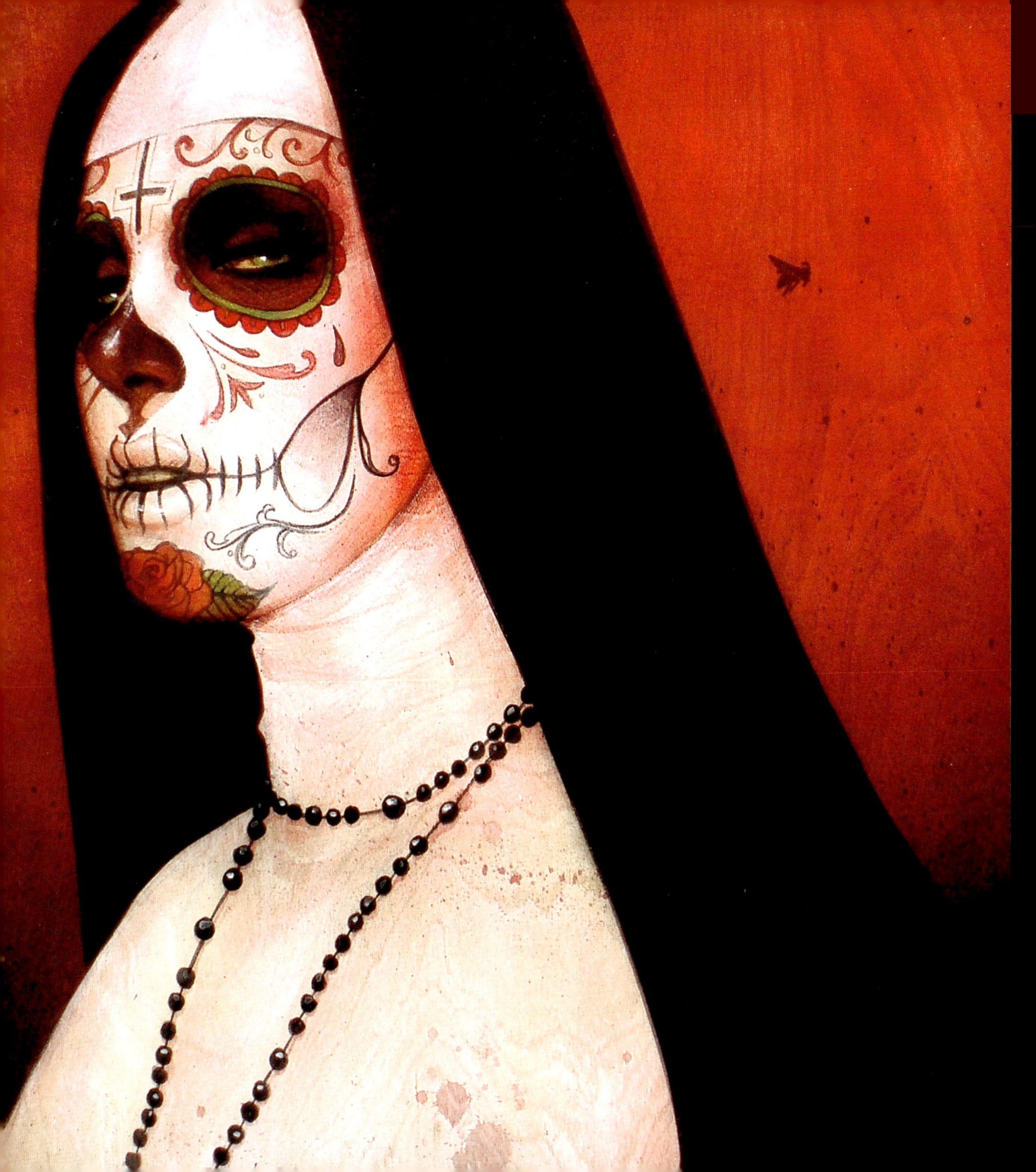

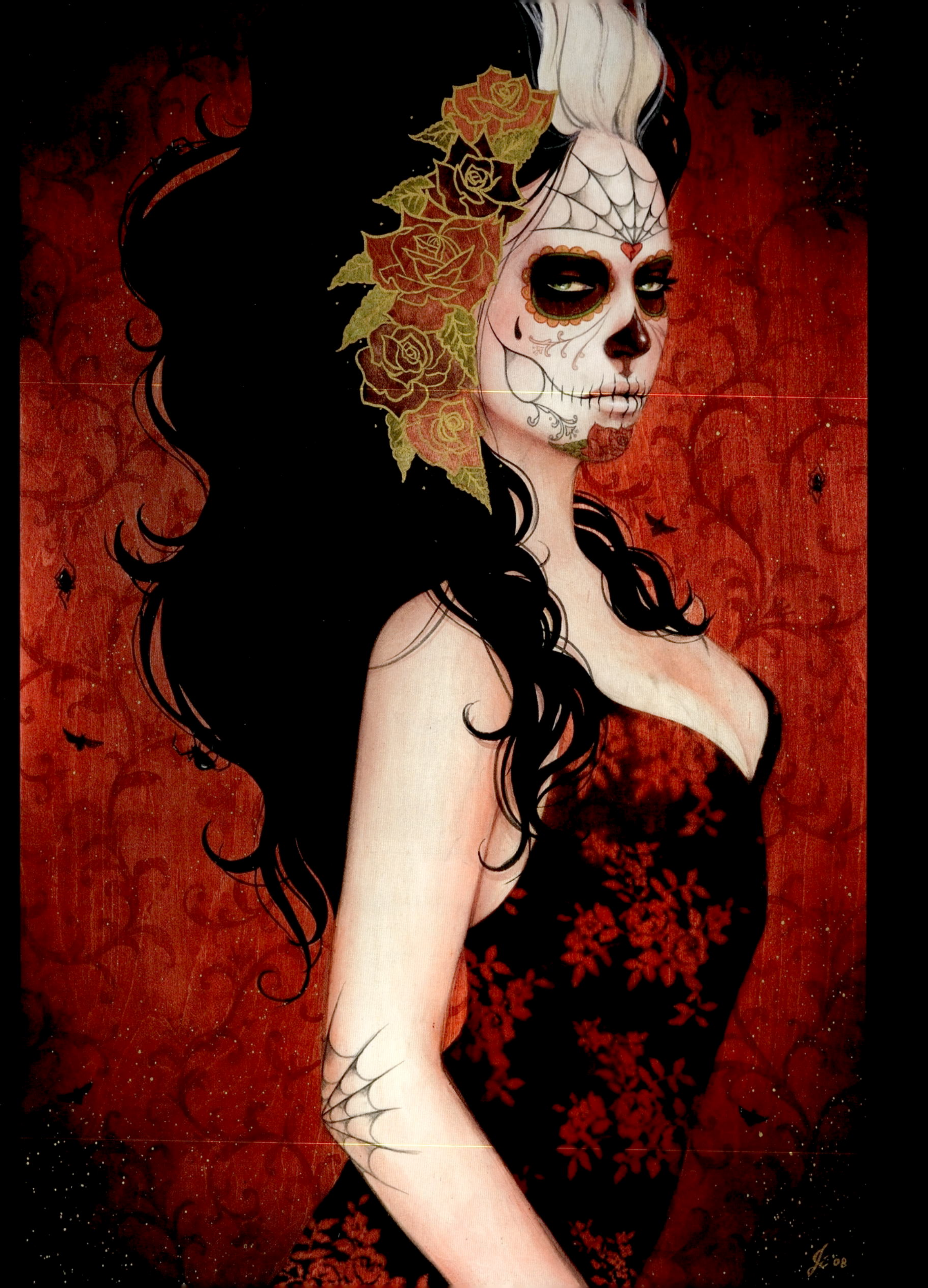

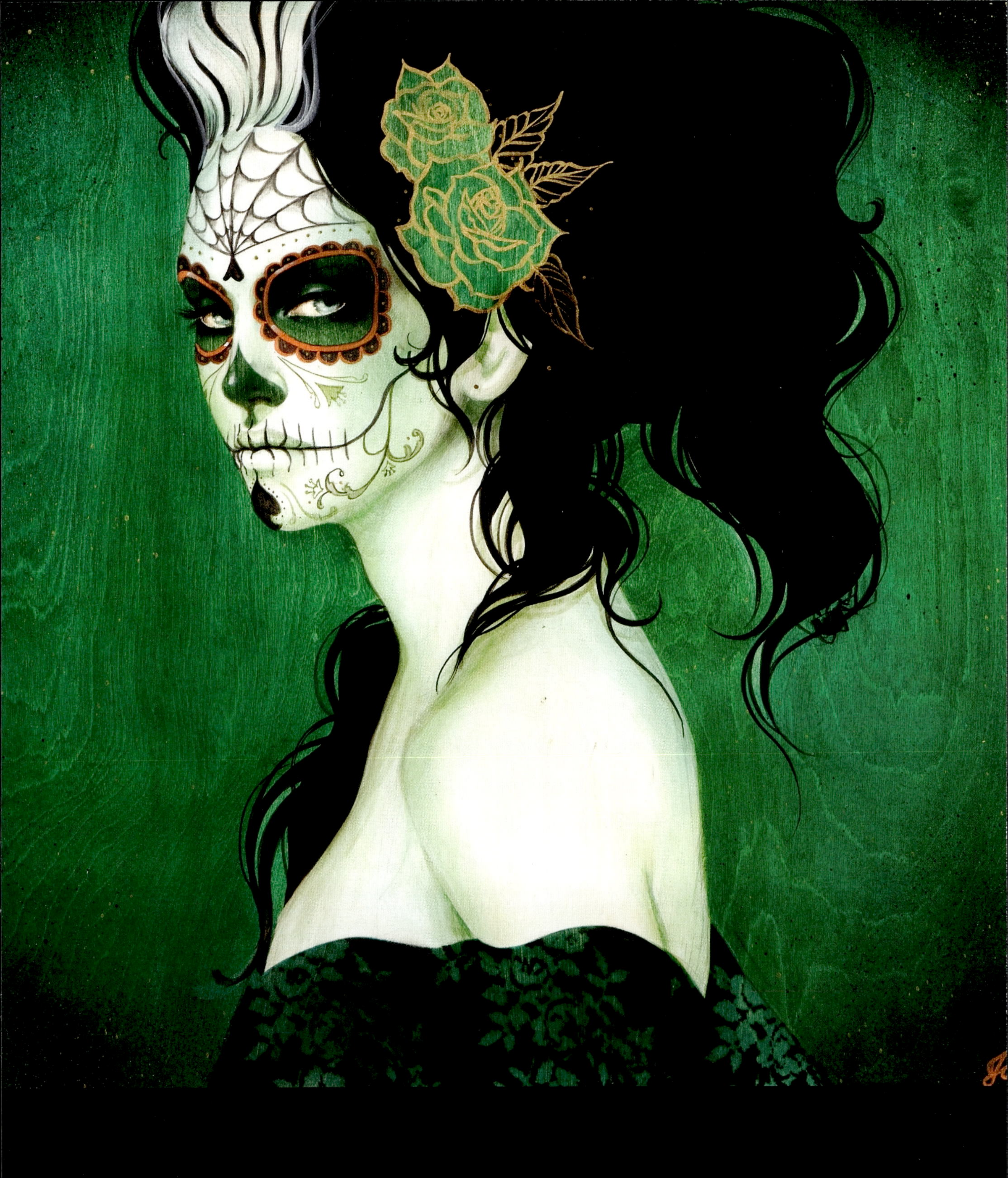

Black Domina; 24 x 24 inches; acrylic on wood panel

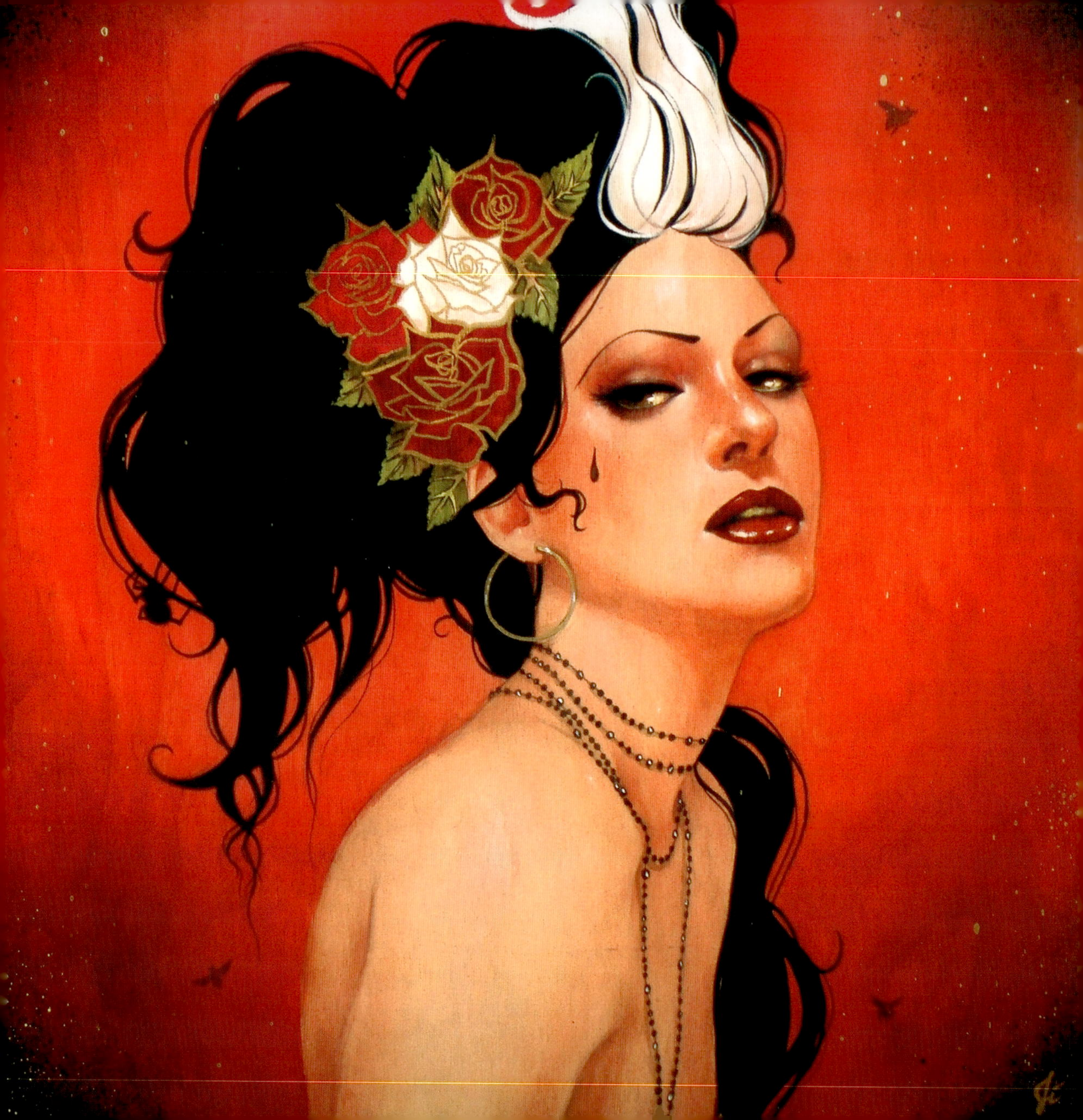

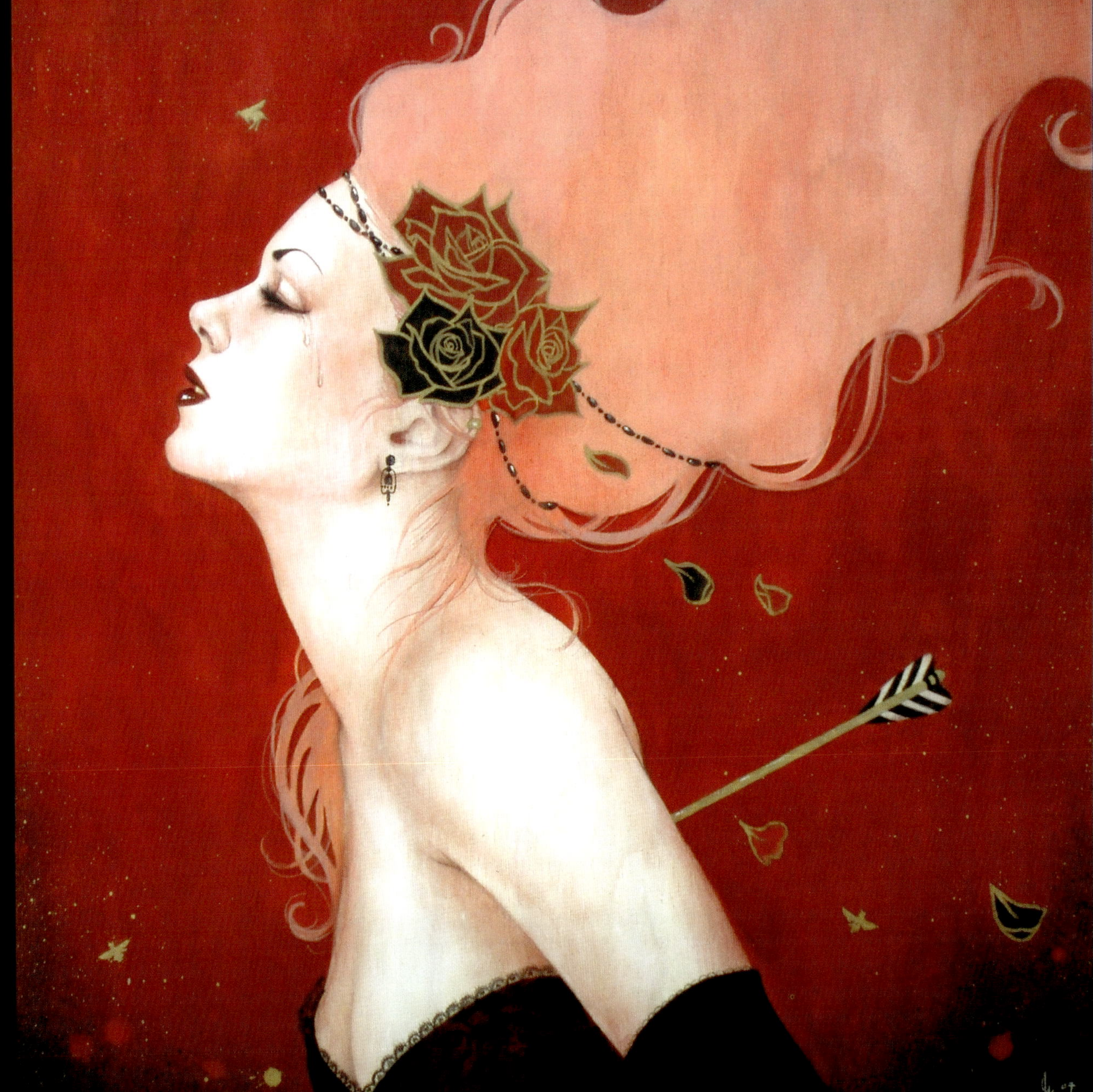

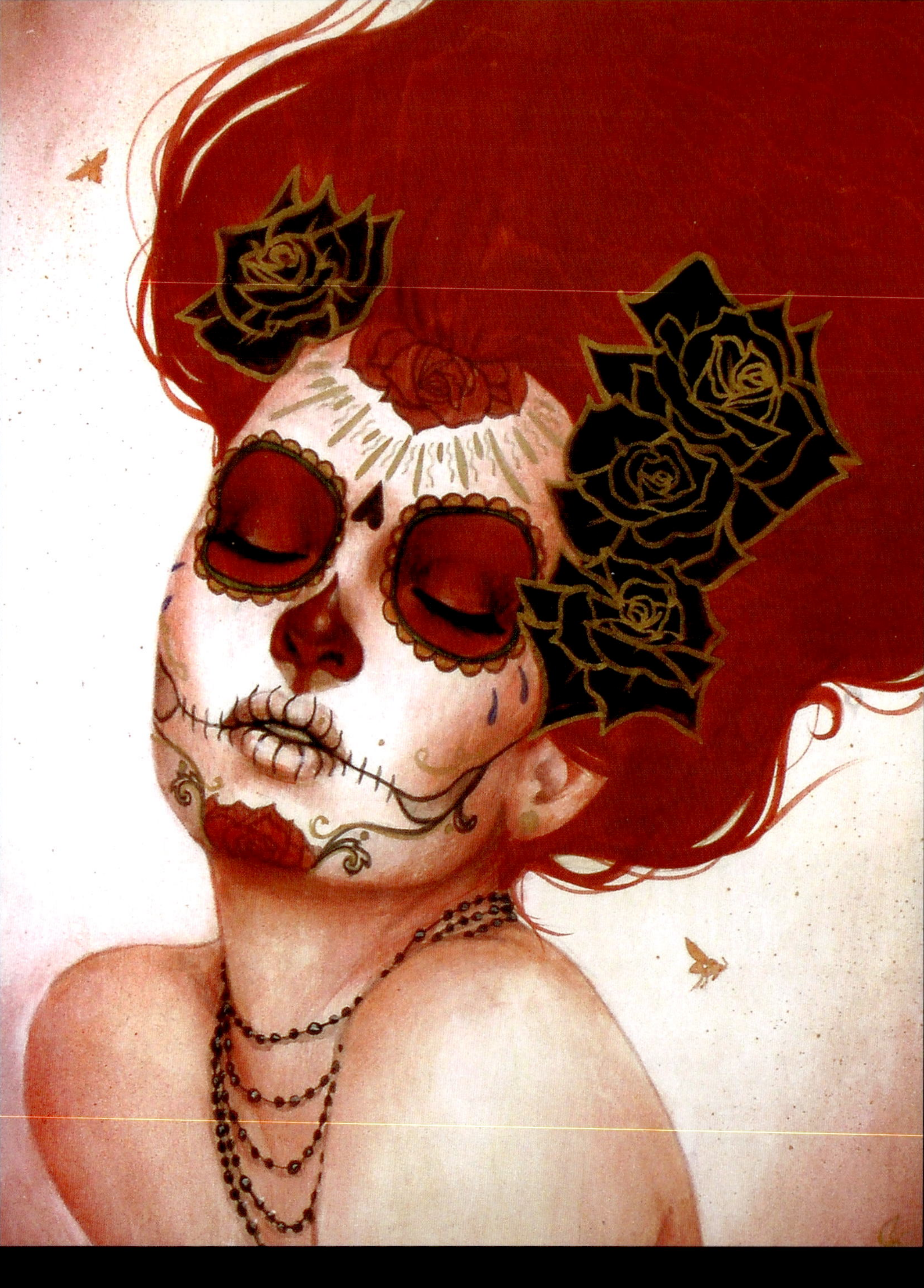

Above: *Untitled;* 8 x 10 inches; acrylic on wood panel

Right: *Panama Red;* 24 x 24 inches; acrylic/mixed media on wood panel

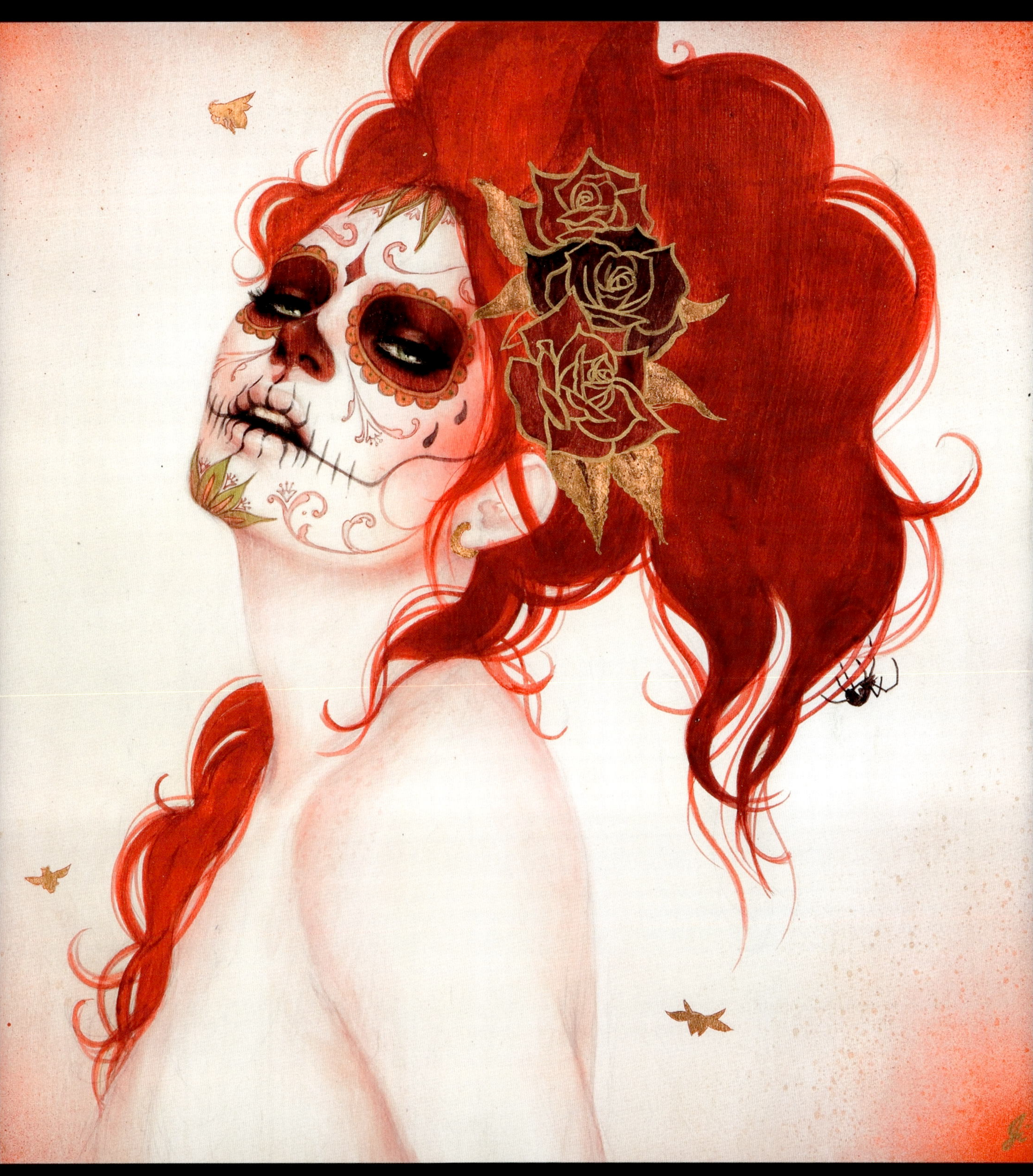

Sylvia Ji

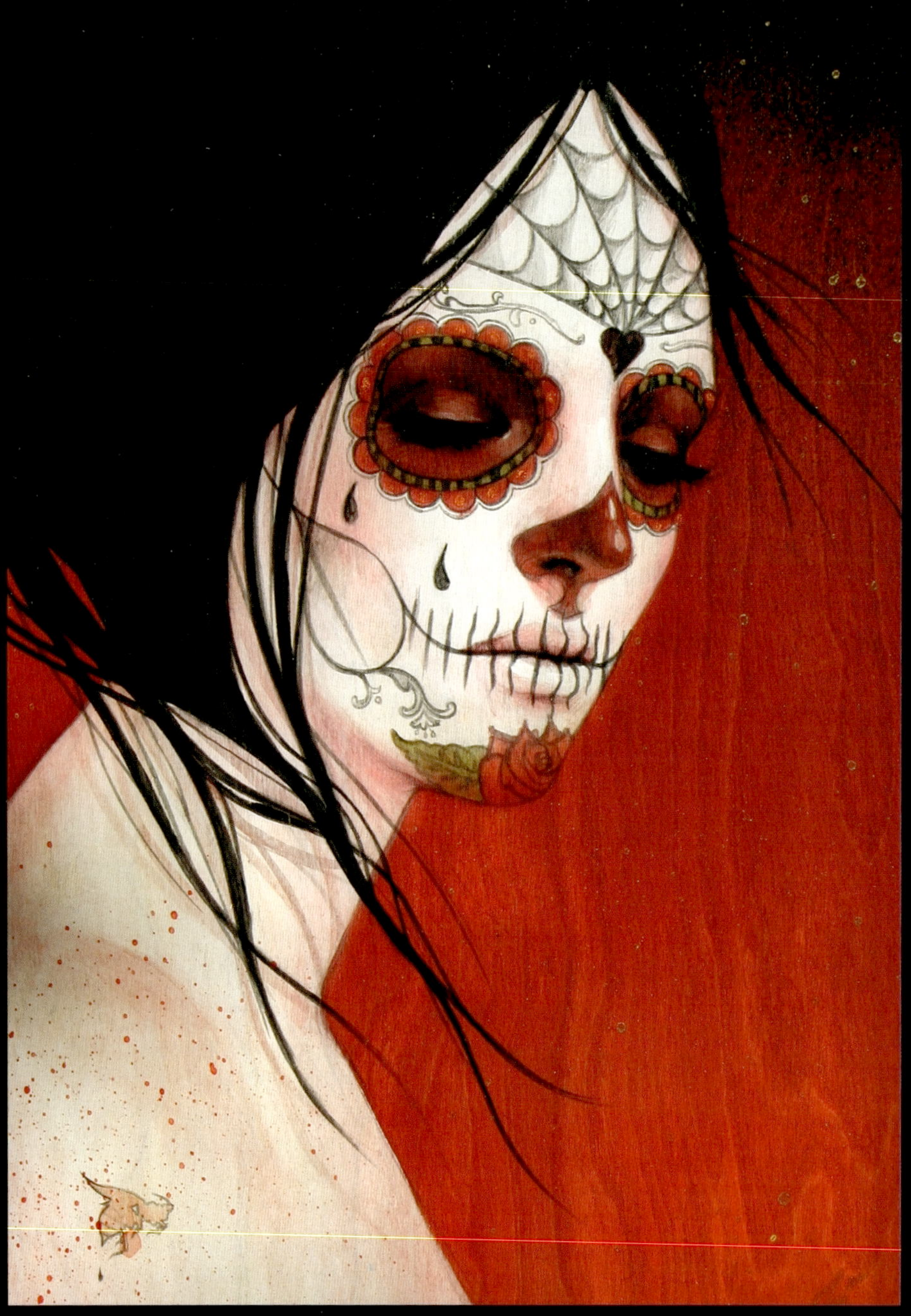

Above: *In My Sorry Way, I Love You;* 10 x 7 inches; acrylic/mixed media on wood panel

Right top: *Rose Catrina;* 48 x 24 inches; acrylic on wood panel

Right below: *Delfina y Maria (las Poquianchis);* 48 x 32 inches; acrylic/mixed media on wood panel

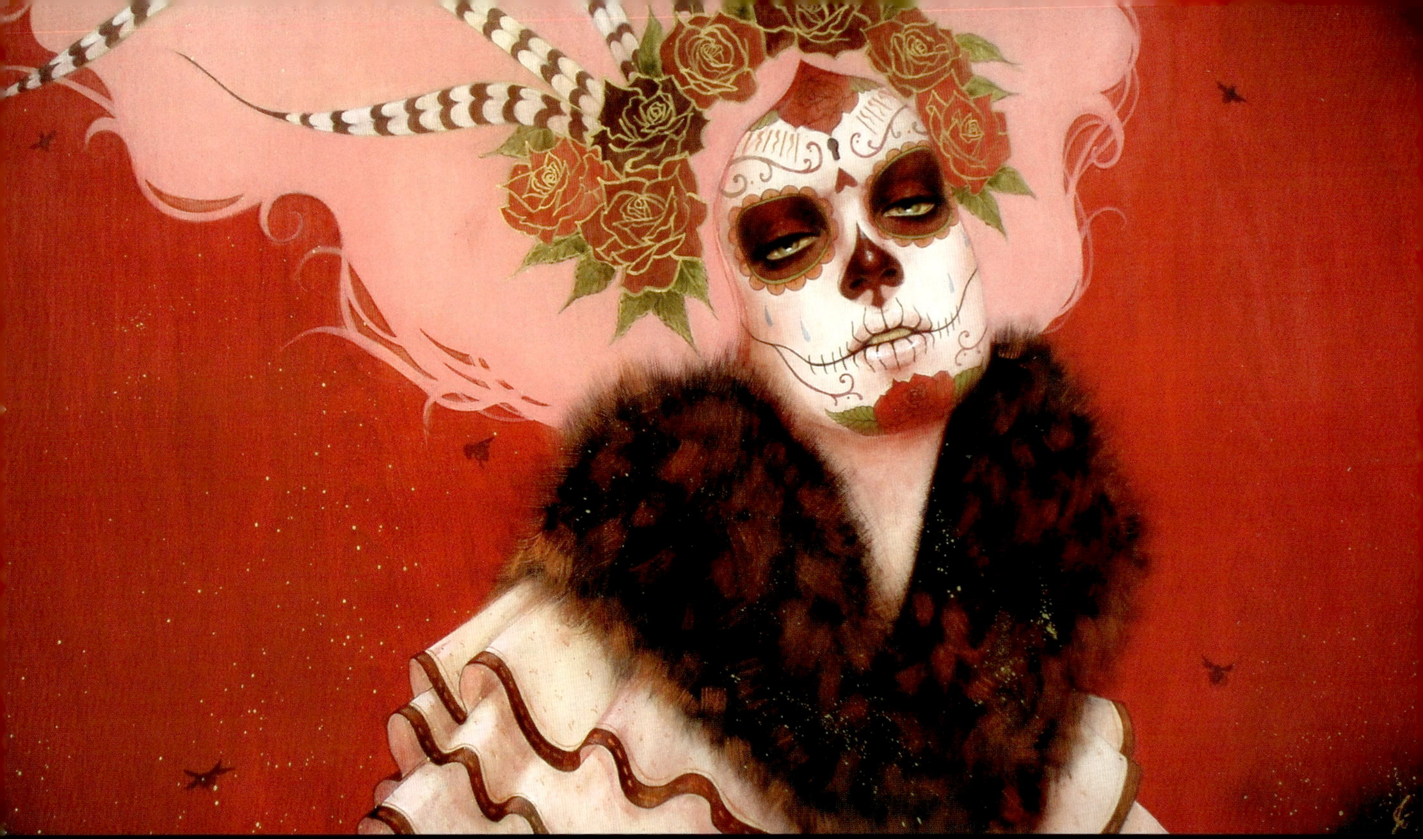

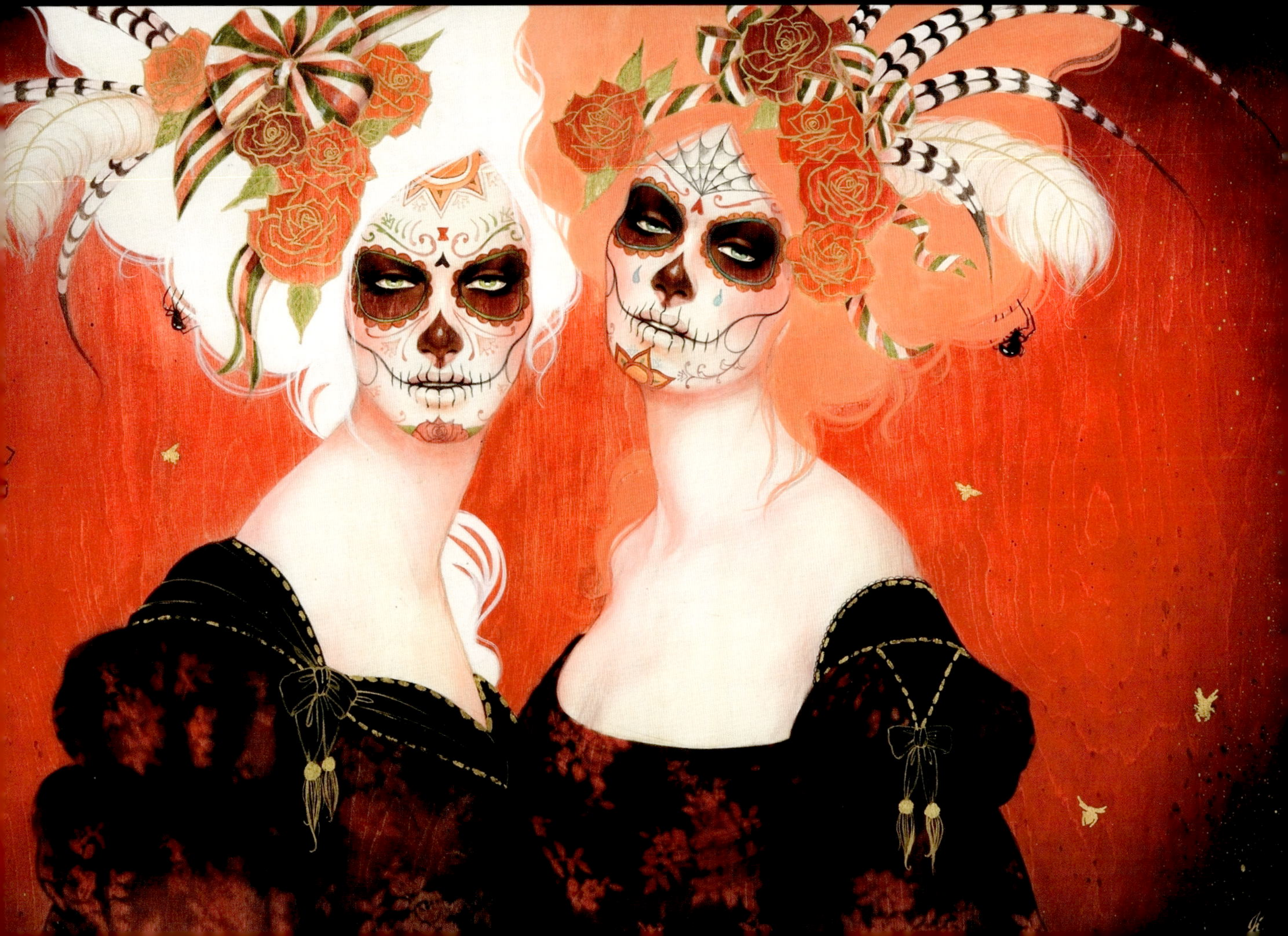

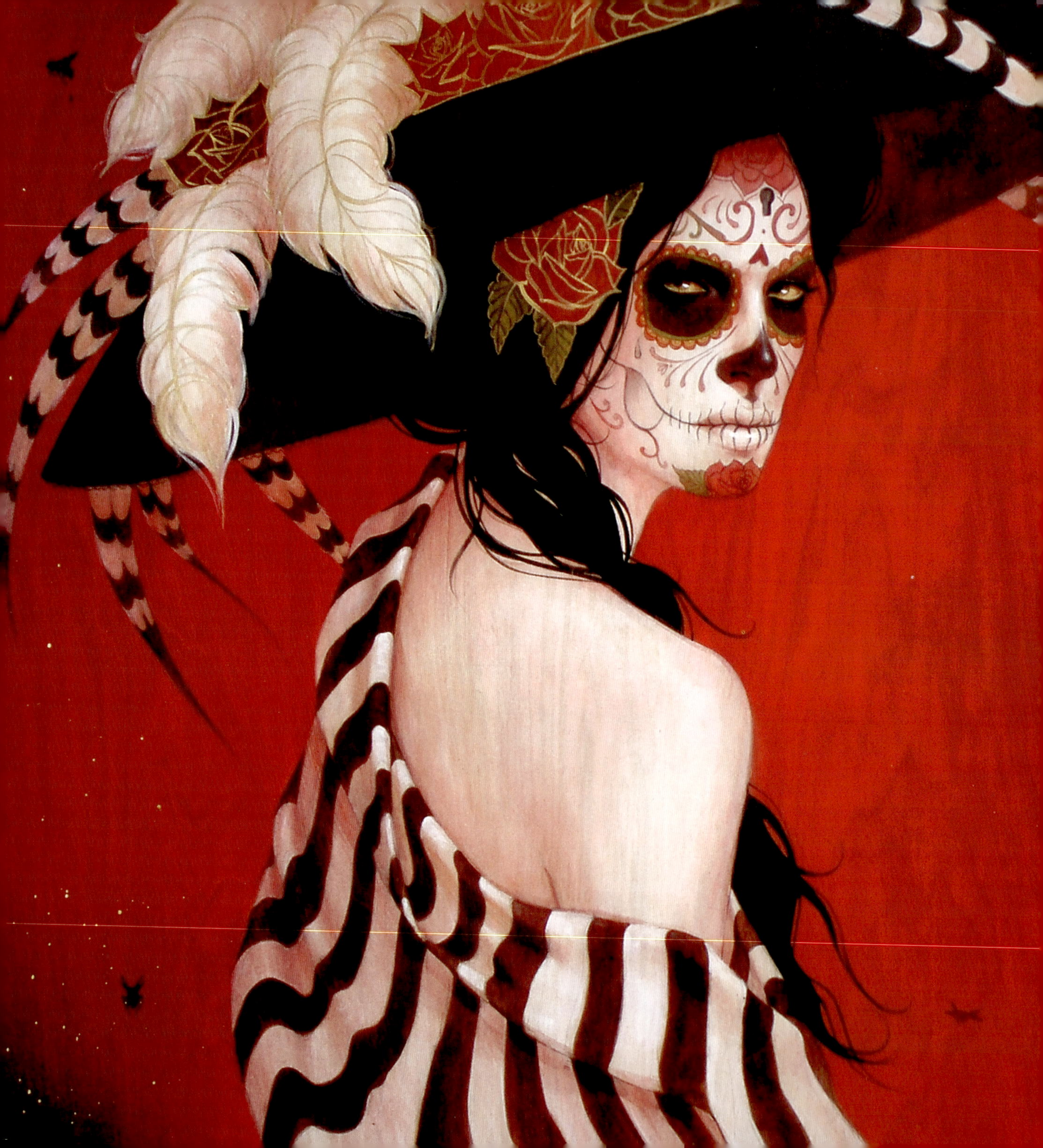

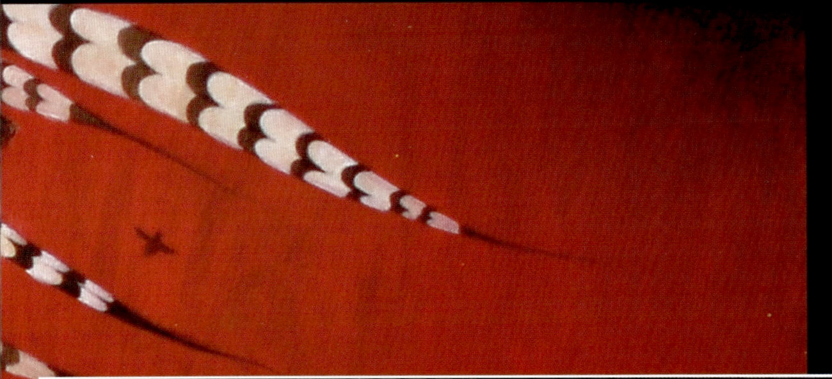

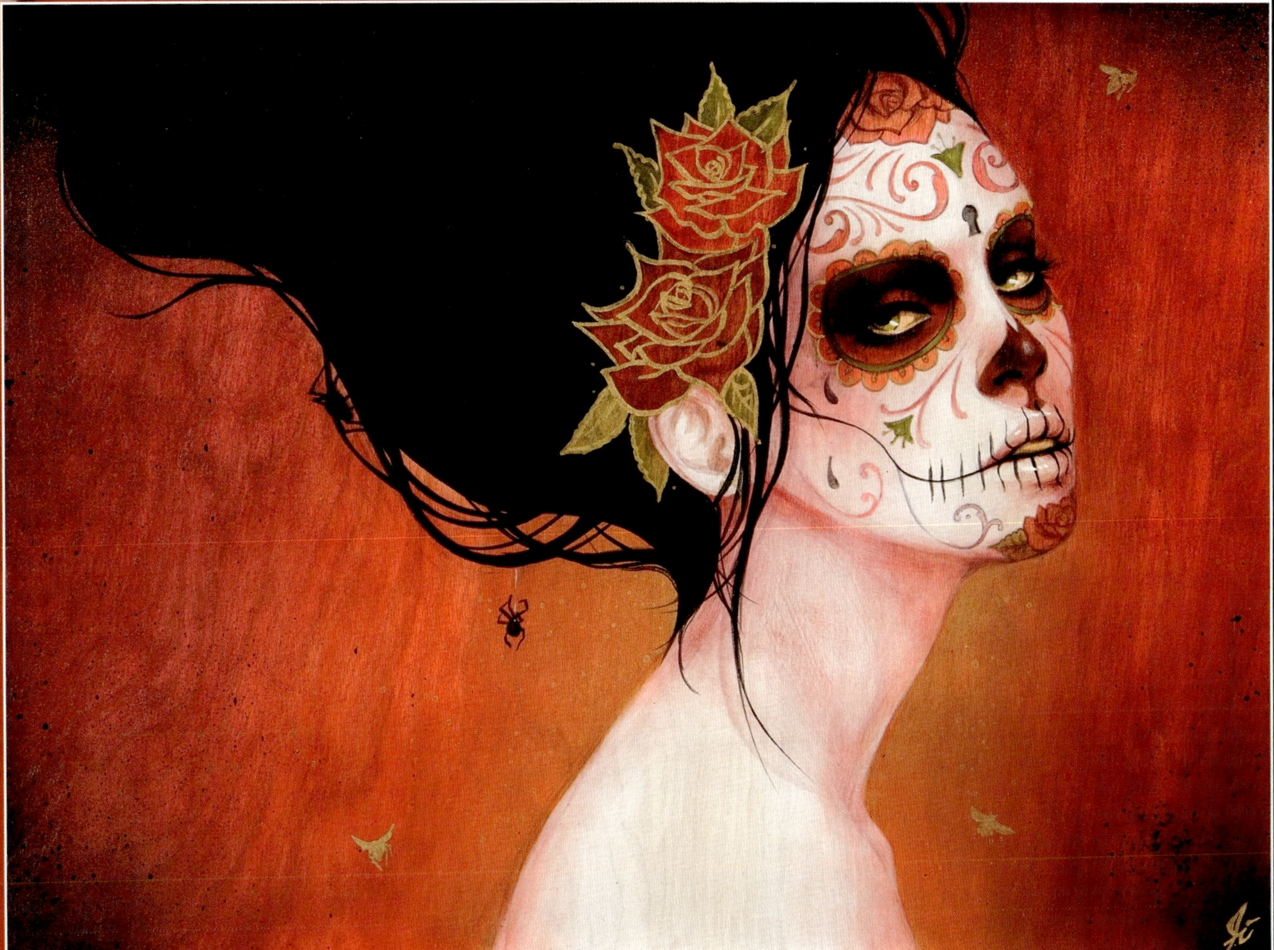

Left: *Catrina in Stripes;* 48 x 32 inches; acrylic/mixed media on wood panel

Above: *Untitled;* 18 x 24 inches; acrylic on wood panel

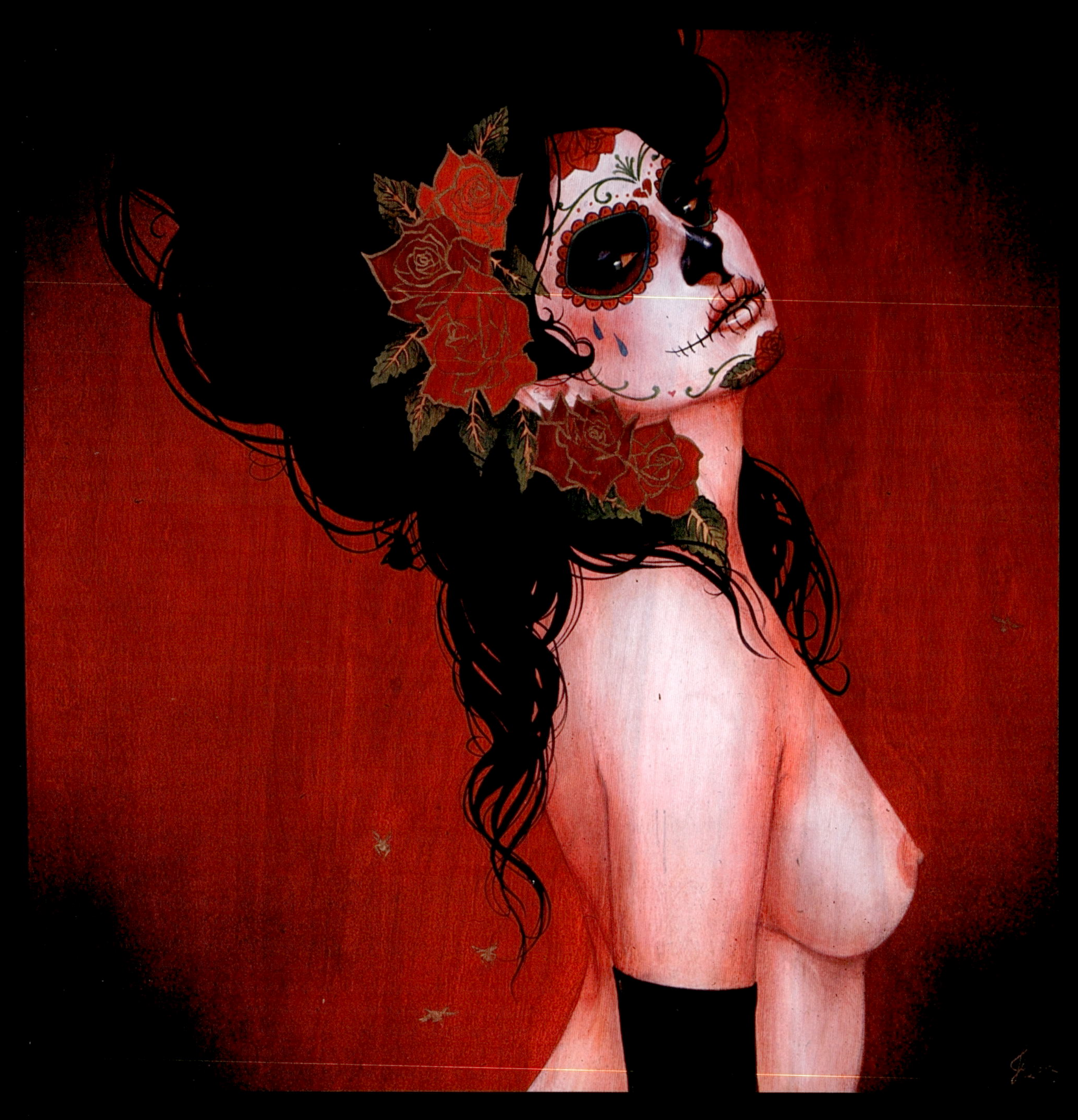

Rosa; 24 x 24 inches; acrylic on wood panel

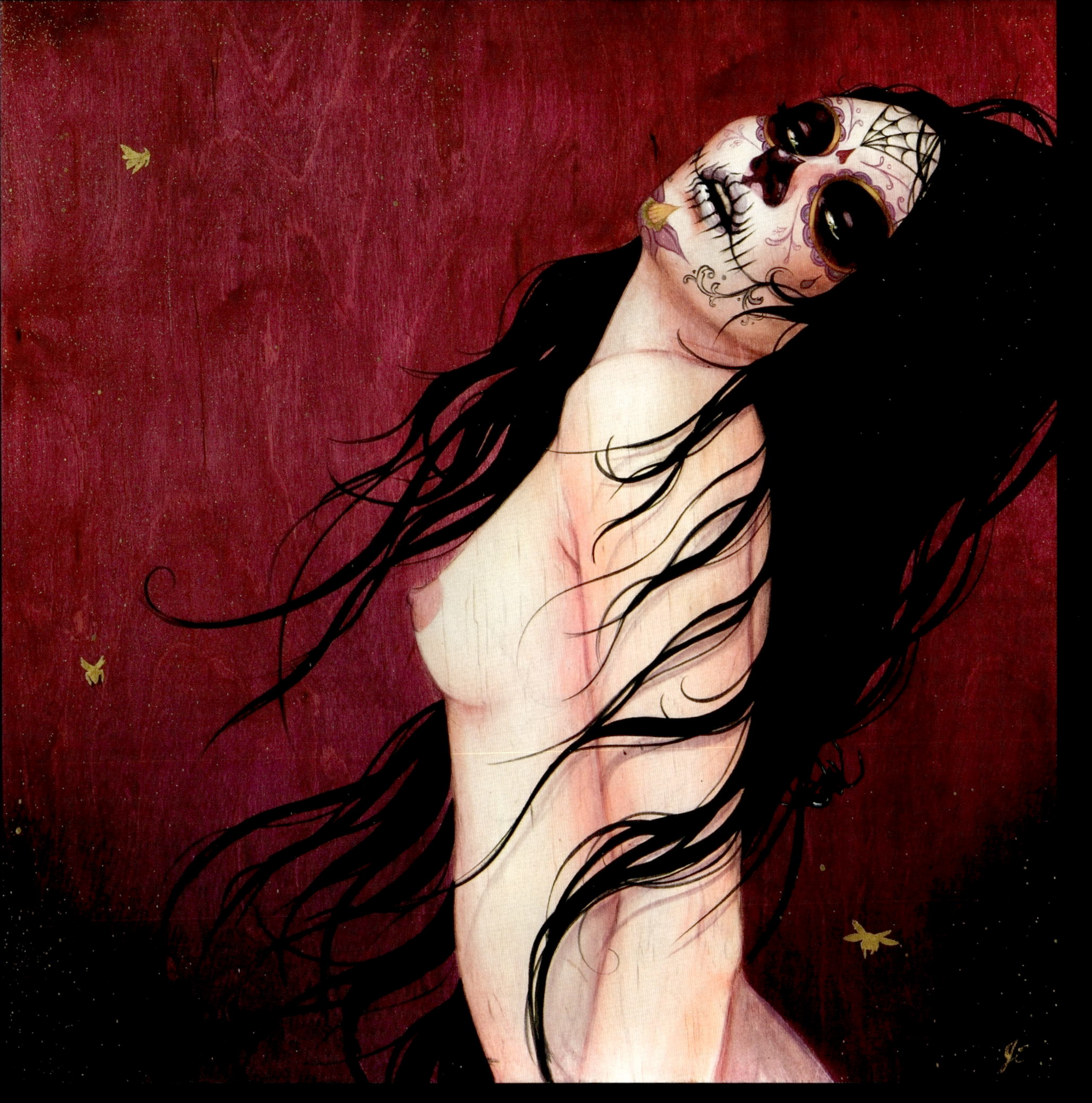

Purple Crush; 24 x 24 inches; acrylic/mixed media on wood panel

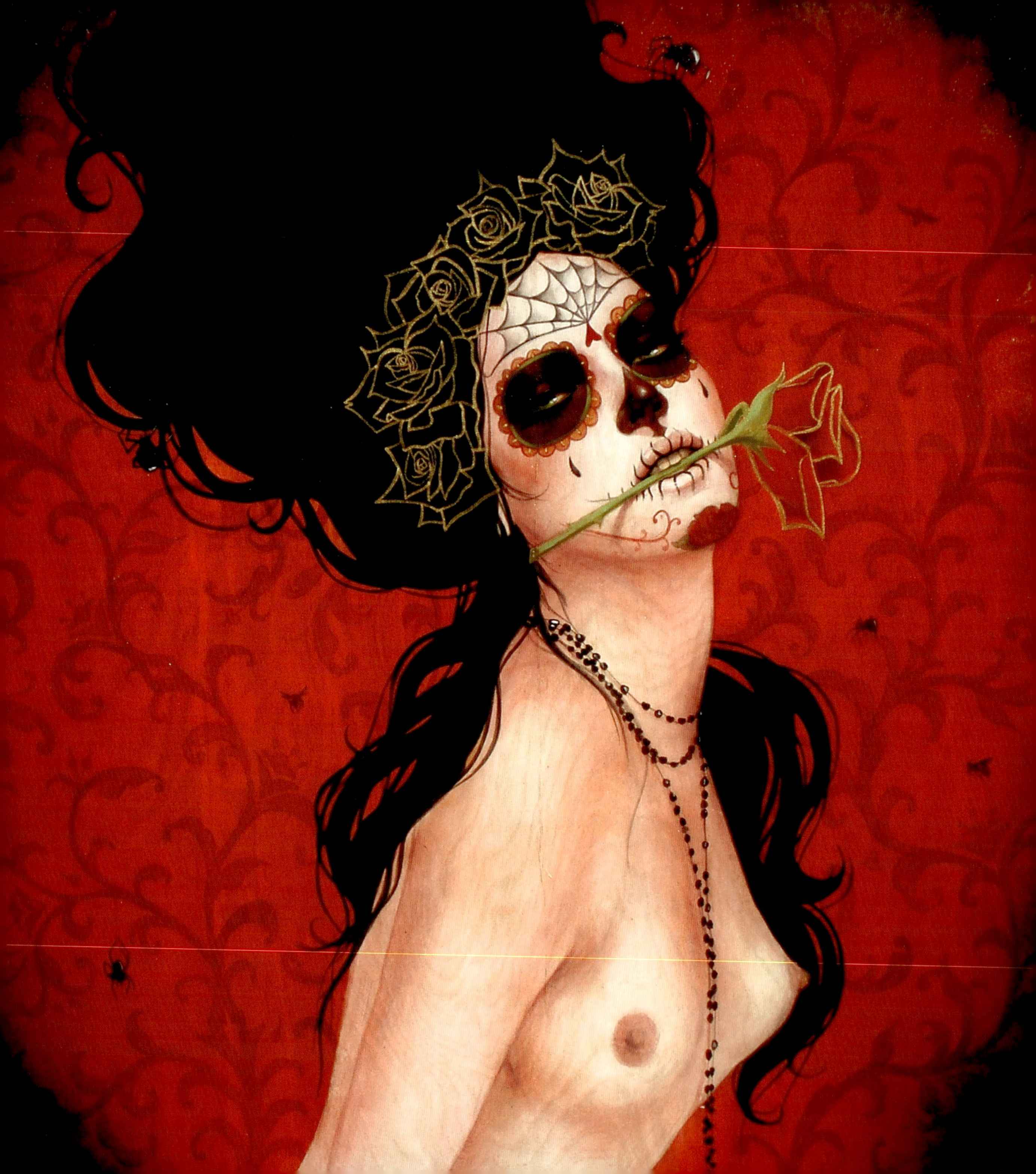

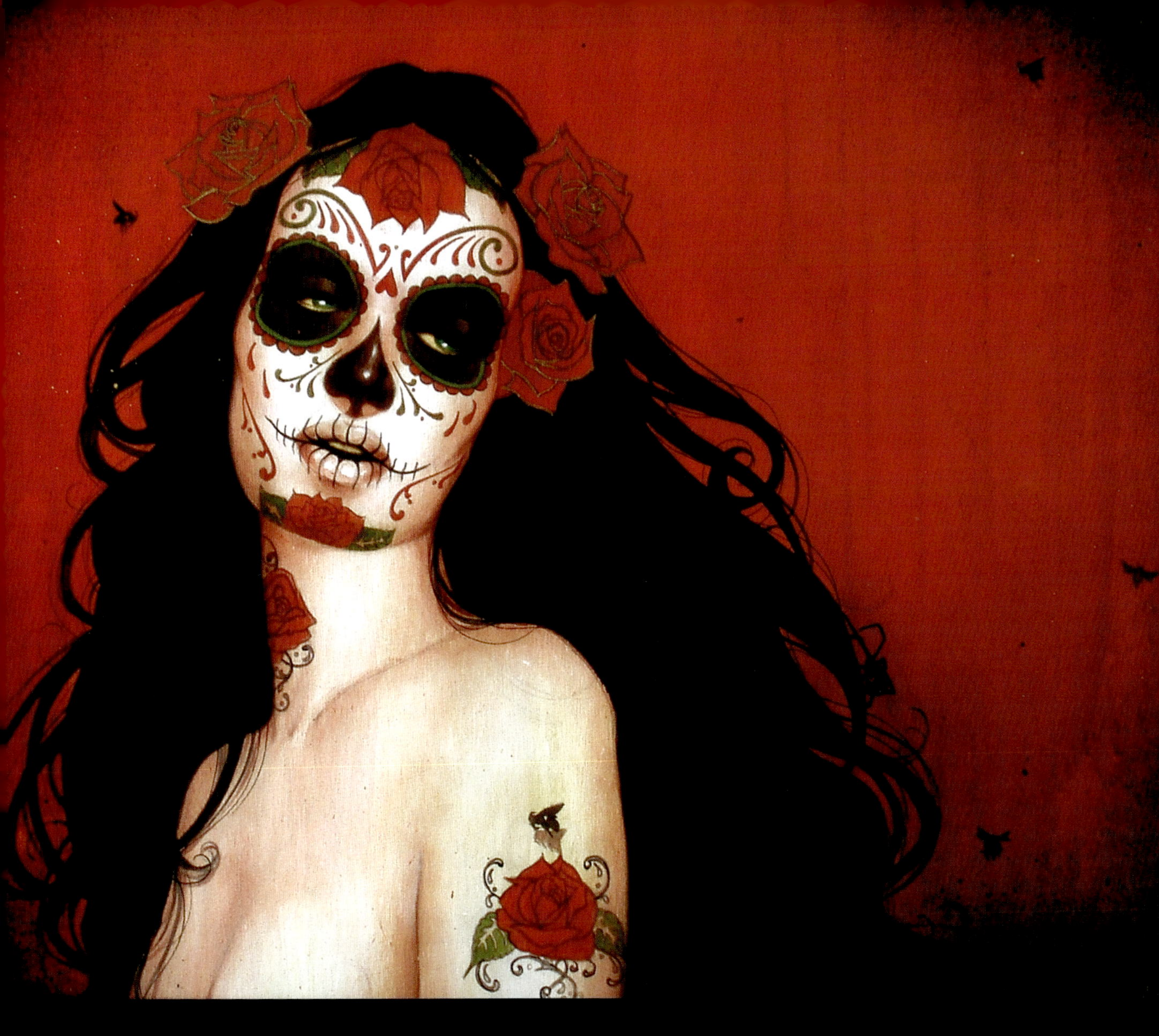

Left: *Por Vida;* 28 x 30 inches; acrylic on wood panel

Above: *There's Nothing Like Living in a Bottle;* 18 x 24 inches; acrylic/mixed media on wood panel

2009–2010
BEAUTY AND DECAY

The next body of "Catrina" works evolved with a more distinct sense of textile patterns and ornamental motifs, but they remained awash with red; I also increased my use of gold leaf.

It was during this time that I moved away for a while from the "Day of the Dead" images and began to explore other areas. However, the pull towards this subject matter remains constant, and though I may sometimes reject it, it creeps back into my thoughts and work.

Sylvia Ji

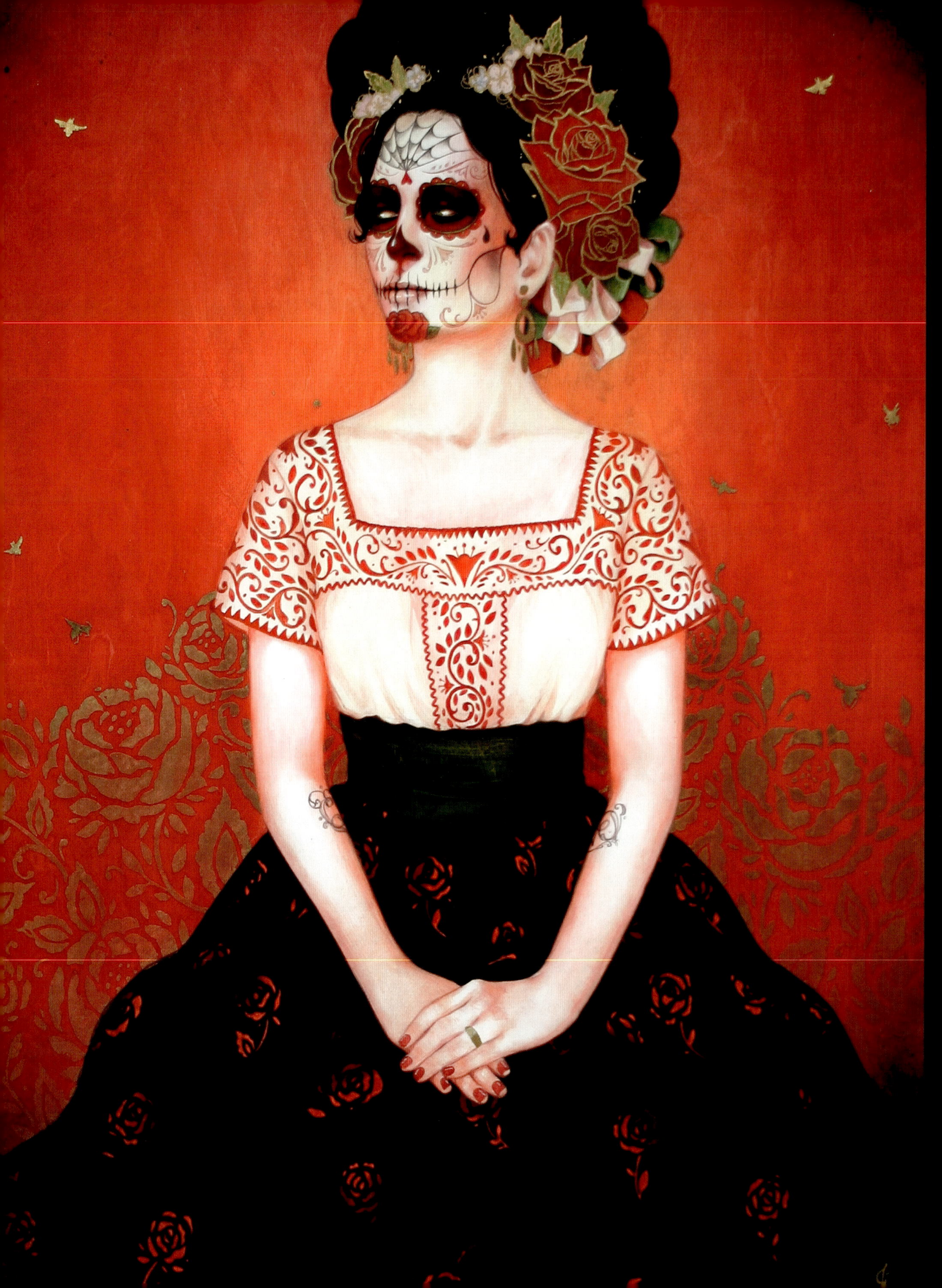

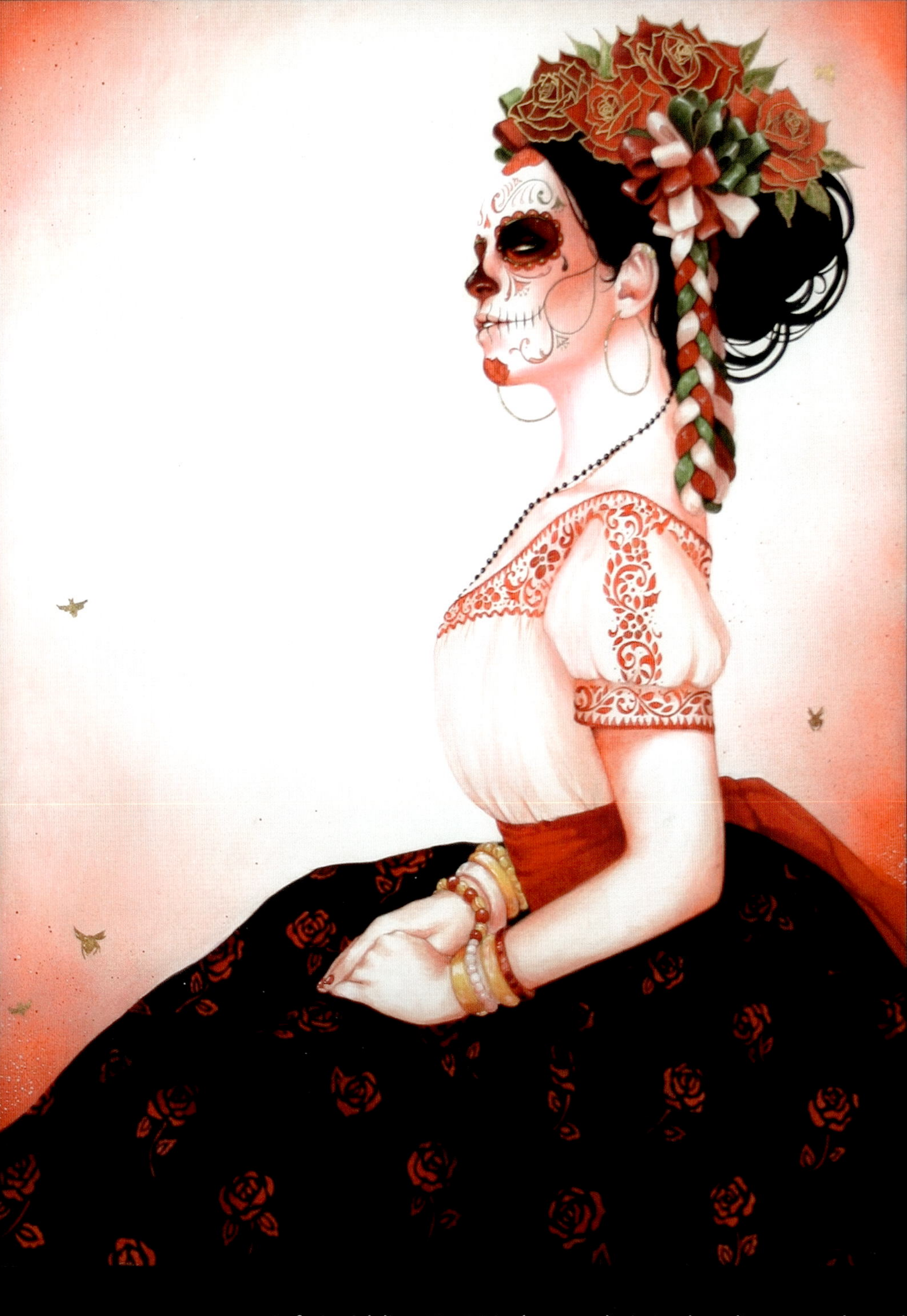

Left: *La Adelita;* 40 x 30 inches; acrylic/mixed media on wood panel

Above: *La Dama de Honor;* 40 x 30 inches; acrylic/mixed media on wood panel

Sylvia Ji

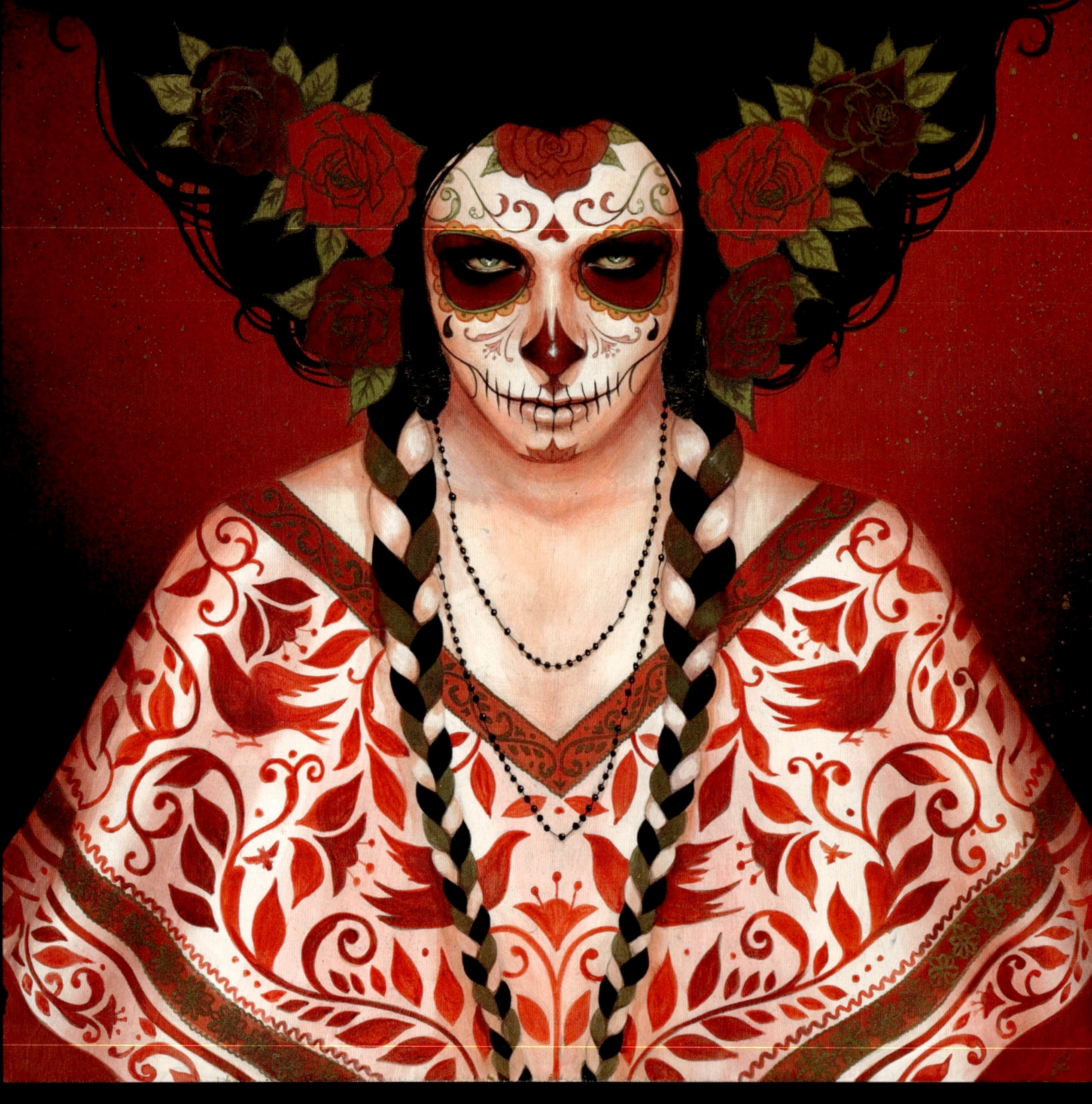

Above: *Red Quechquemitis;* 24 x 24 inches; acrylic/mixed media on wood panel

Right: *Catarina*; 80 x 36 inches; acrylic/mixed media on wood panel

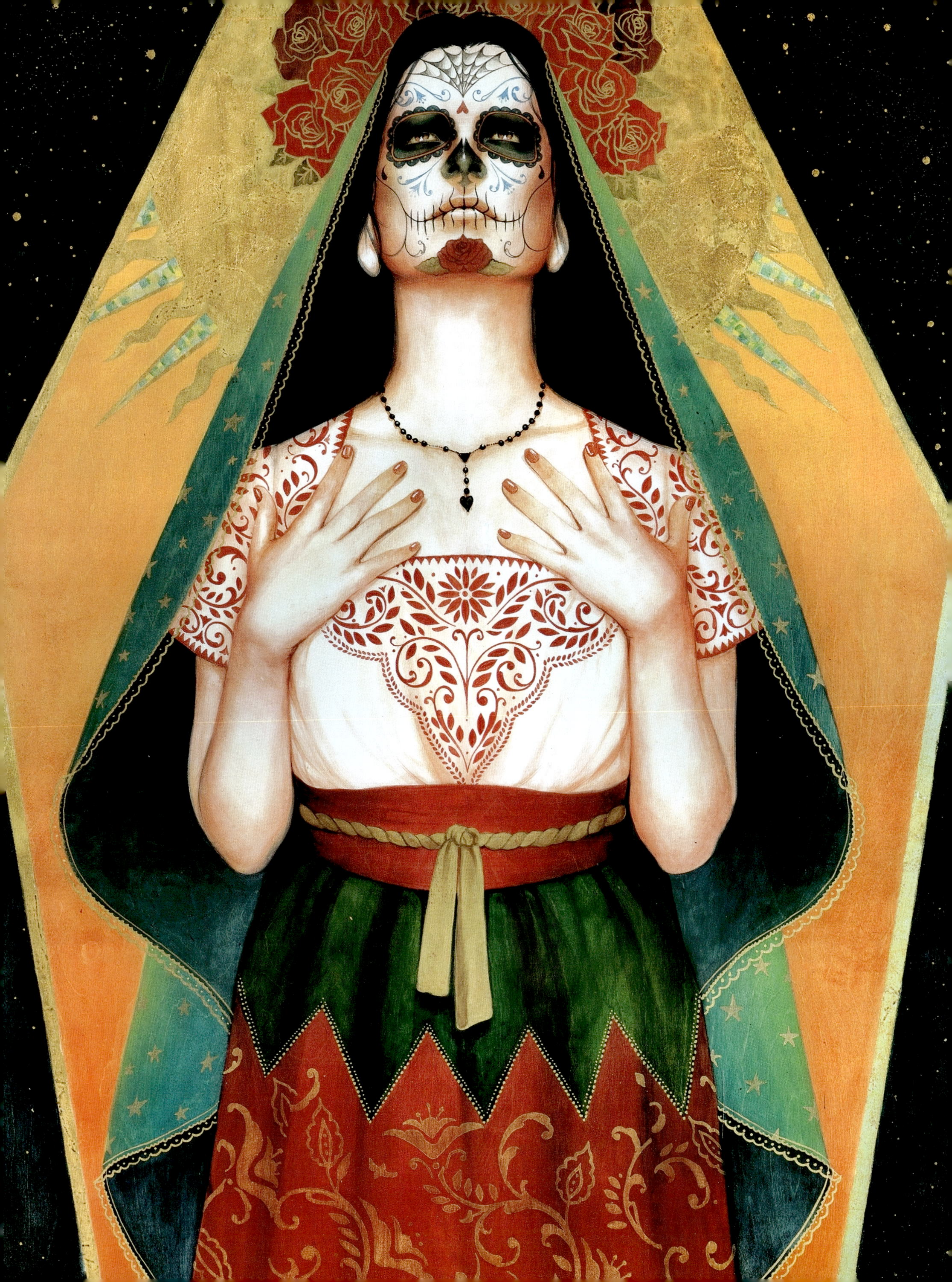

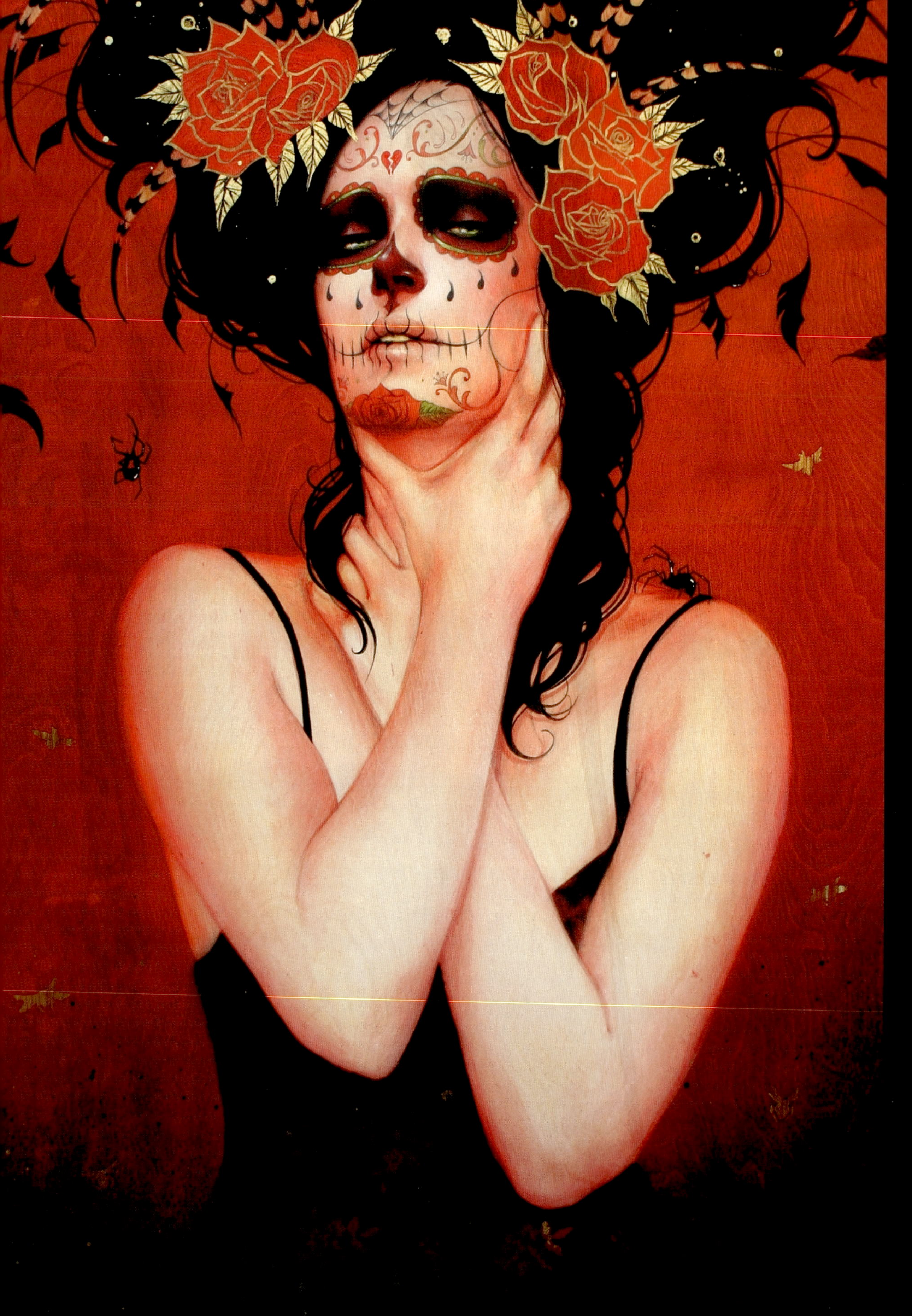

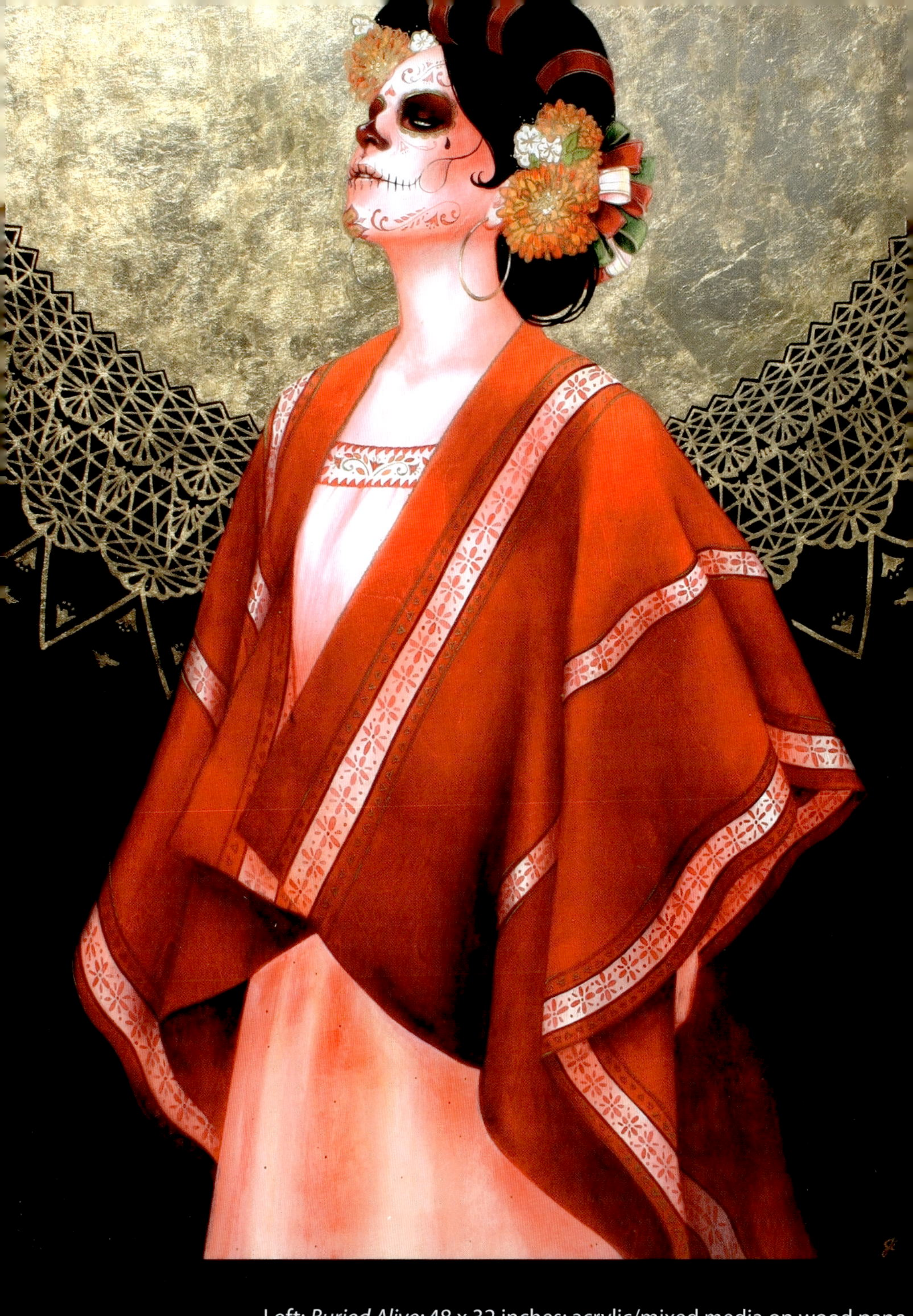

Left: *Buried Alive;* 48 x 32 inches; acrylic/mixed media on wood pane[l]

Above: *Red Serape;* 40 x 30 inches; acrylic/mixed media on wood pane[l]

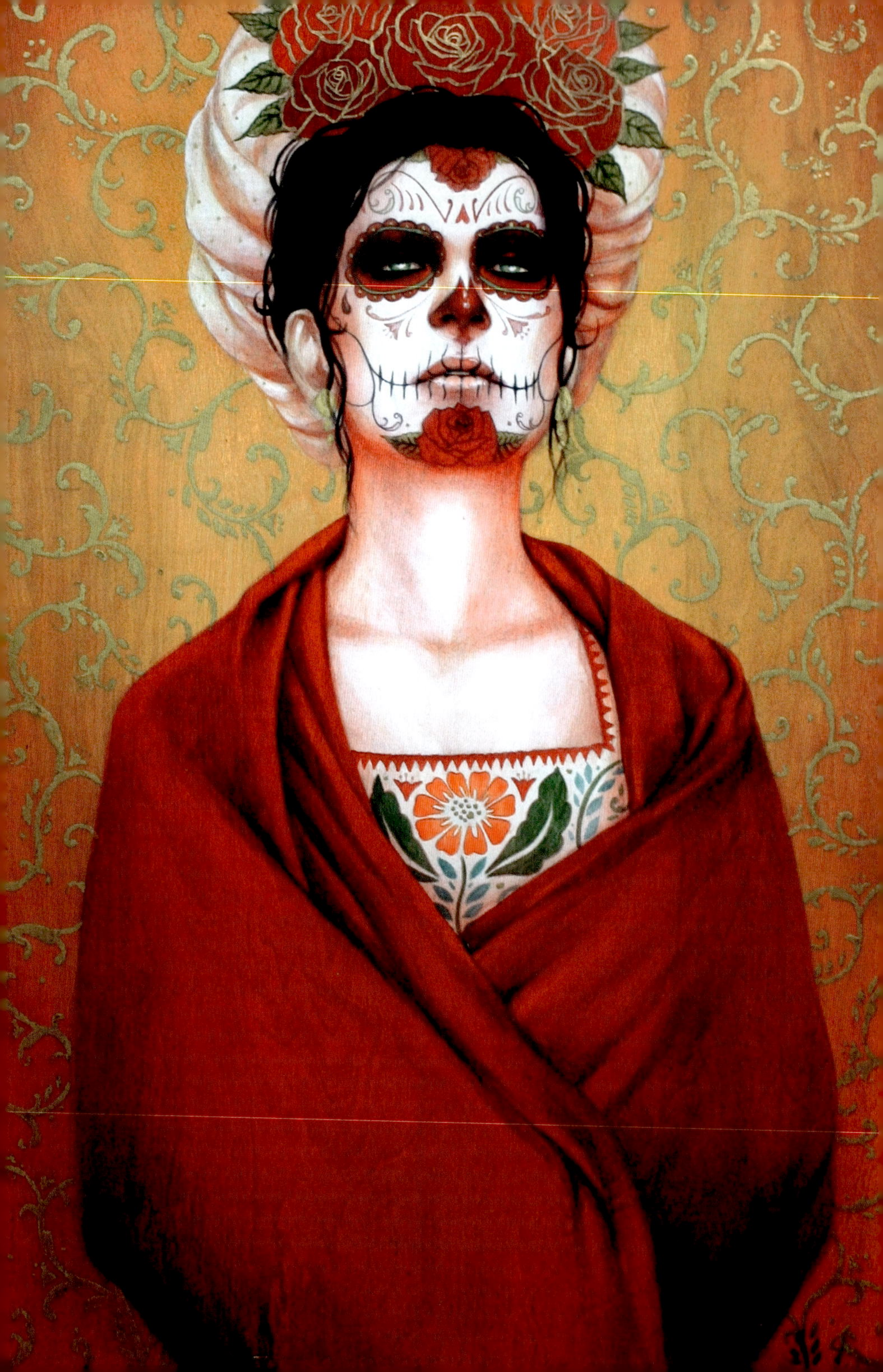

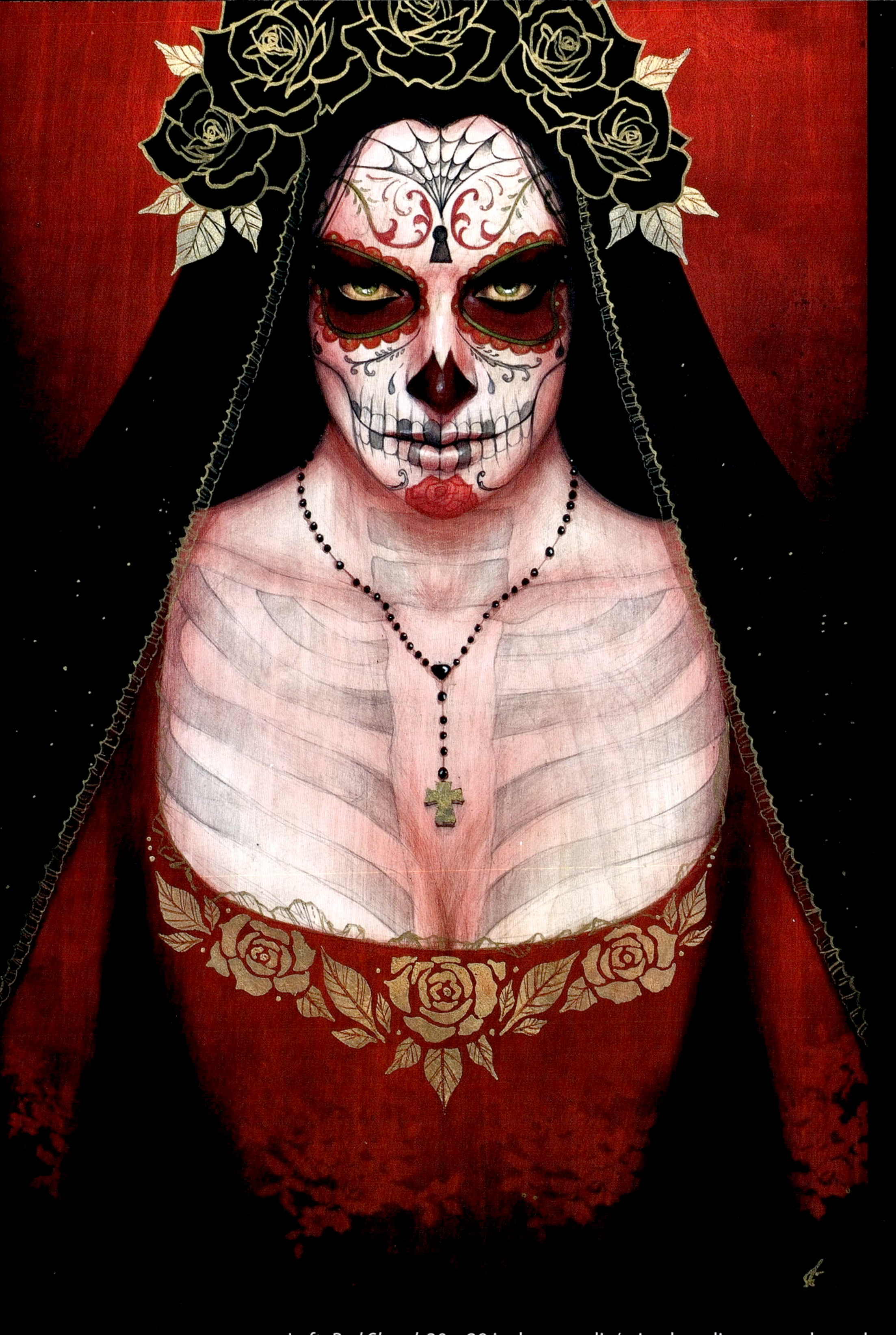

Left: *Red Shawl;* 30 x 20 inches; acrylic/mixed media on wood panel

Above: *Santa Muerte;* 30 x 20 inches; acrylic/mixed media on wood panel

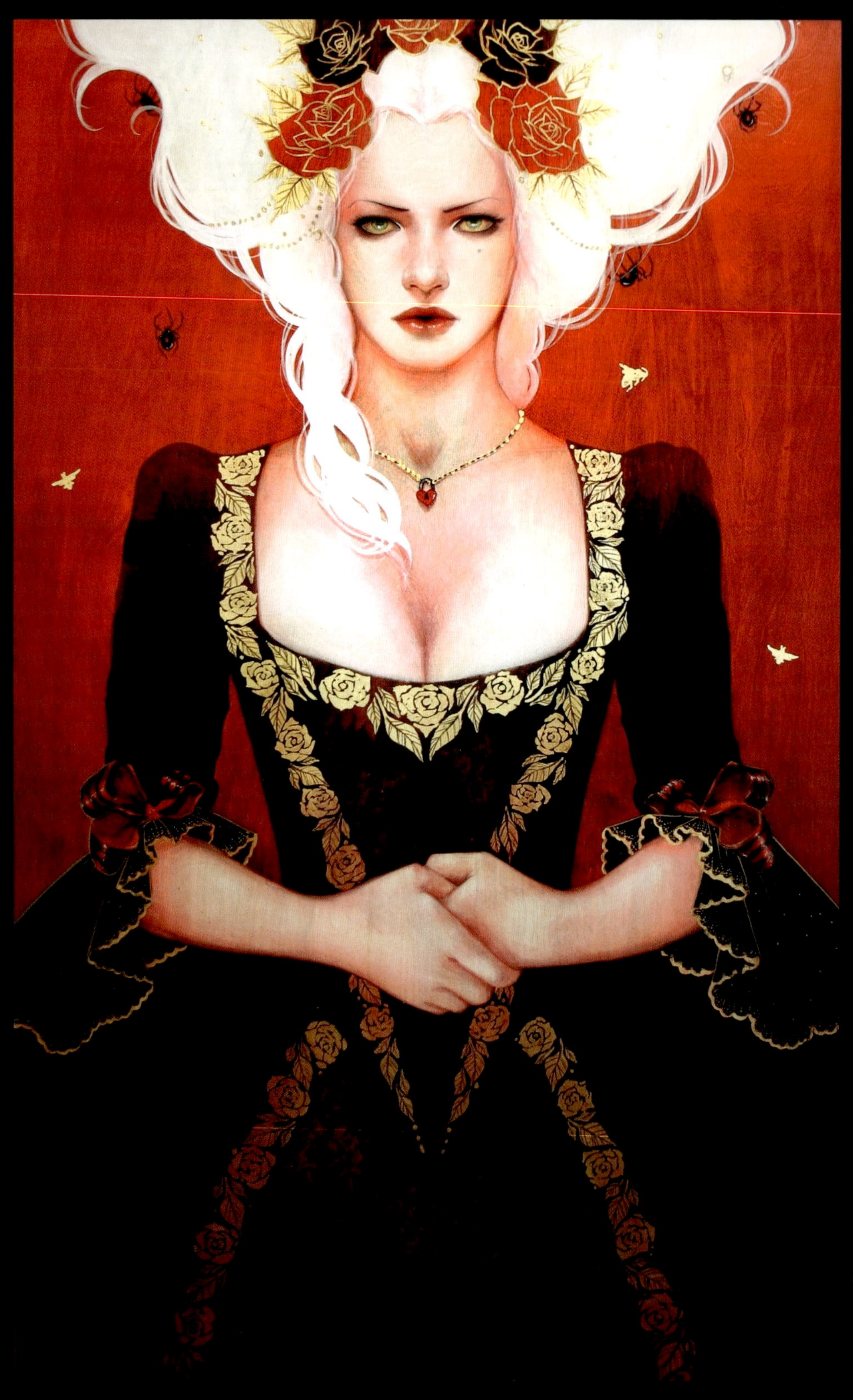

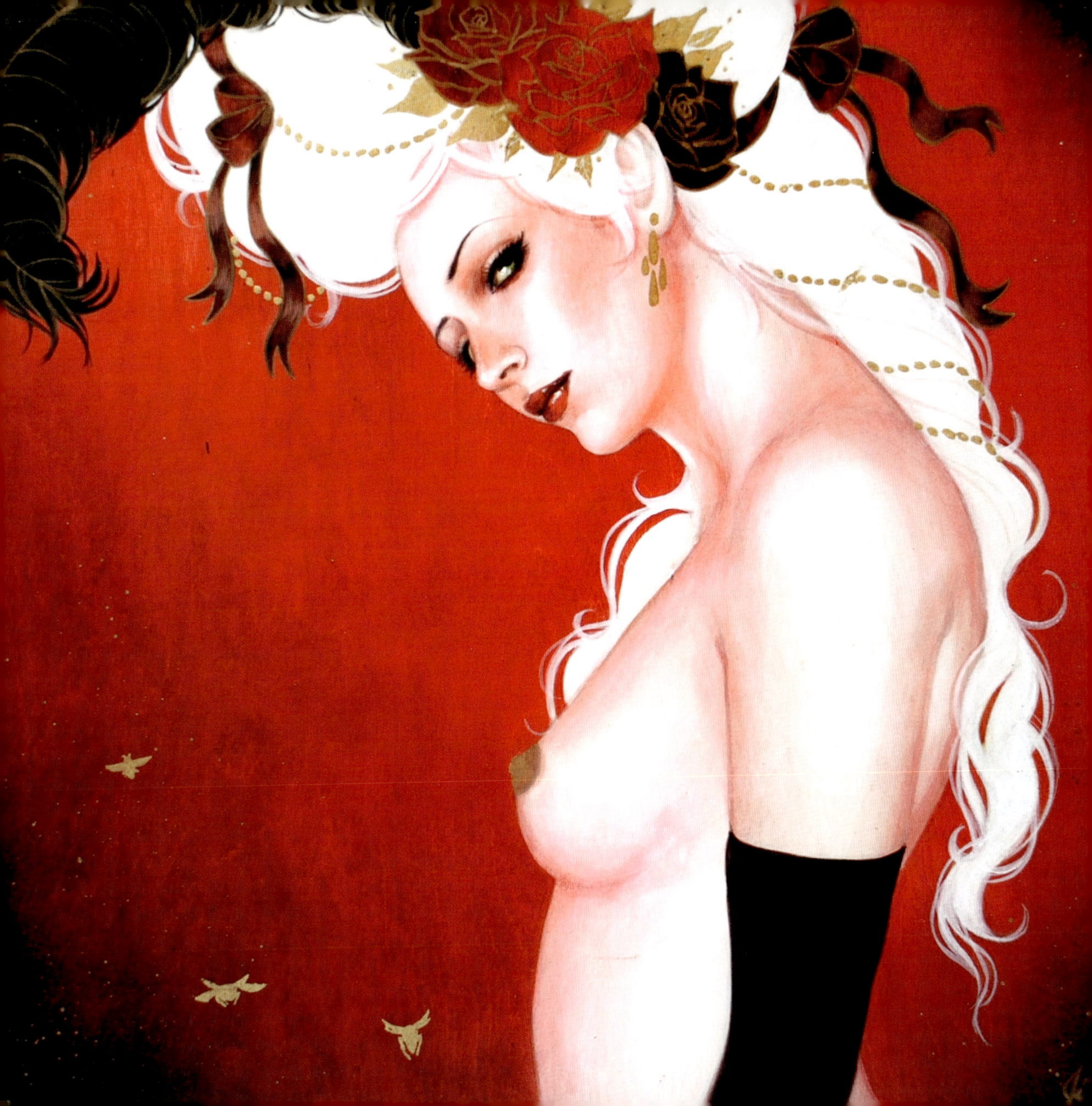

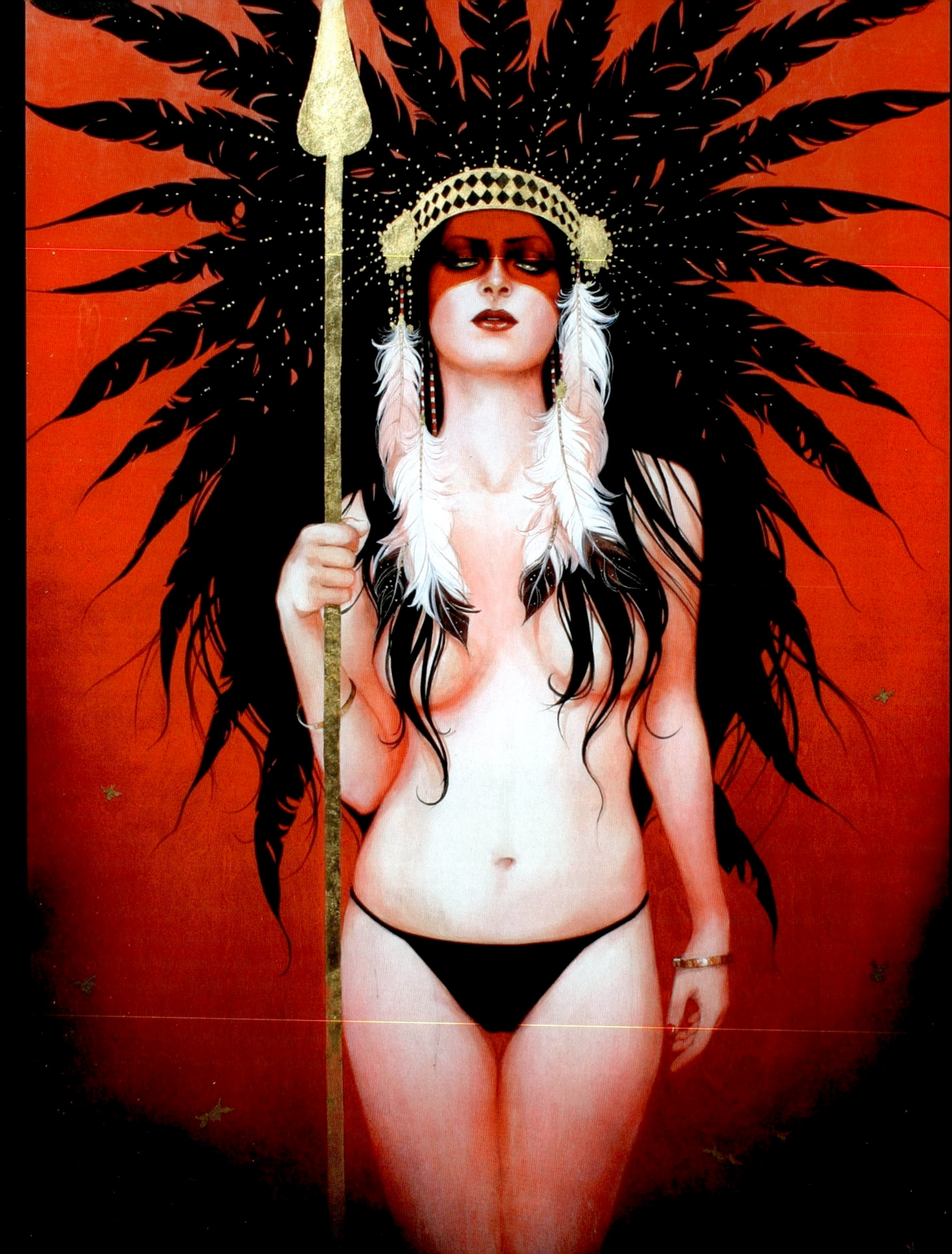

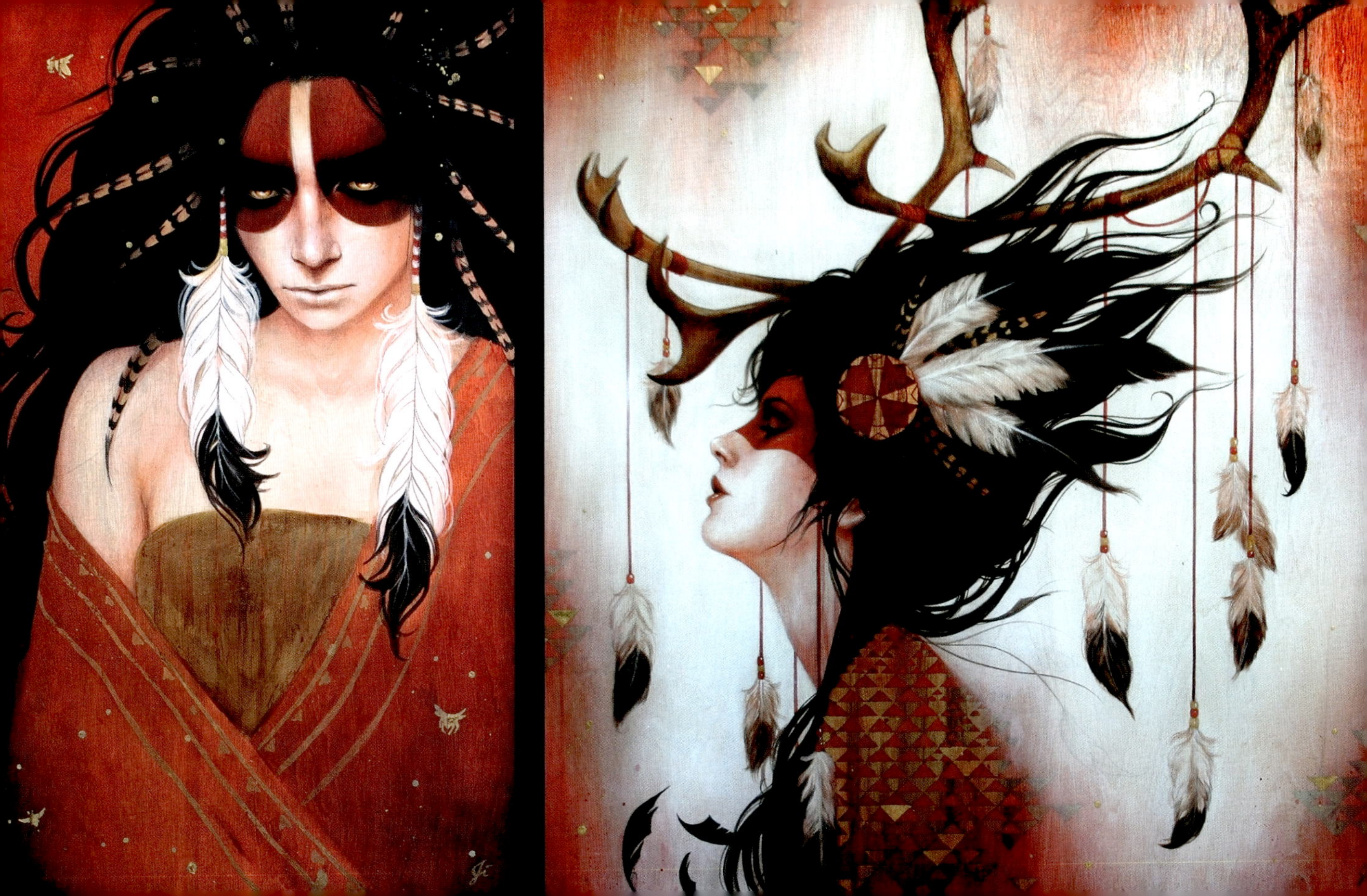

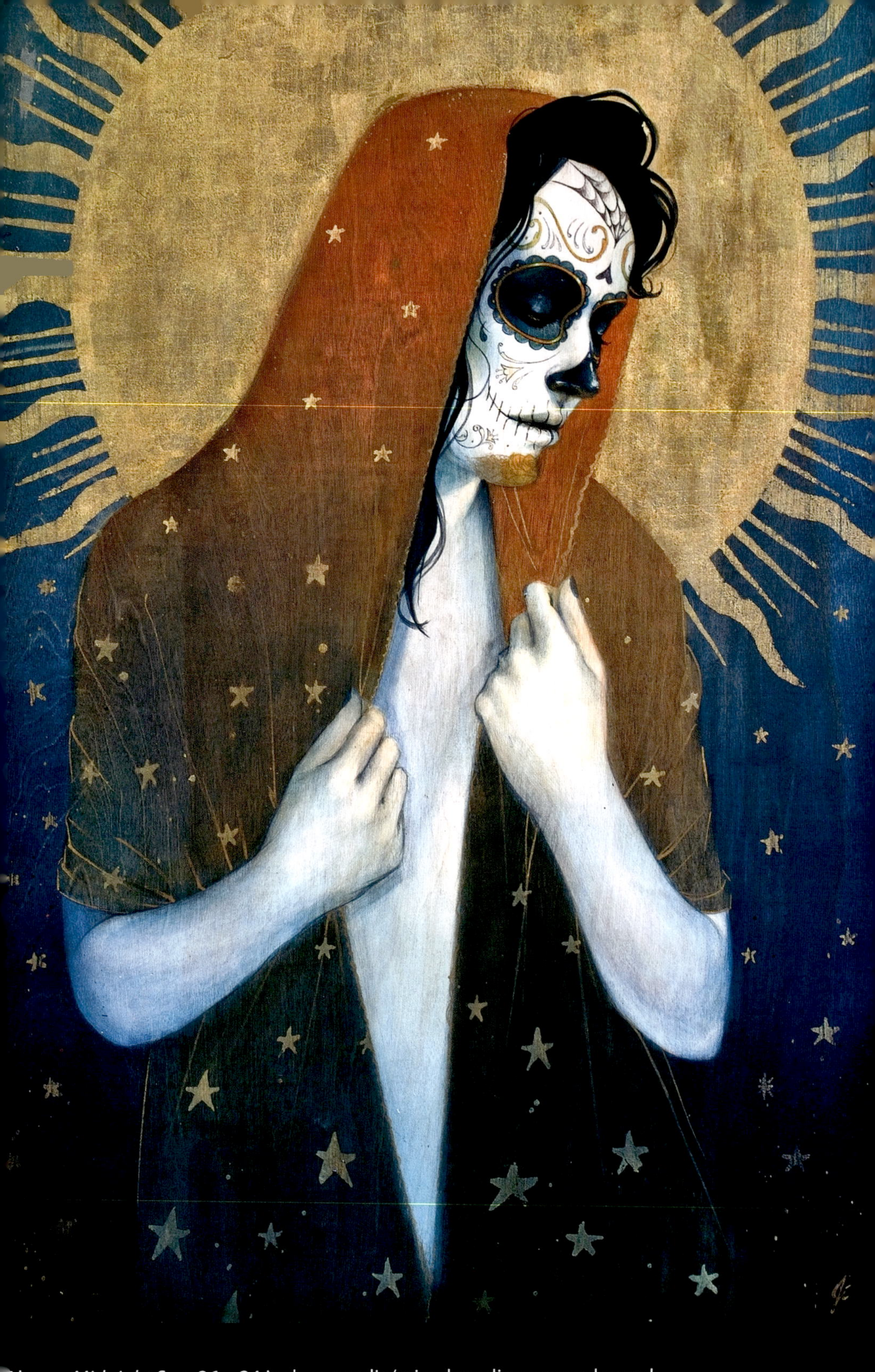

Above: *Midnight Sun*; 36 x 24 inches; acrylic/mixed media on wood panel

Right: *Flor del Muerto*; 32 x 18 inches; acrylic/mixed media on wood panel

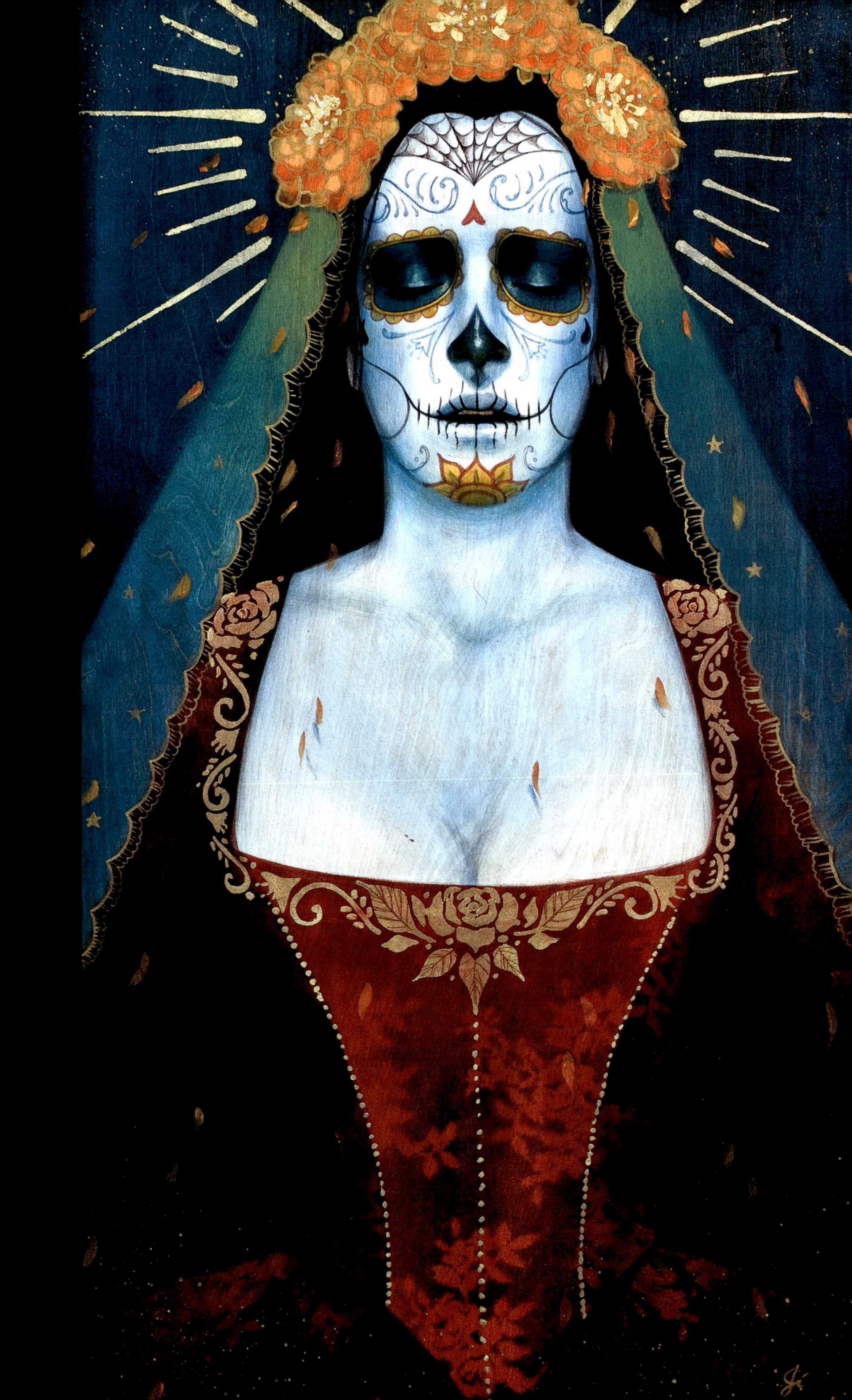

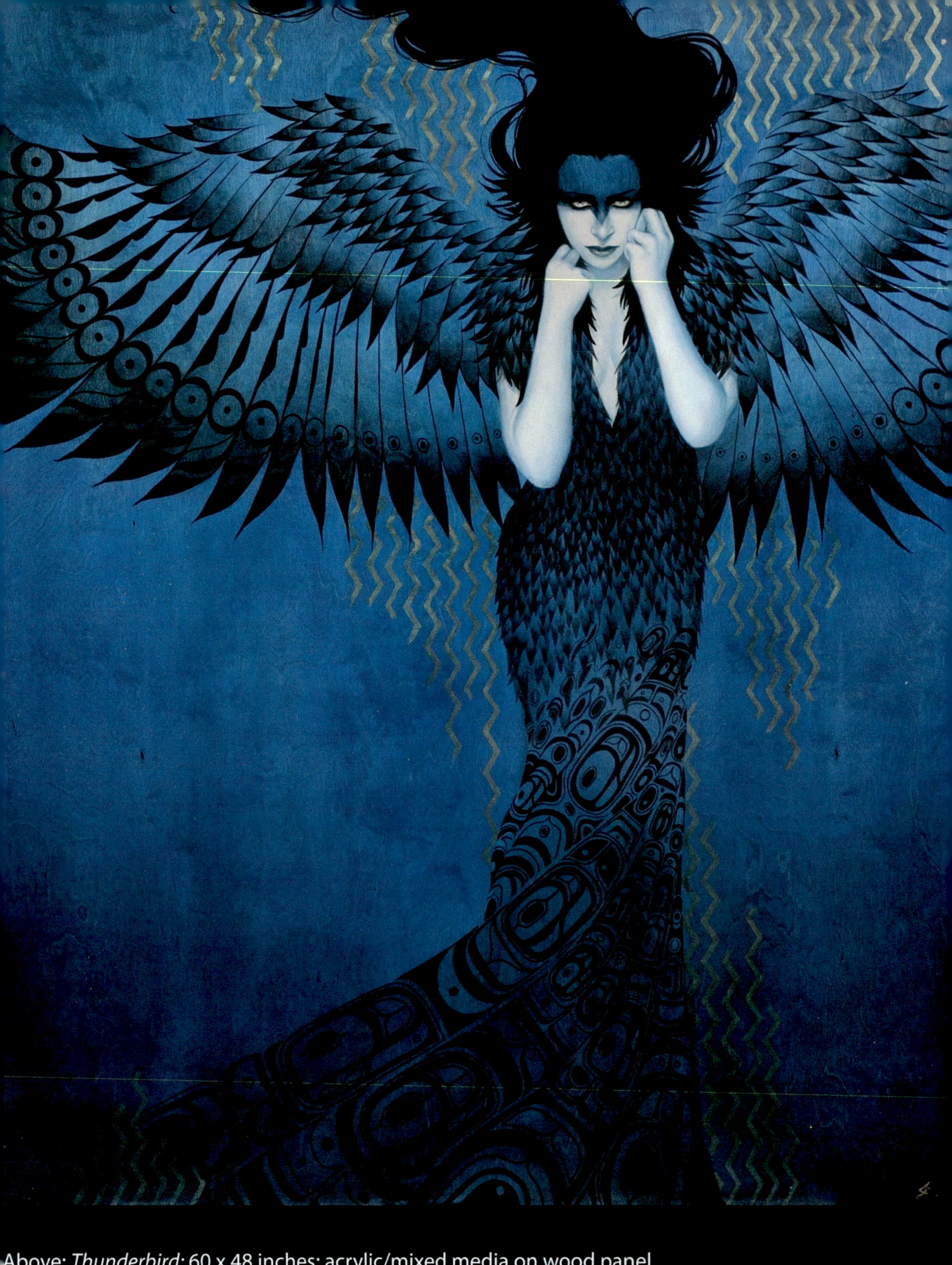

Above: *Thunderbird*; 60 x 48 inches; acrylic/mixed media on wood panel

Right: *The Bandit*; 48 x 36 inches; acrylic/mixed media on wood panel

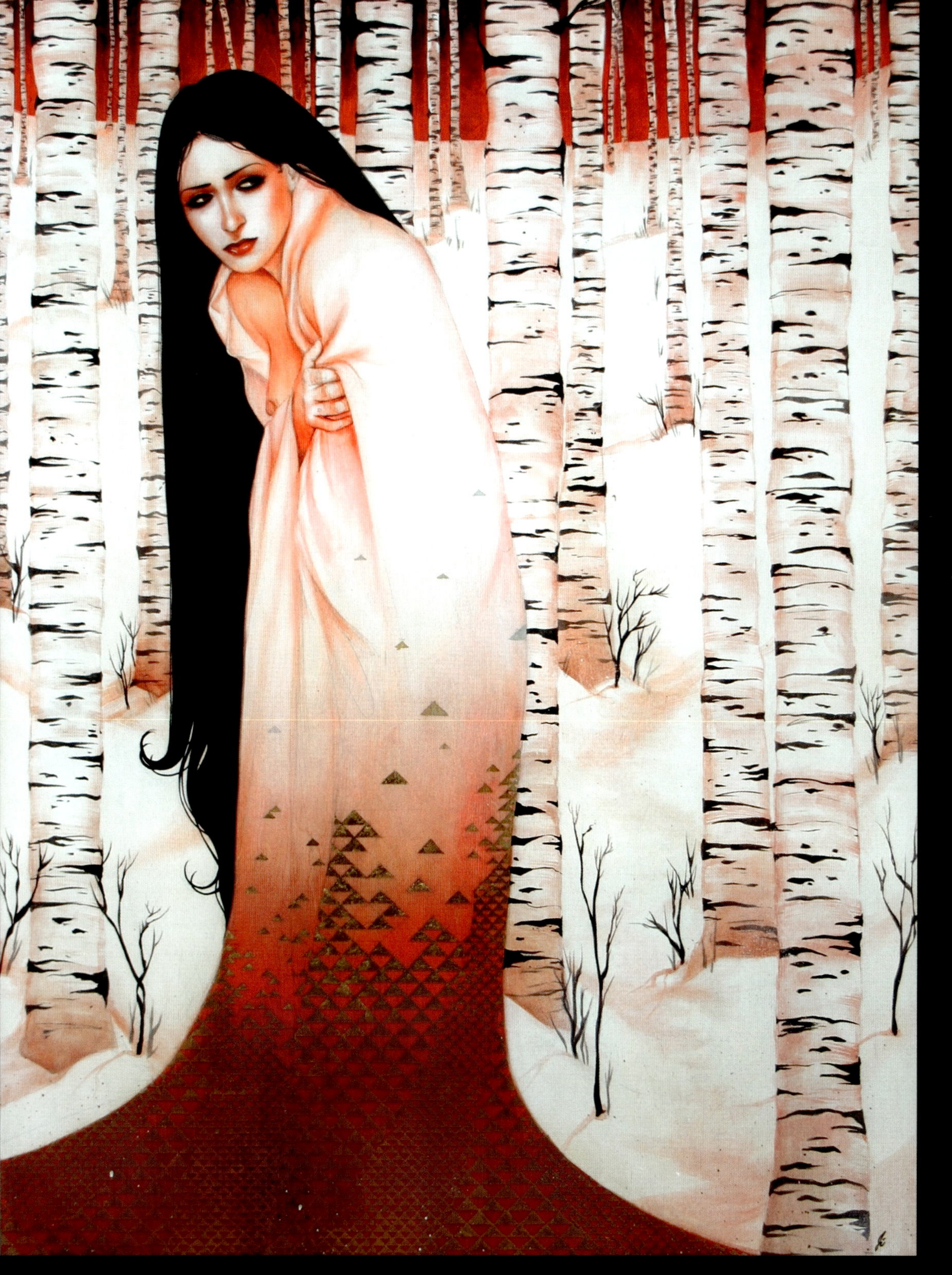

Sylvia Ji

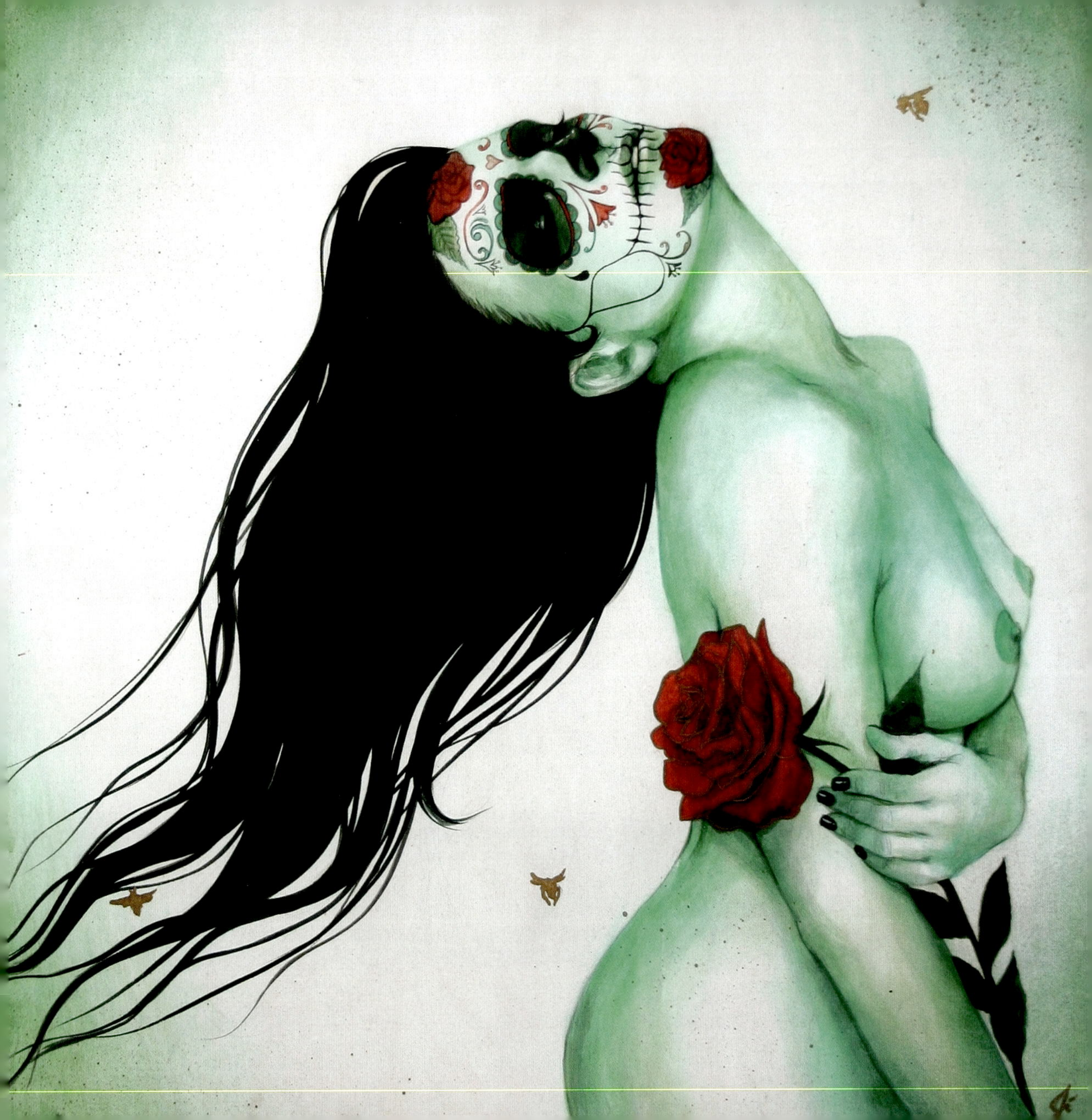

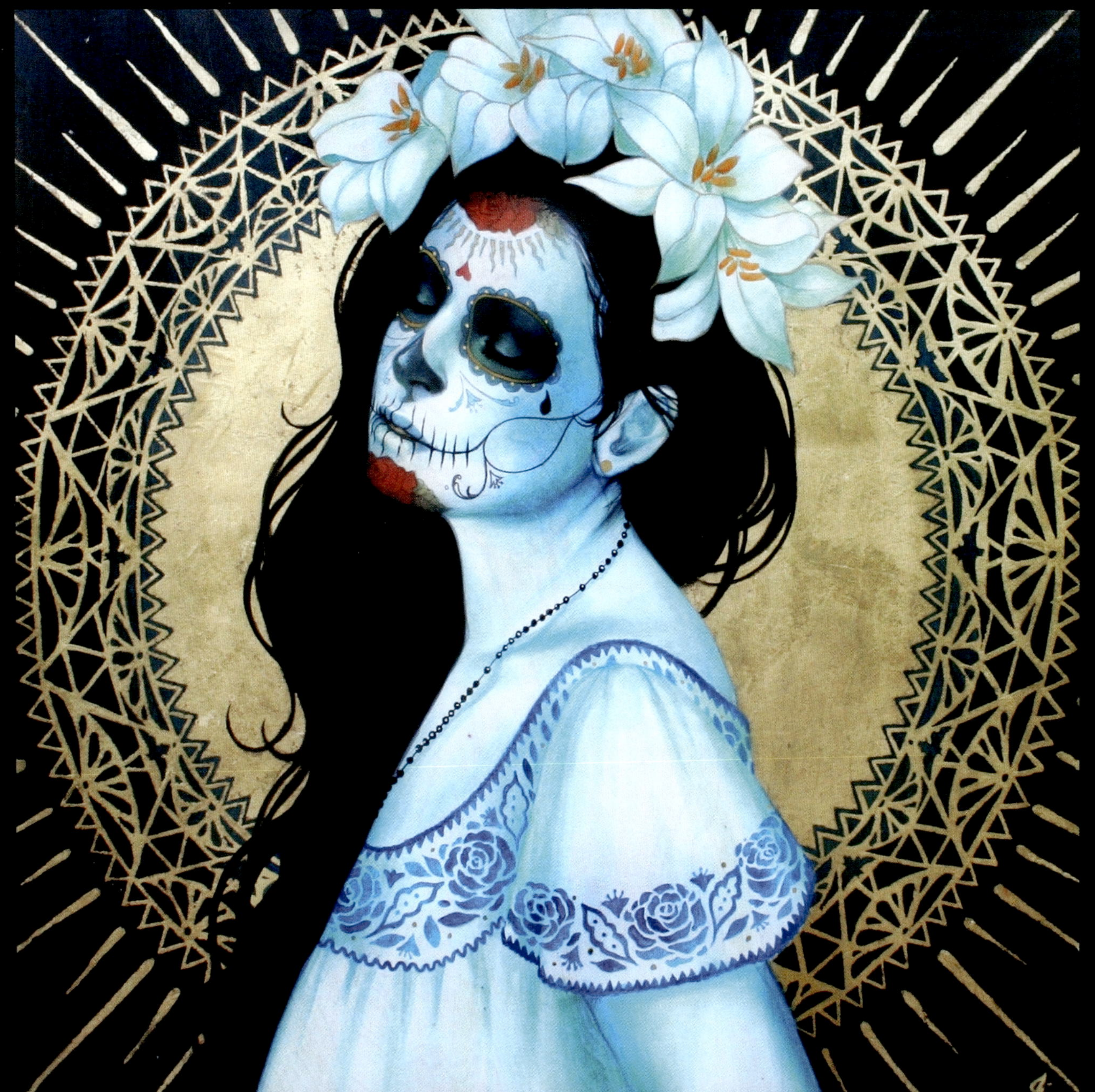

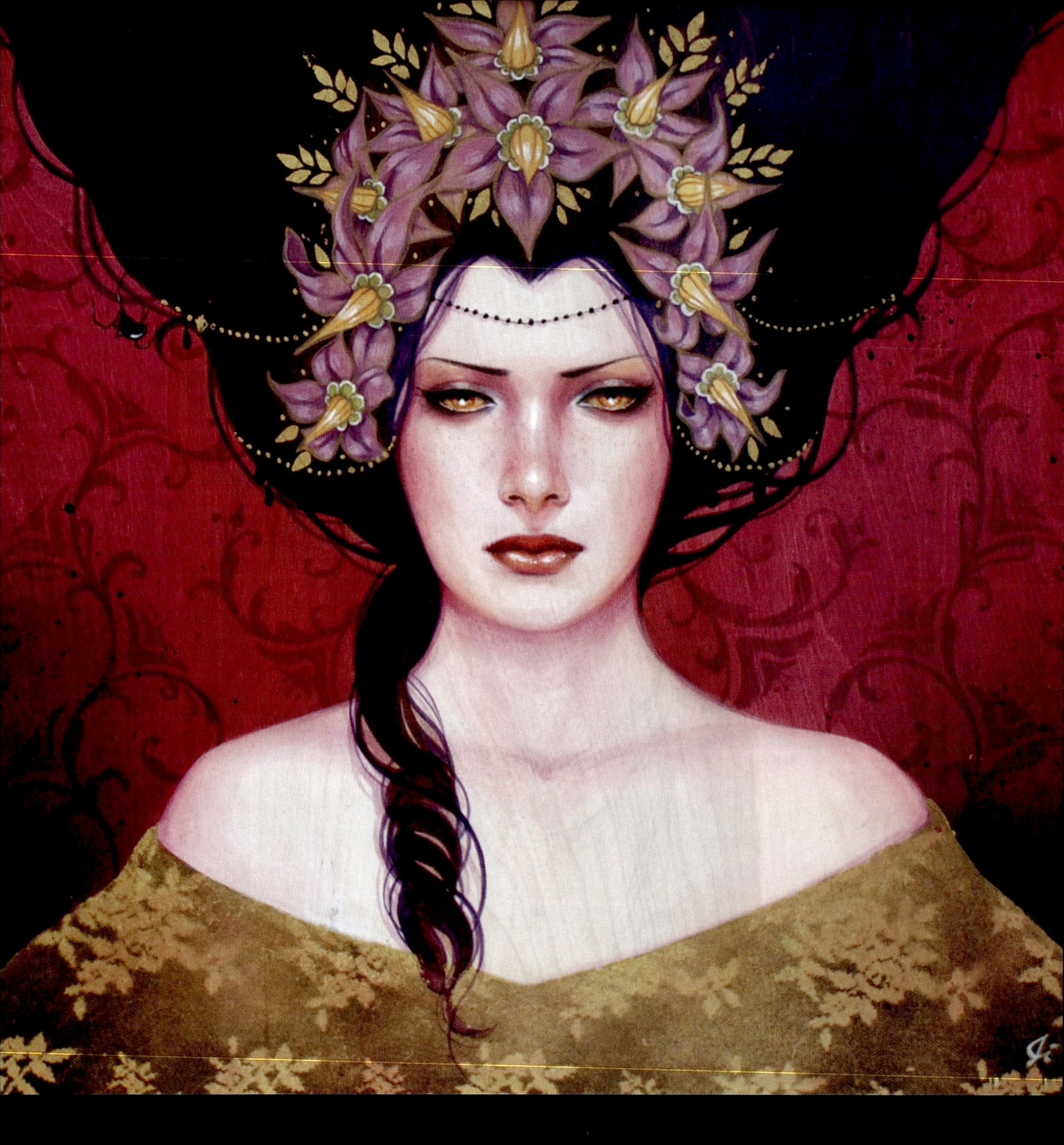

Atropa Bella Donna; 24 x 24 inches; acrylic/mixed media on wood panel

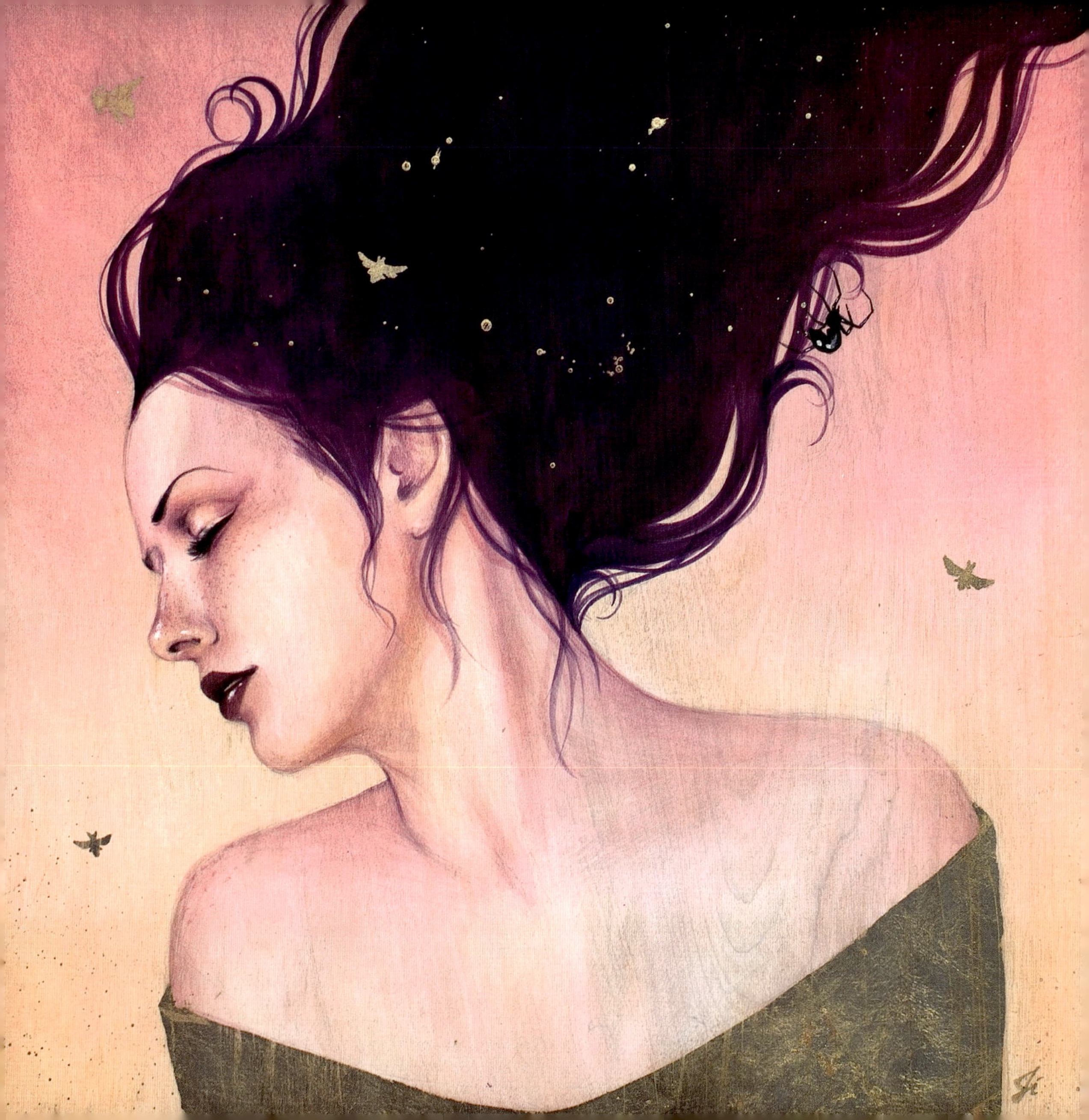

2011
GILDED ROSES

I have always loved and been drawn to the costumes and fashion of the past. This sartorial escapism is an undeniable passion that has formed an undercurrent in all my work. The bygone eras of corsets, crinolines, silks, and satins, are all gilded to a state of heightened beauty and elegance, and intricate patterns, fine textures, jewel tones, and historical silhouettes define the subjects of this body of work.

Sylvia Ji

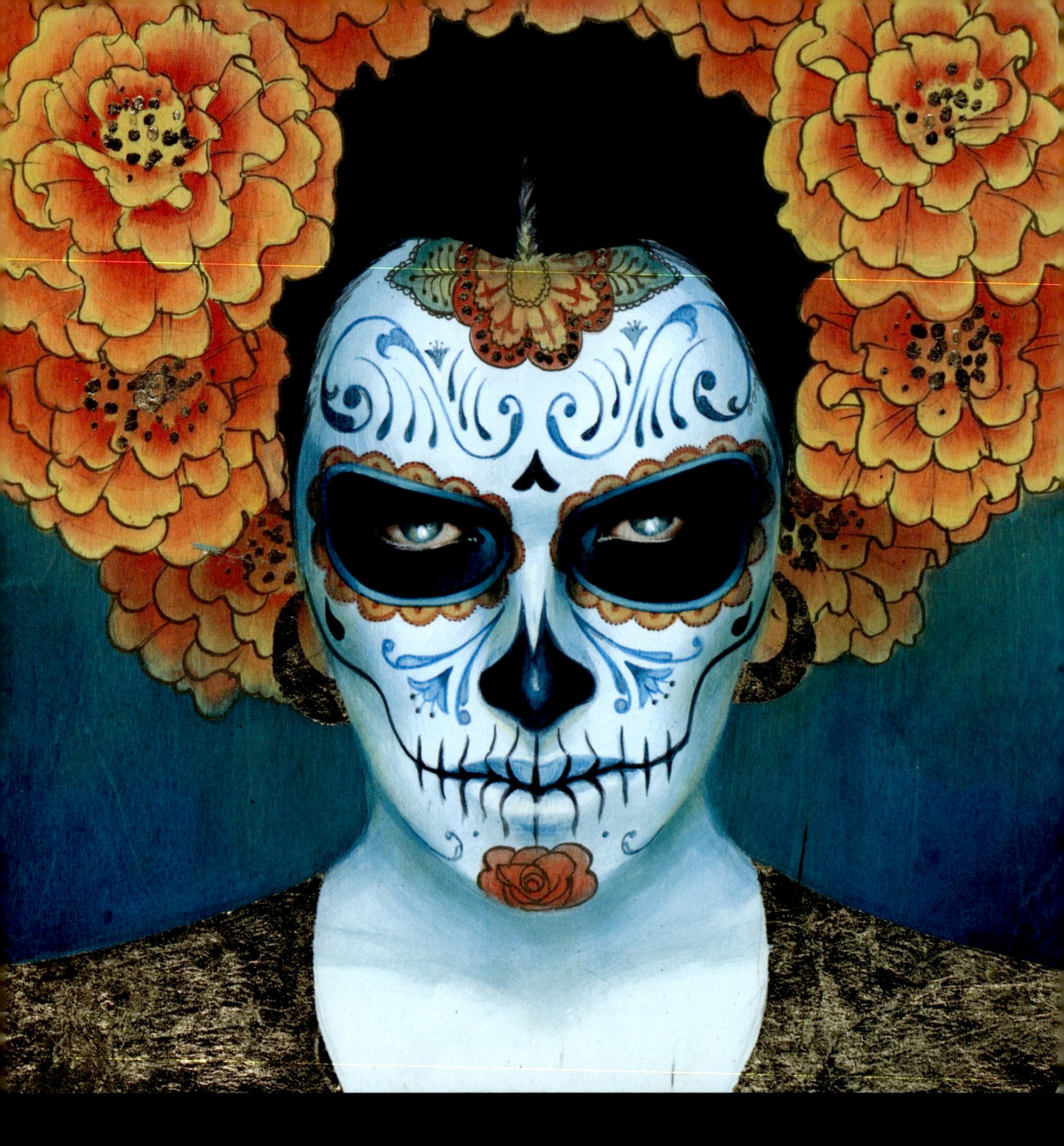

Above: *Caléndula;* 12 x 12 inches; acrylic/mixed media on wood panel

Right: *Immaculada;* 24 x 36 inches; acrylic/mixed media on wood panel

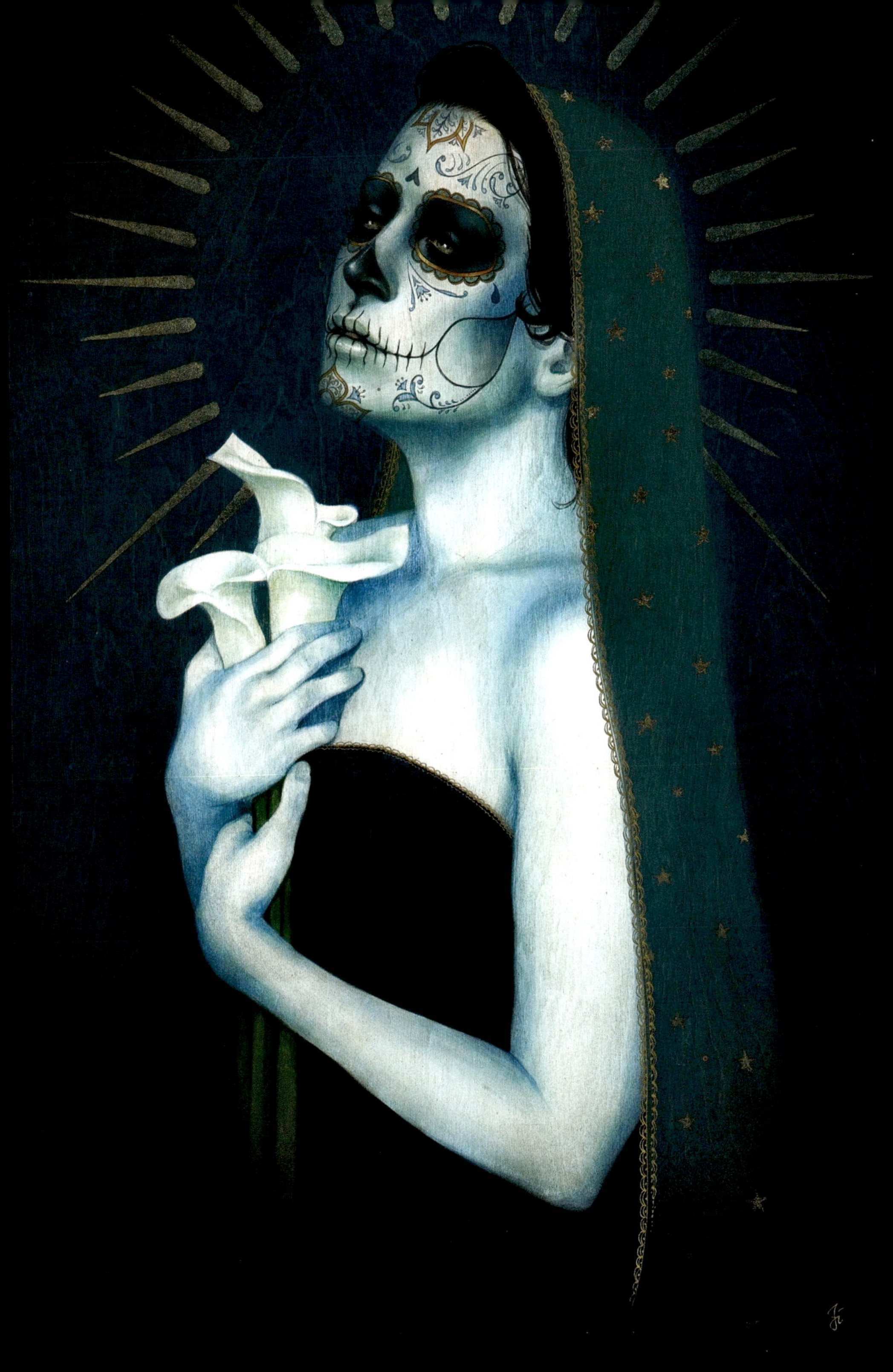

Sylvia Ji

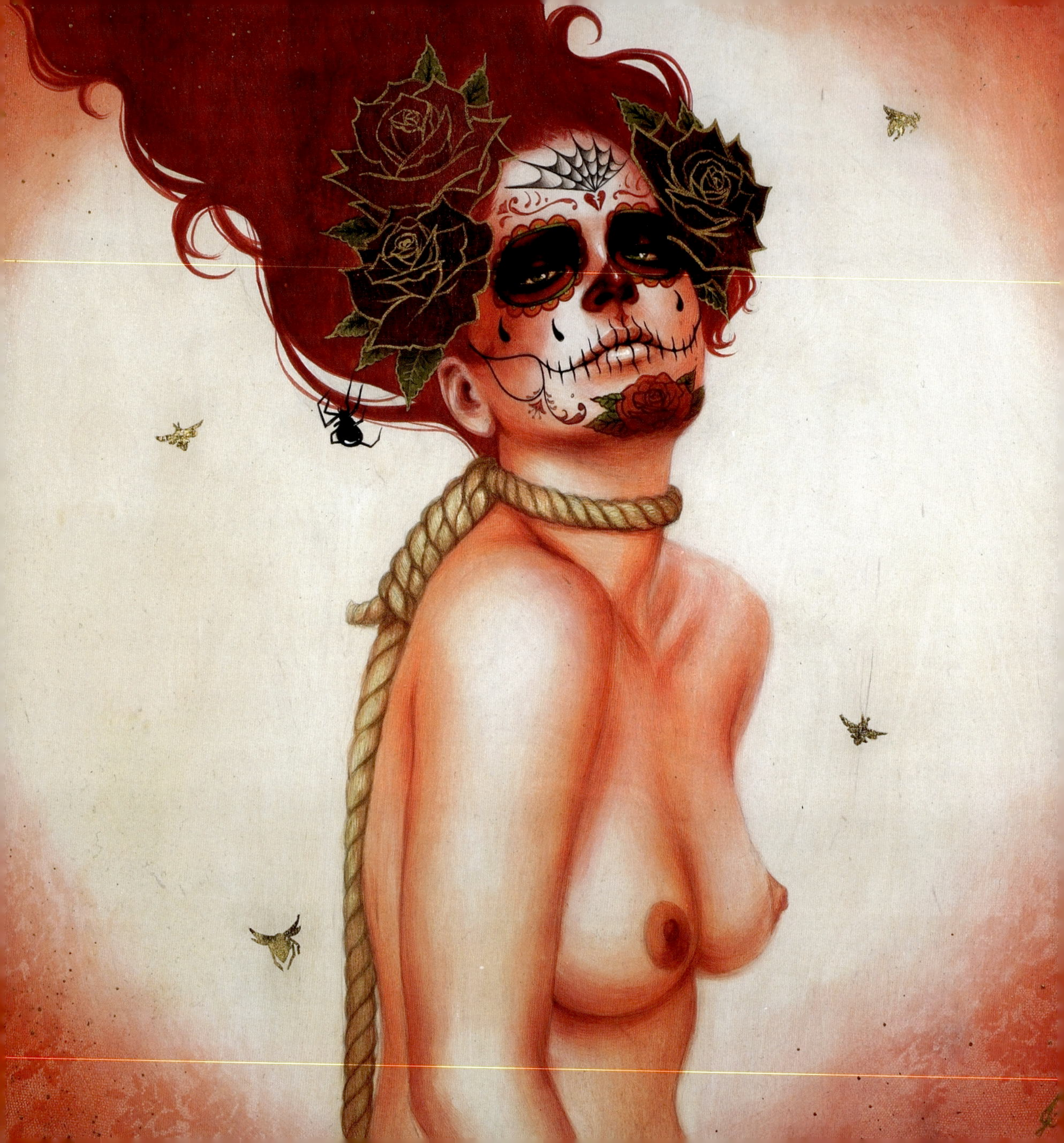

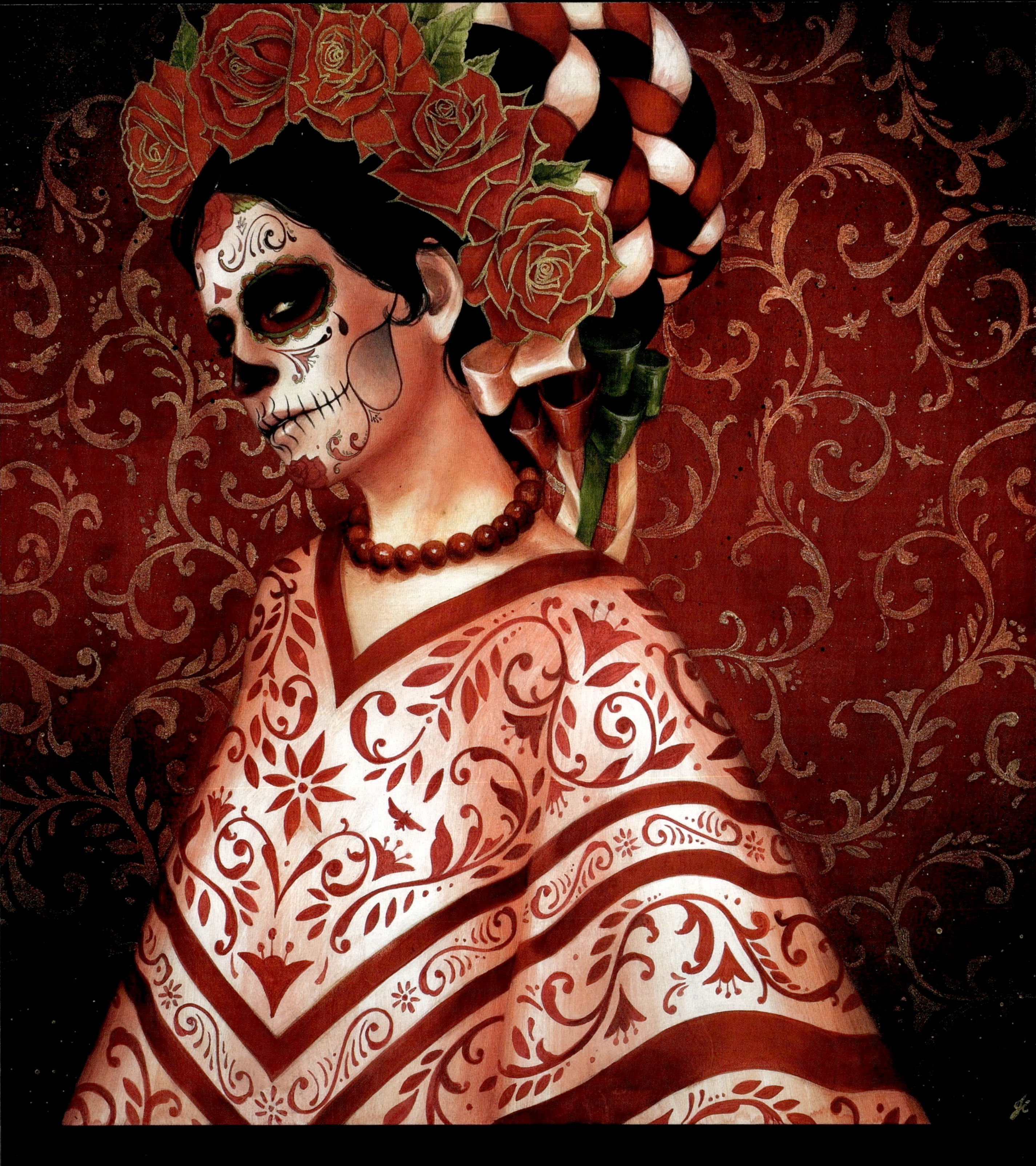

Rosario; 24 x 24 inches; acrylic/mixed media on wood panel

Sylvia Ji

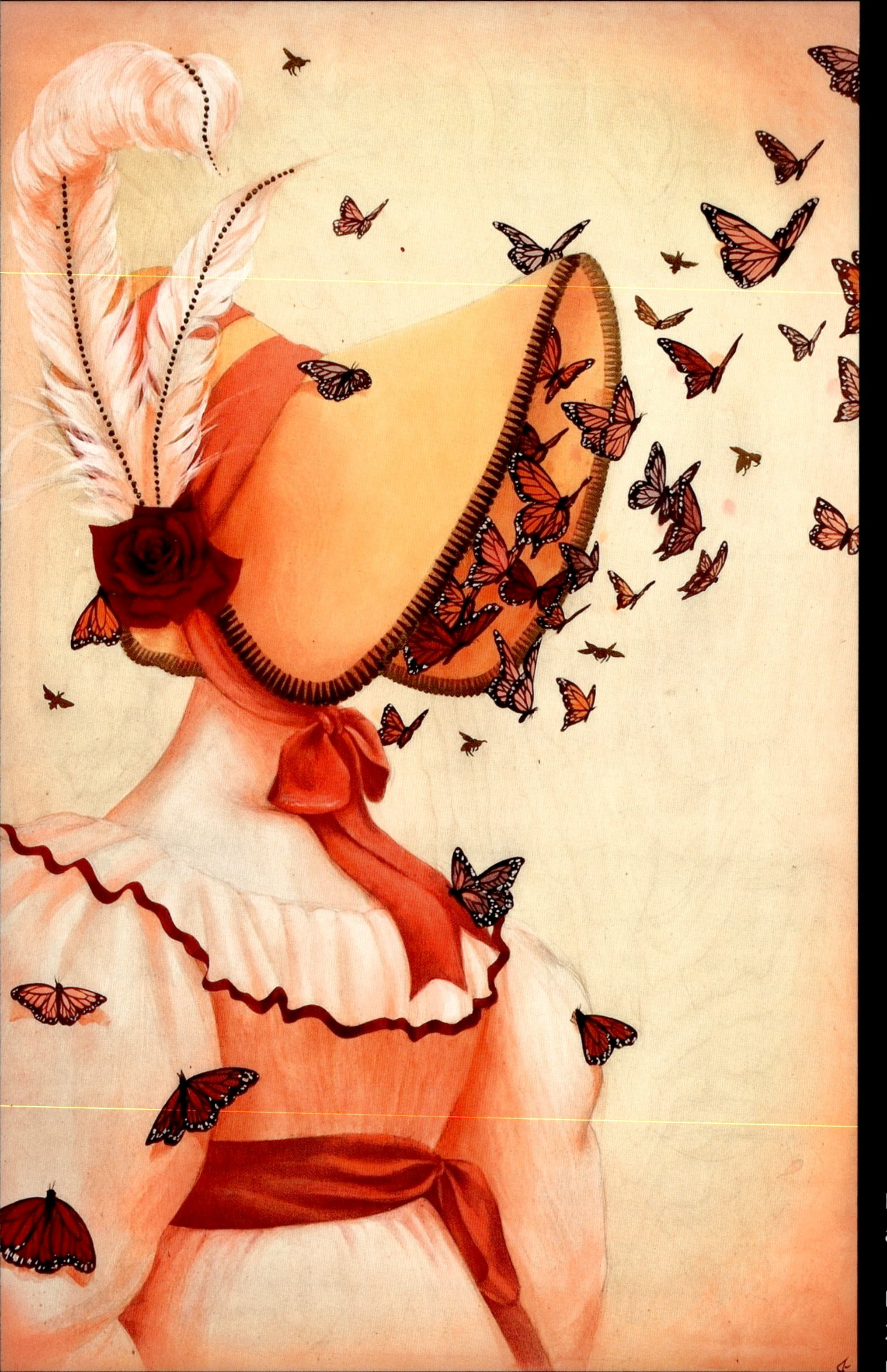

Left: *Spring Bonnet;* 24 x 32 inches; acrylic/mixed media on wood panel

Right: *La Belle Papillonne;* 24 x 36 inches; acrylic/mixed media on wood panel

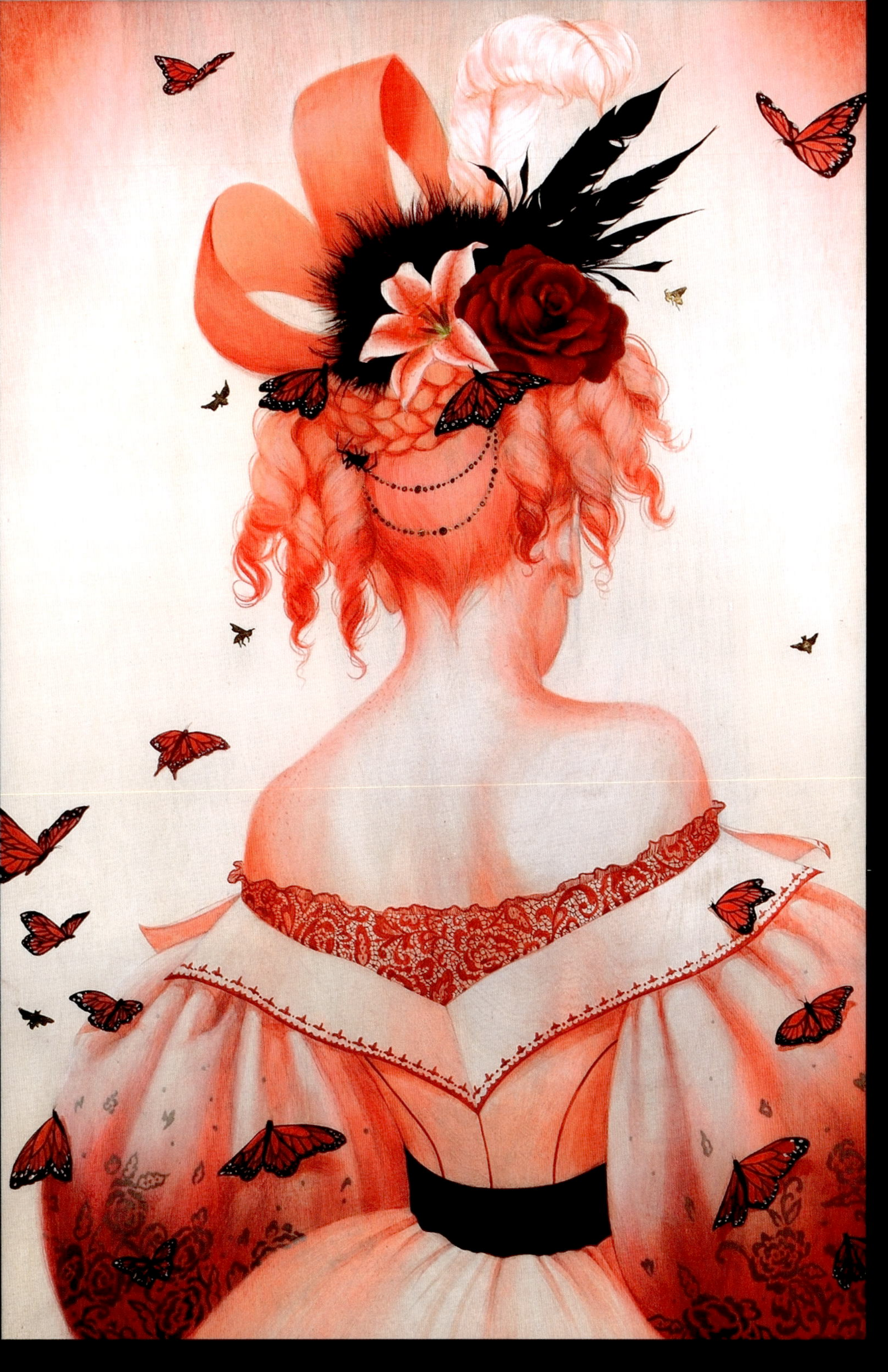

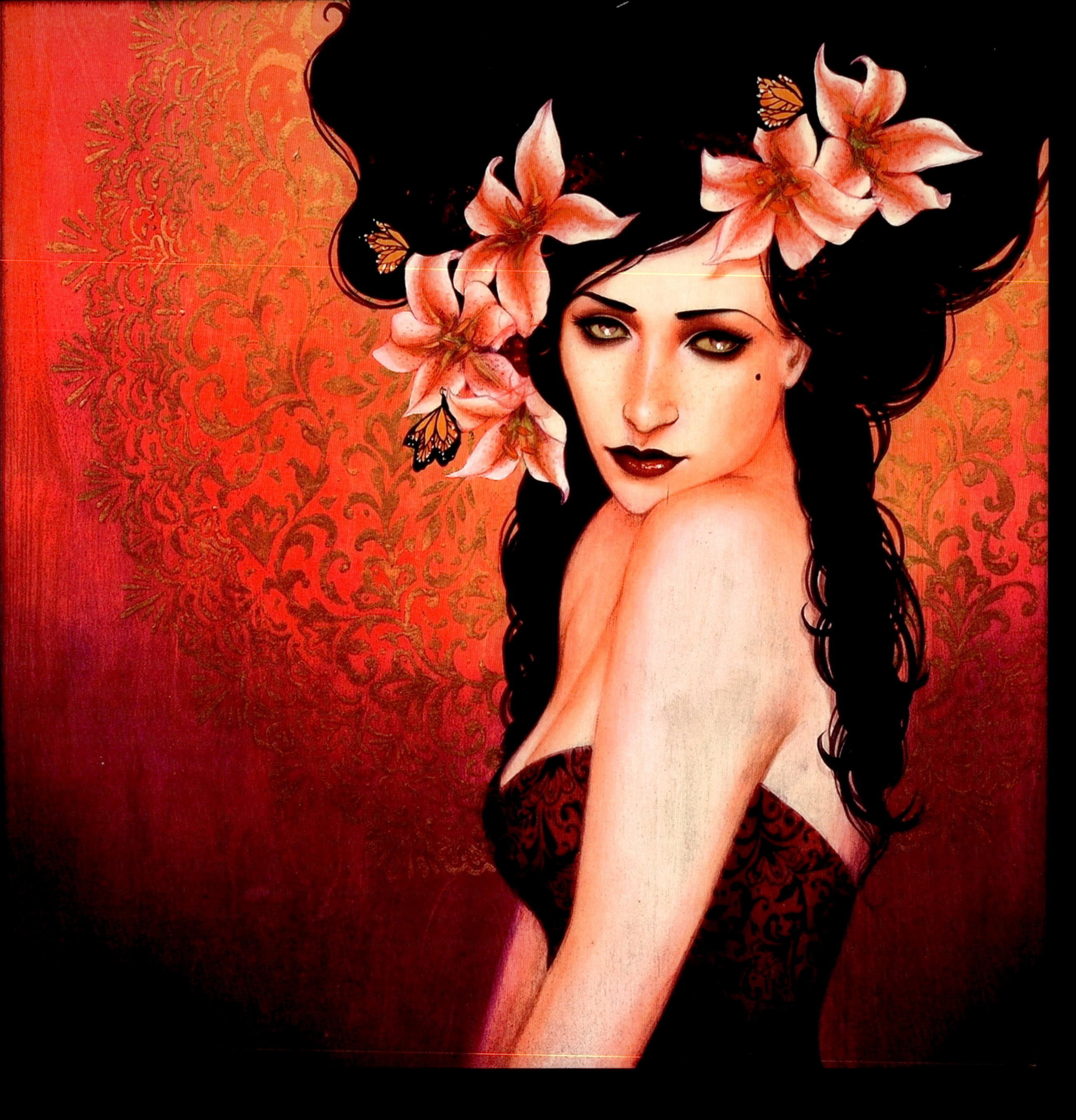

Above: *Lilac Lily;* 24 x 24 inches; acrylic/mixed media on wood panel

Right: *La Fee Verte;* 48 x 60 inches; acrylic/mixed media on wood panel

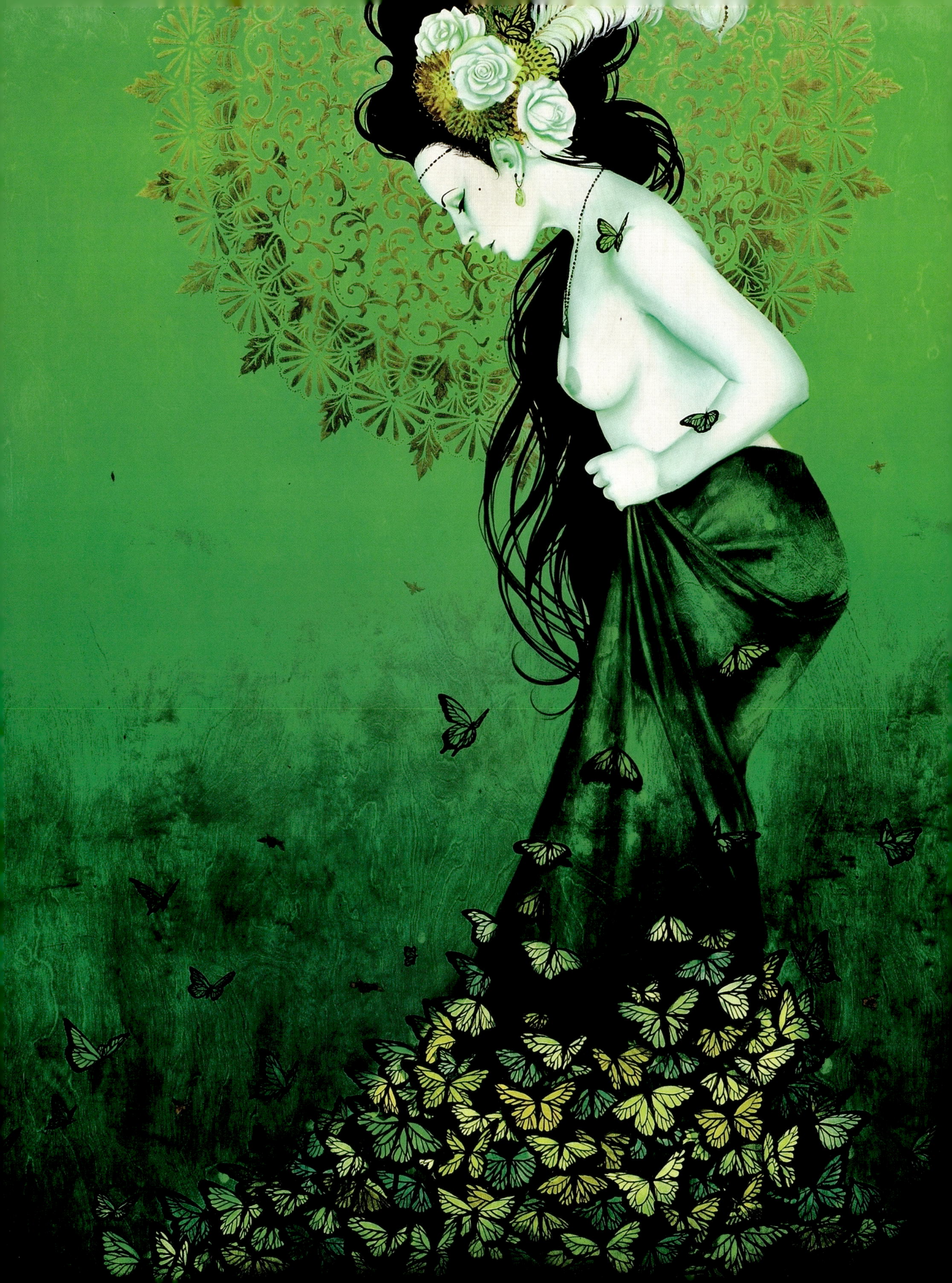

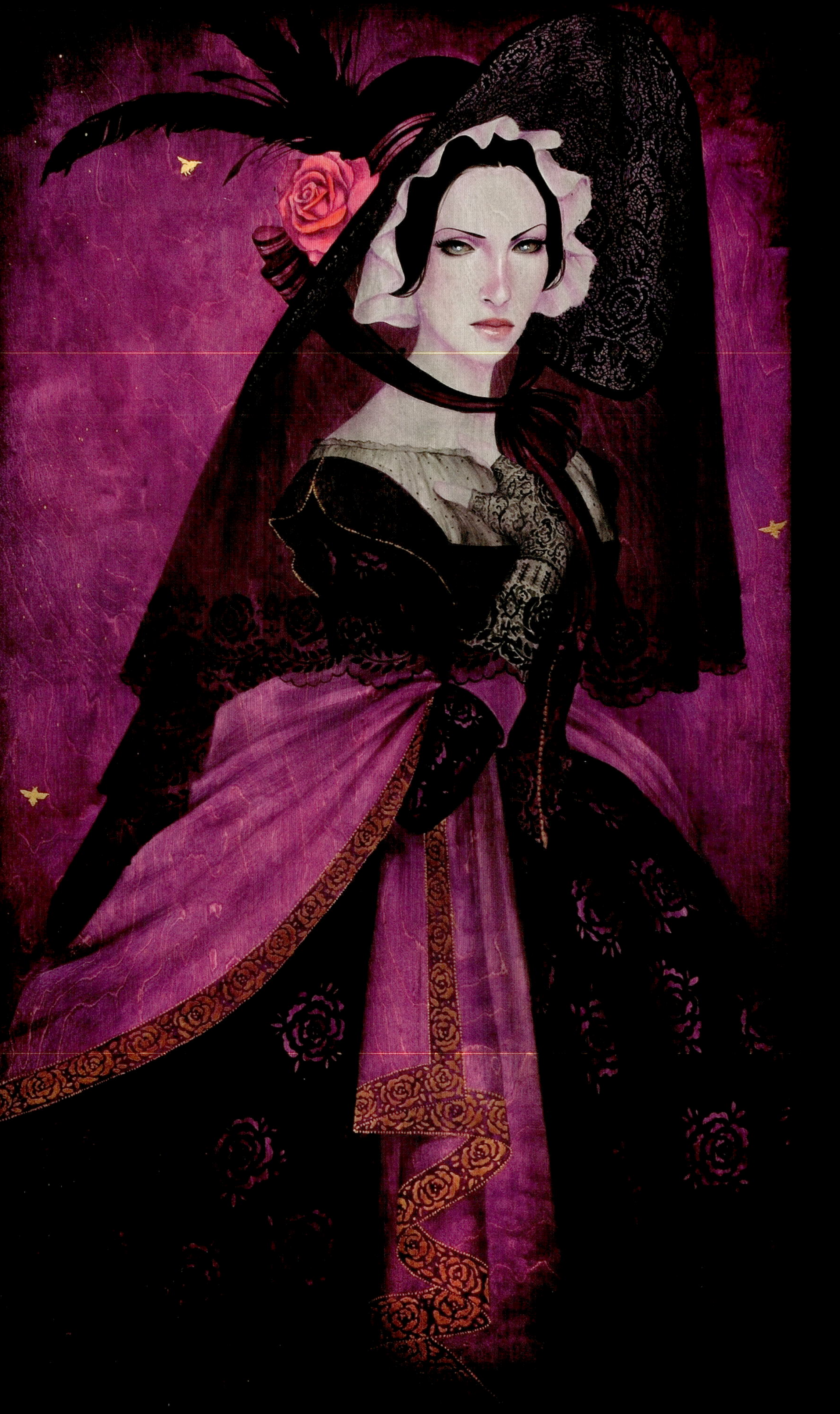

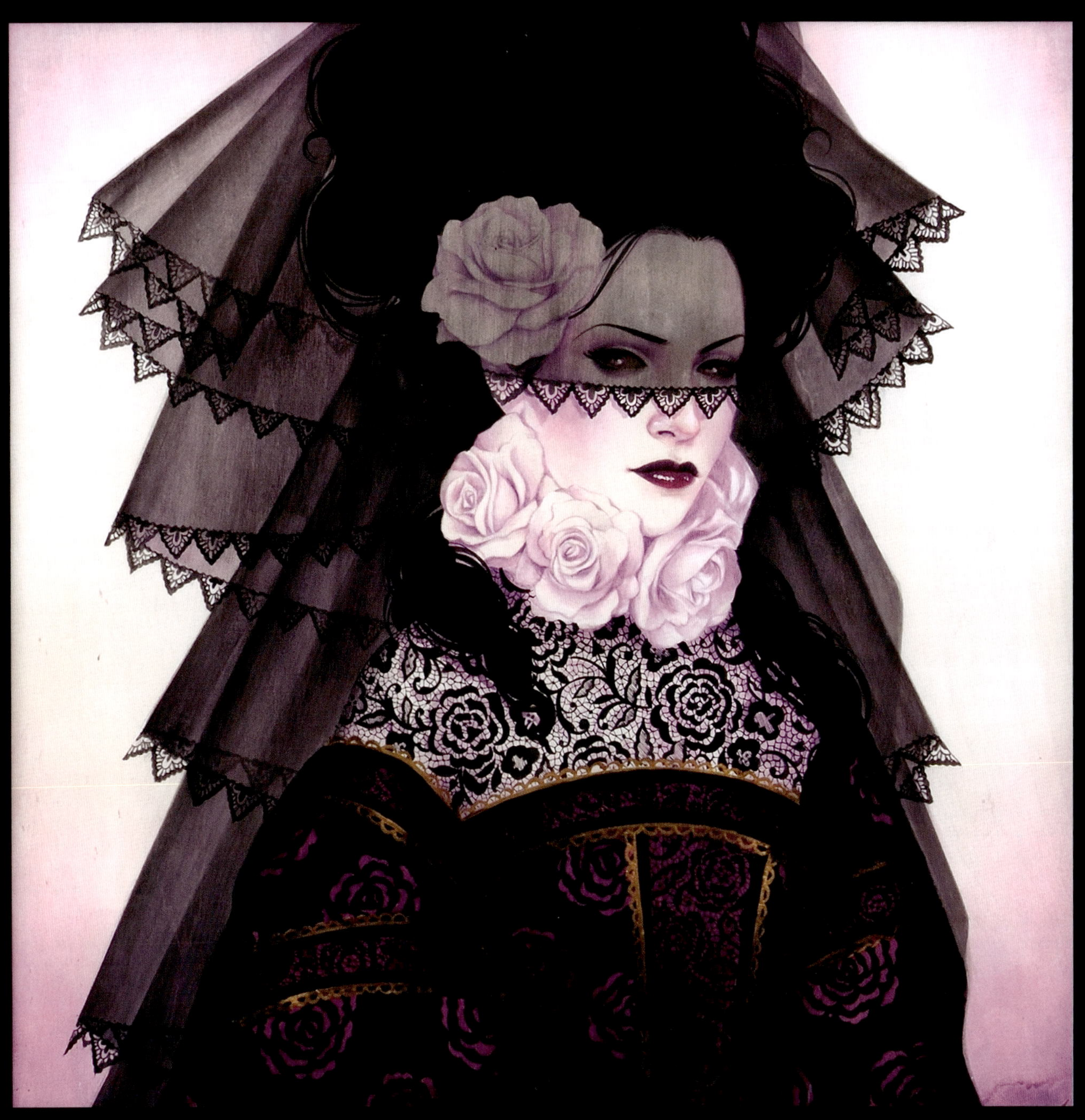

Left: *Mourning Dress in Violet;* 30 x 48 inches; acrylic/mixed media on wood panel

Above: *Violet Rose;* 24 x 24 inches; acrylic/mixed media on wood panel

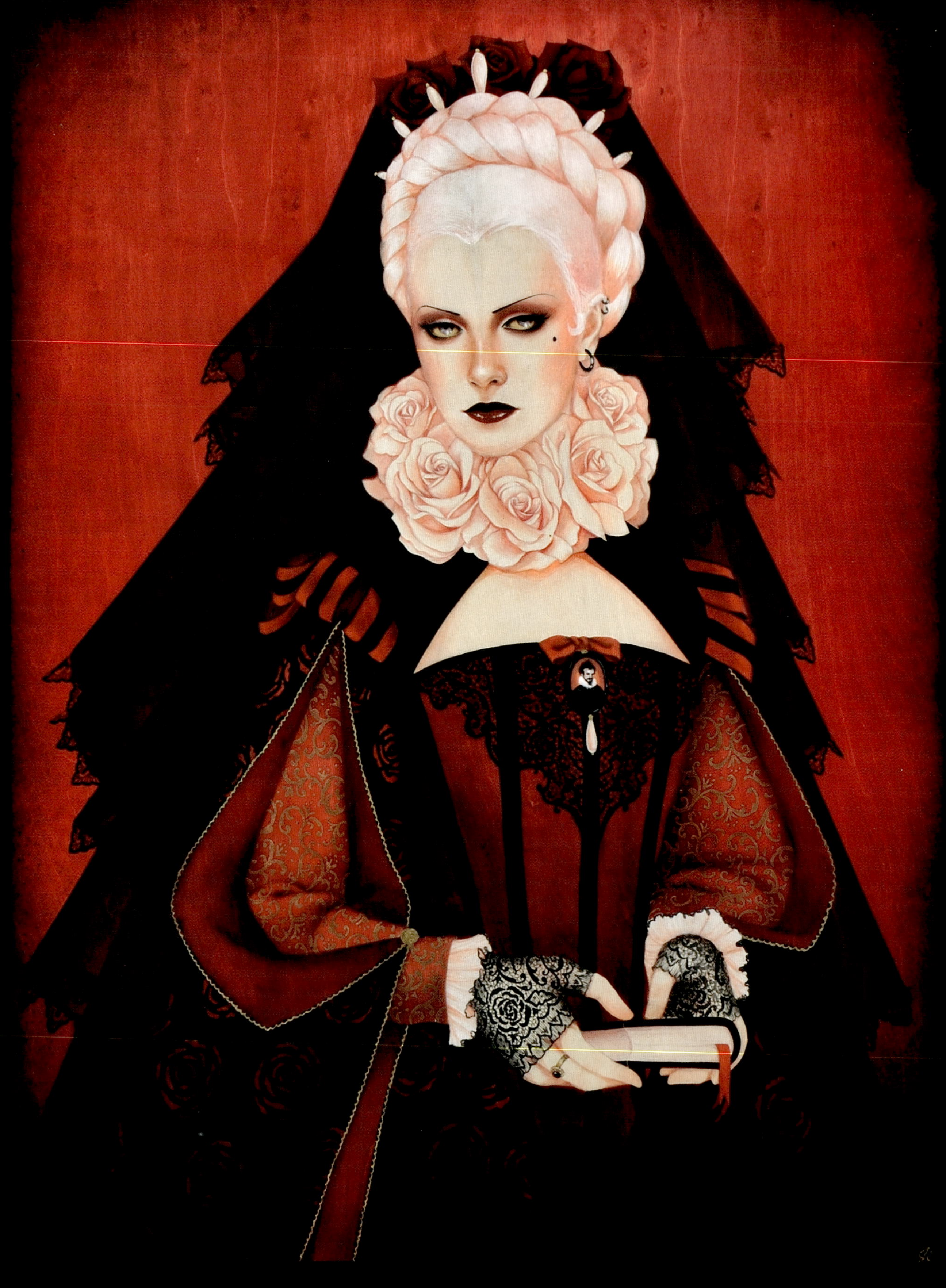

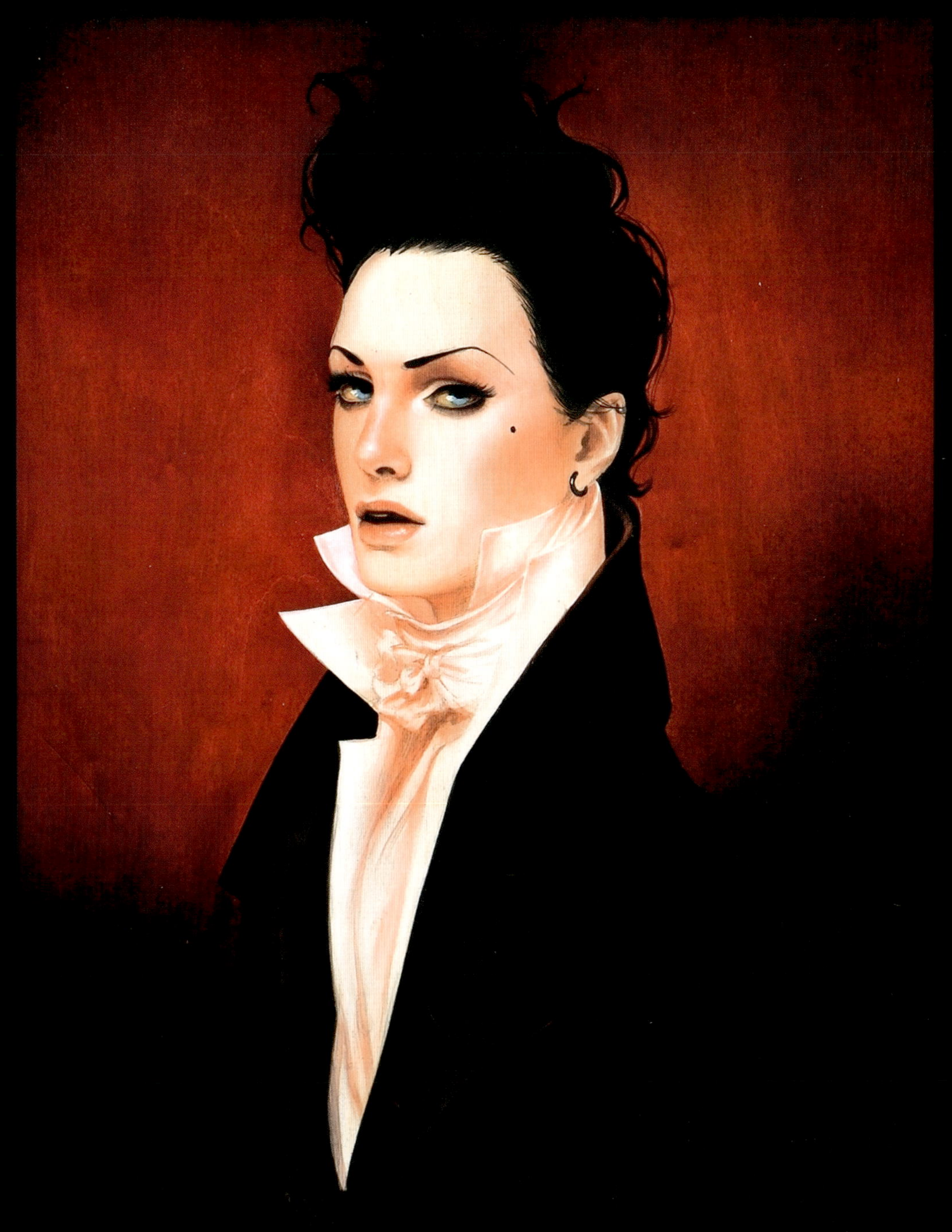

Left: *Tudor Rose;* 30 x 40 inches; acrylic/mixed media on wood panel

Above: *White Cravat;* 18 x 24 inches; acrylic on wood panel

2012–2015 NIGHT SHADE

The year 2012 saw the return of my "Day of the Dead"-based paintings for a solo exhibition at Corey Helford Gallery in Los Angeles, USA. These, and the work I produced in the years that followed, further blended more ornate textile patterns, and more vibrant colors. I also utilized copper, silver, or gold leaf to embellish details such as faces, hair, and costumes.

Eventually during this period, the figure became displaced by purely ornamental pattern – the golden, orange, and flowery artworks seen in this chapter represent a time of rebirth: a celebration of light, if you will.

  Sylvia Ji

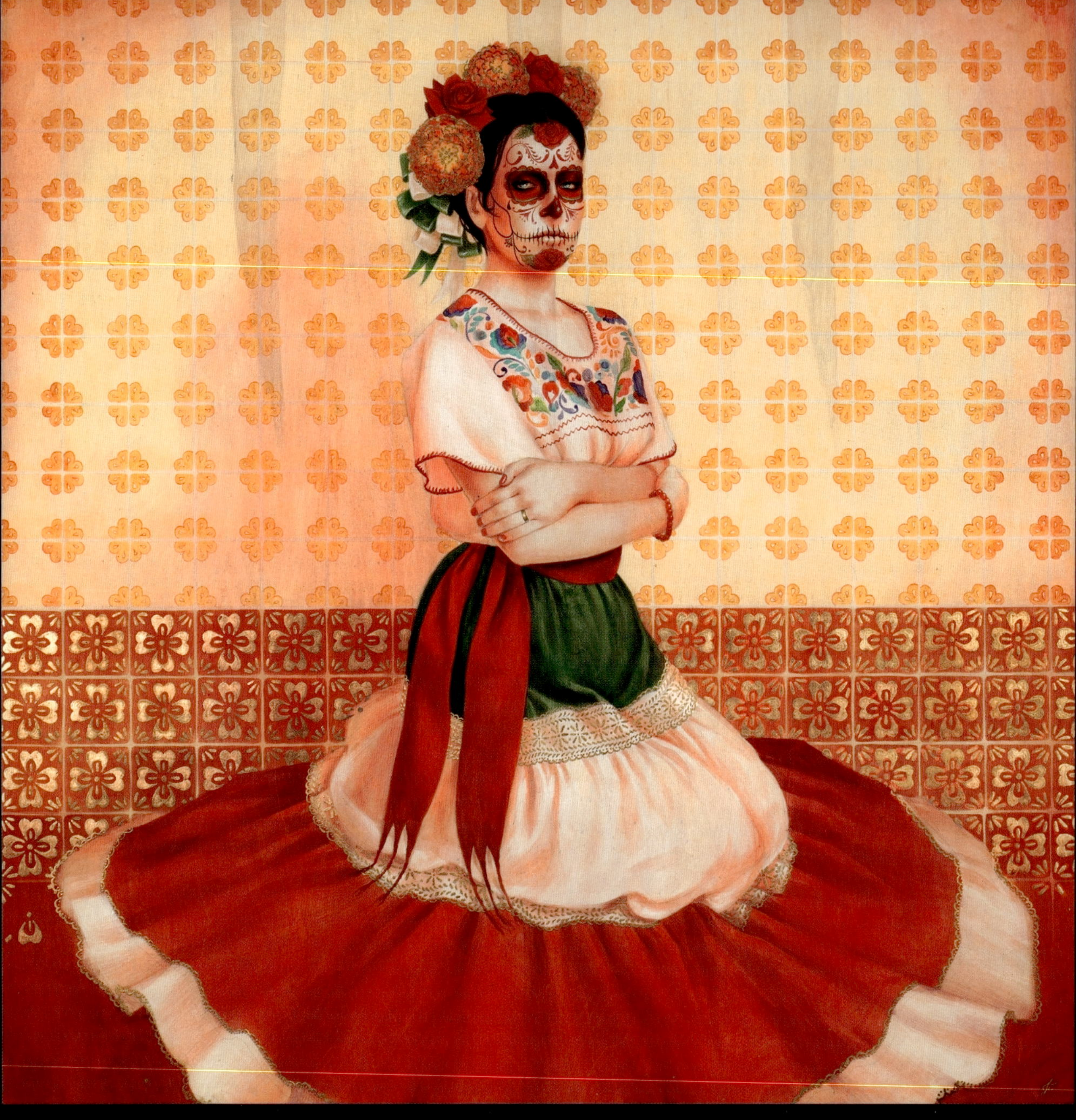

Above: *Catrina in Repose*; 48 x 48 inches; acrylic/gold leaf on wood panel

Right top: *Marigold Catrina;* 24 x 24 inches; acrylic/gold leaf on wood panel

Right below: *Tres Cabezas*; 36 x 16 inches; acrylic/gold leaf on wood panel

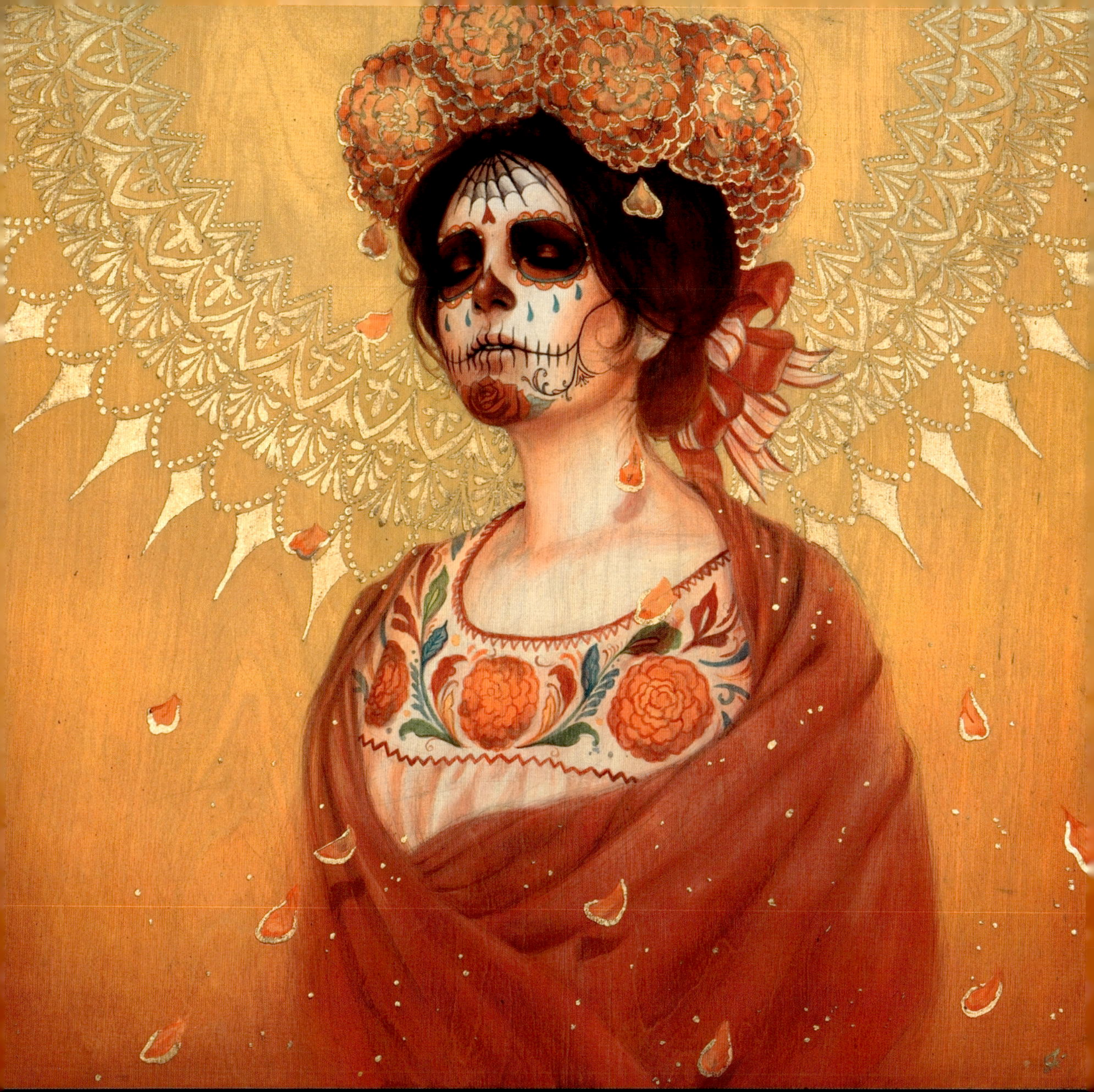

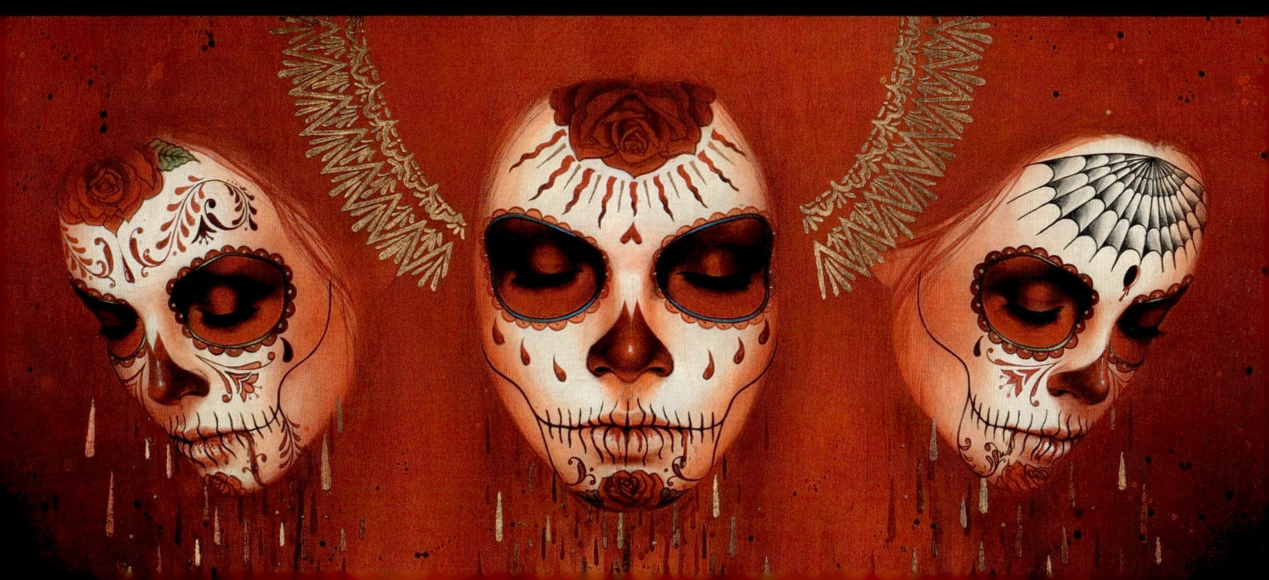

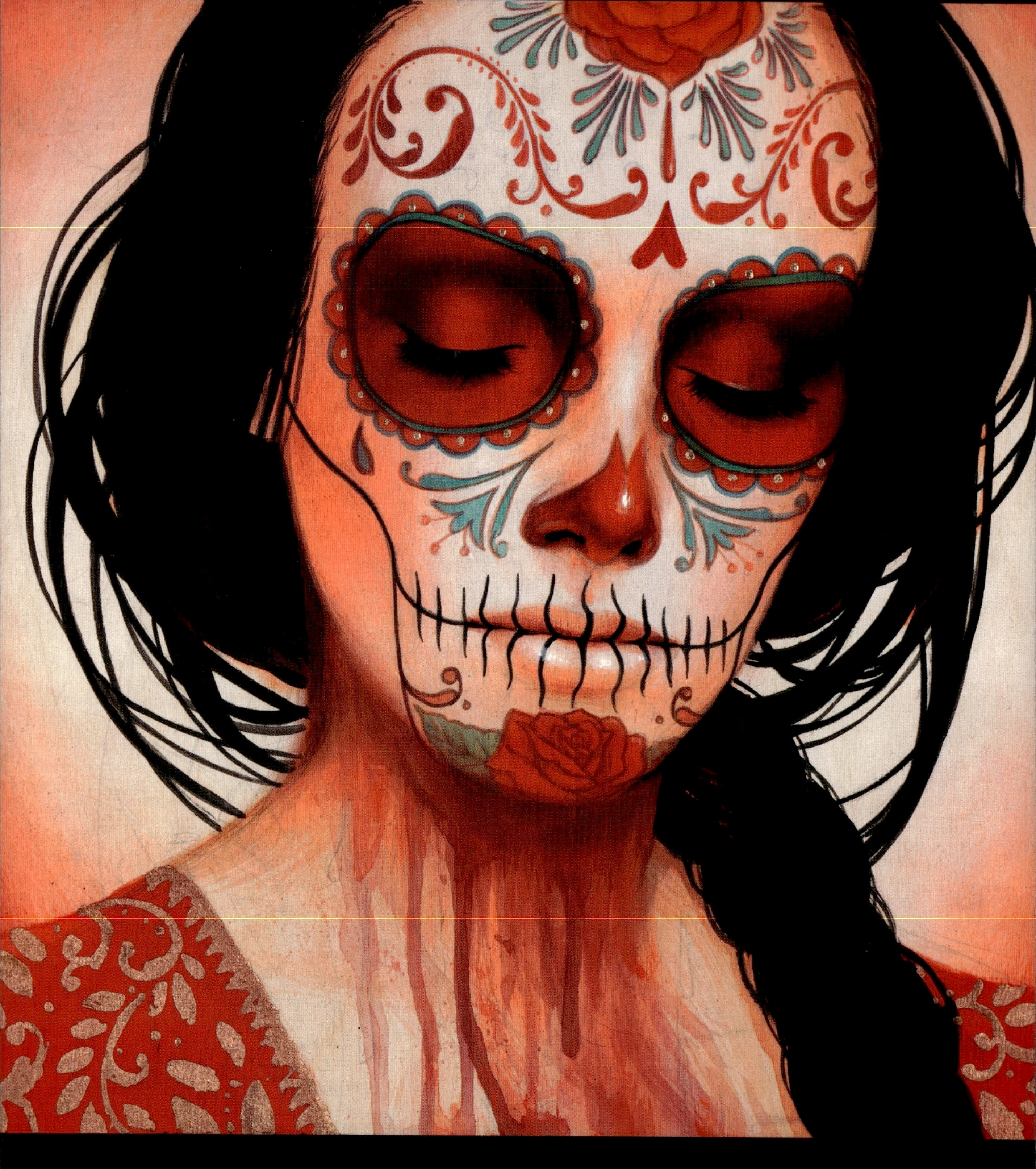

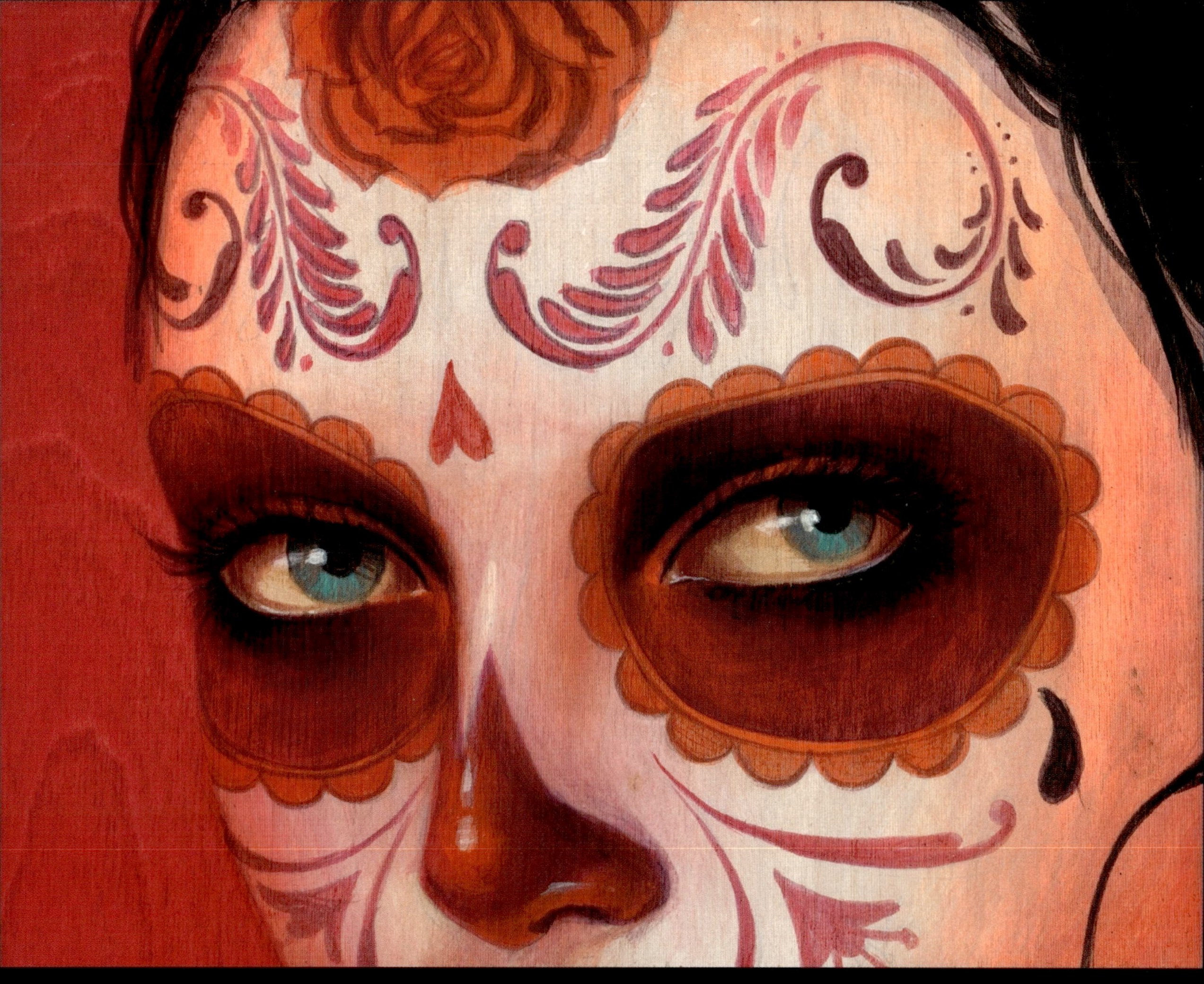

Left: *Alma Errante (Wandering Soul)* ; 10 x 10 inches;
acrylic/copper leaf on wood panel

Above: *Yo te veo (I See You);* 7 x 5.5 inches; acrylic on wood panel

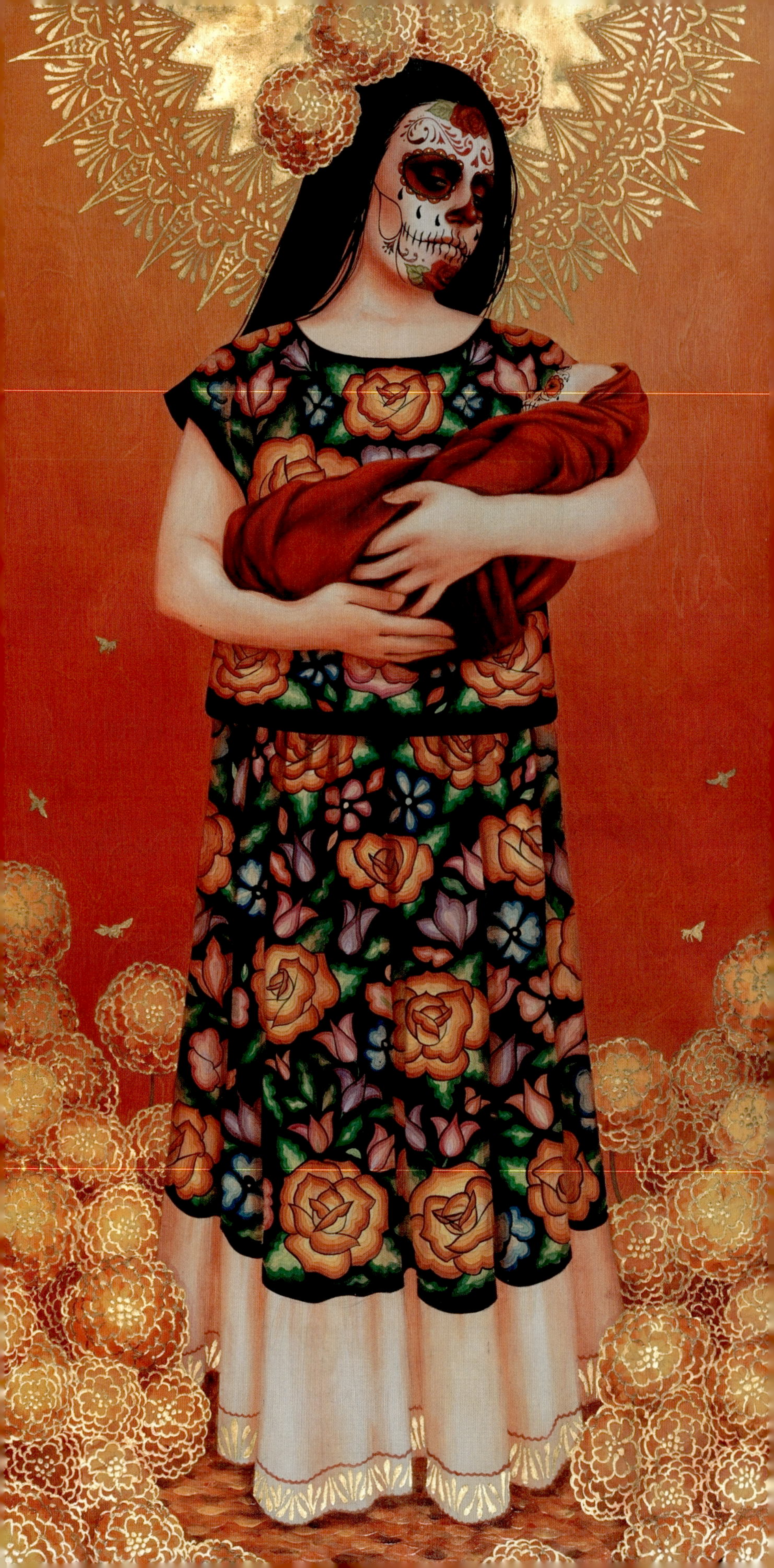

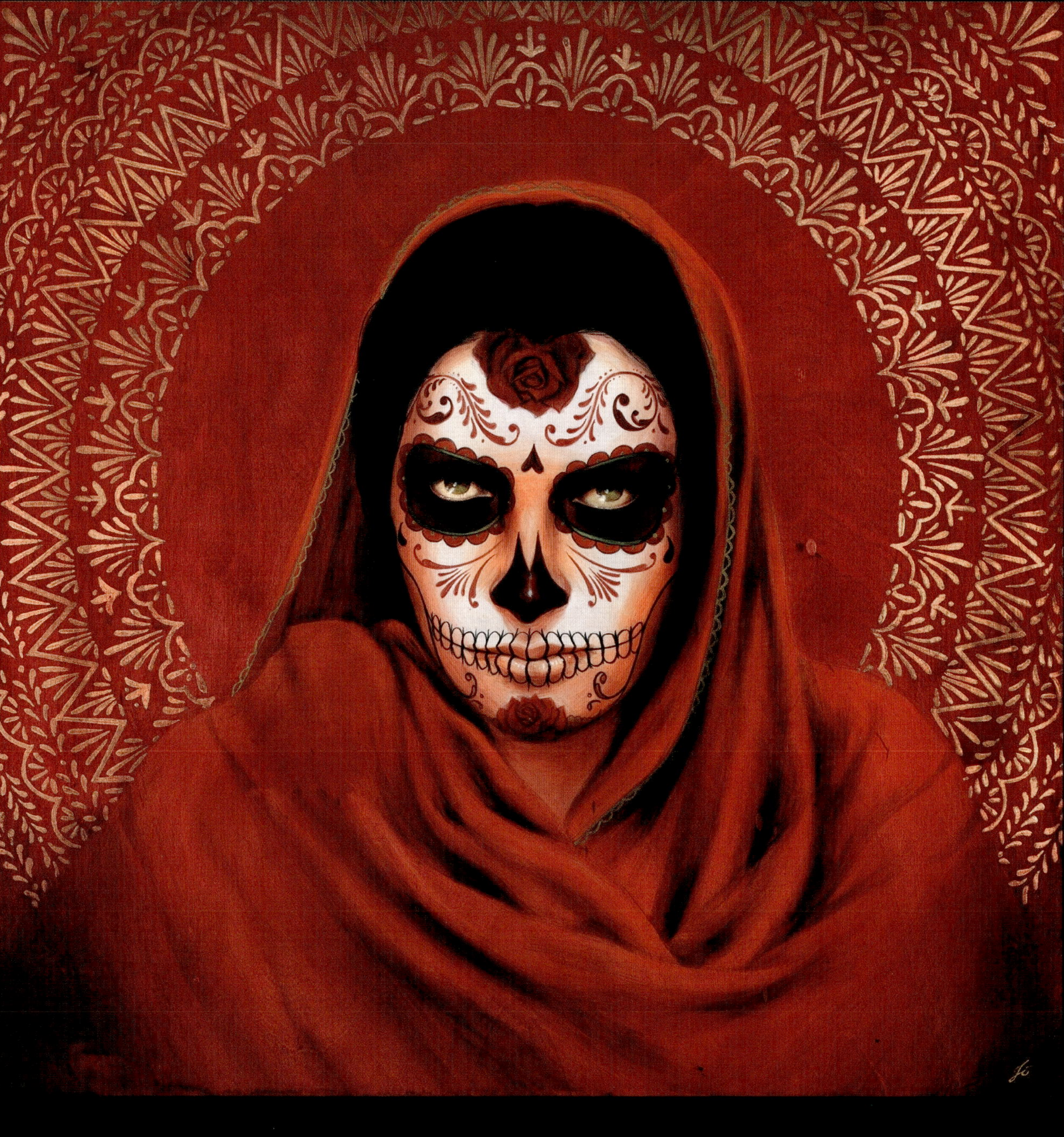

Left: *Madre y Niño;* 48 x 24 inches; acrylic/gold leaf on wood panel

Above: *Rebozo Rojo;* 24 x 24 inches; acrylic/copper leaf on wood panel

Sylvia Ji

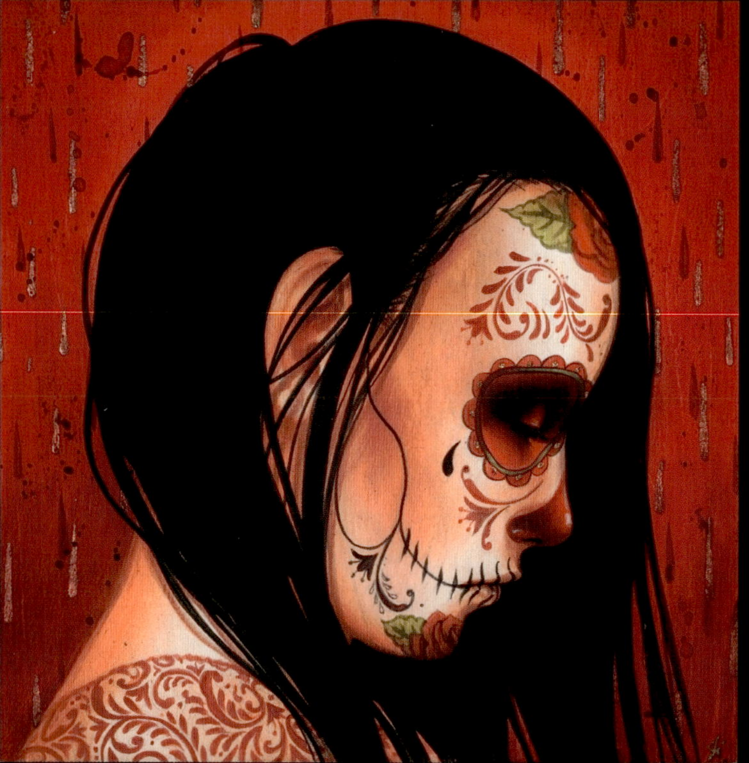

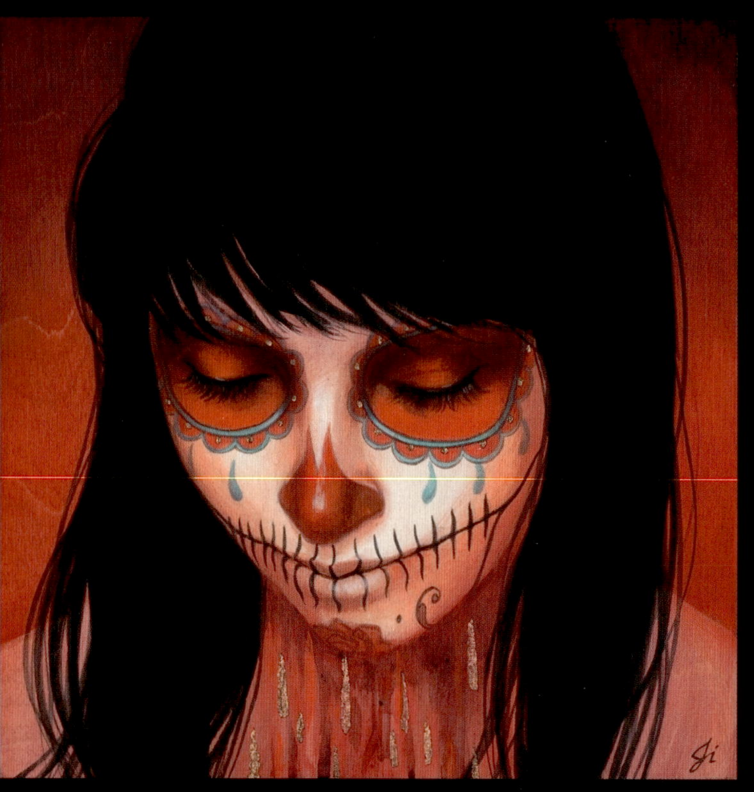

Top: *Alma Perdida;* 10 x 10 inches;
acrylic/copper leaf on wood panel

Below: *Calavera de Escobar;* 10 x 10
acrylic/copper leaf on wood panel

Right: *Blusa Rojo;* 24 x 18 inches;
acrylic on wood panel

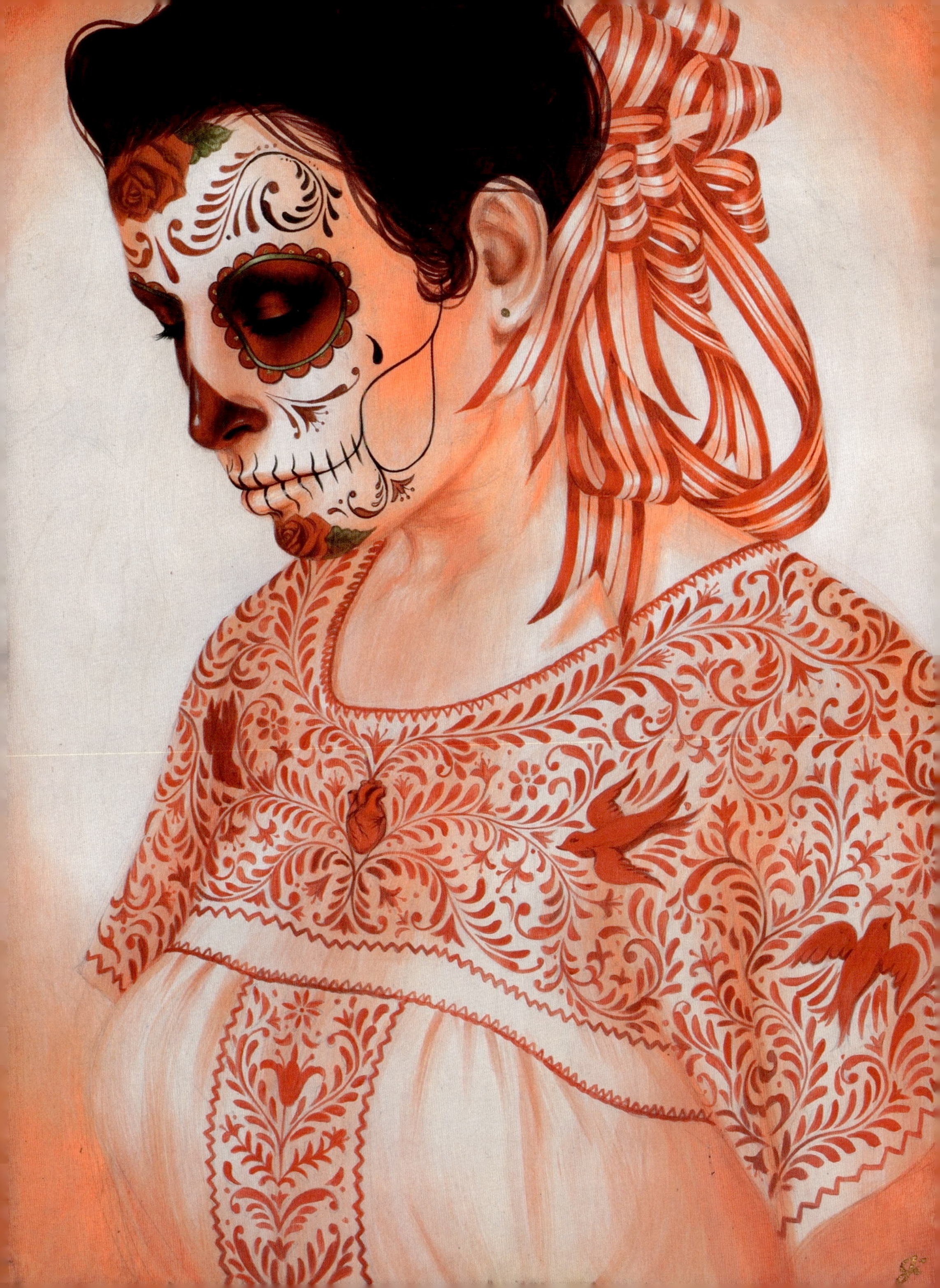

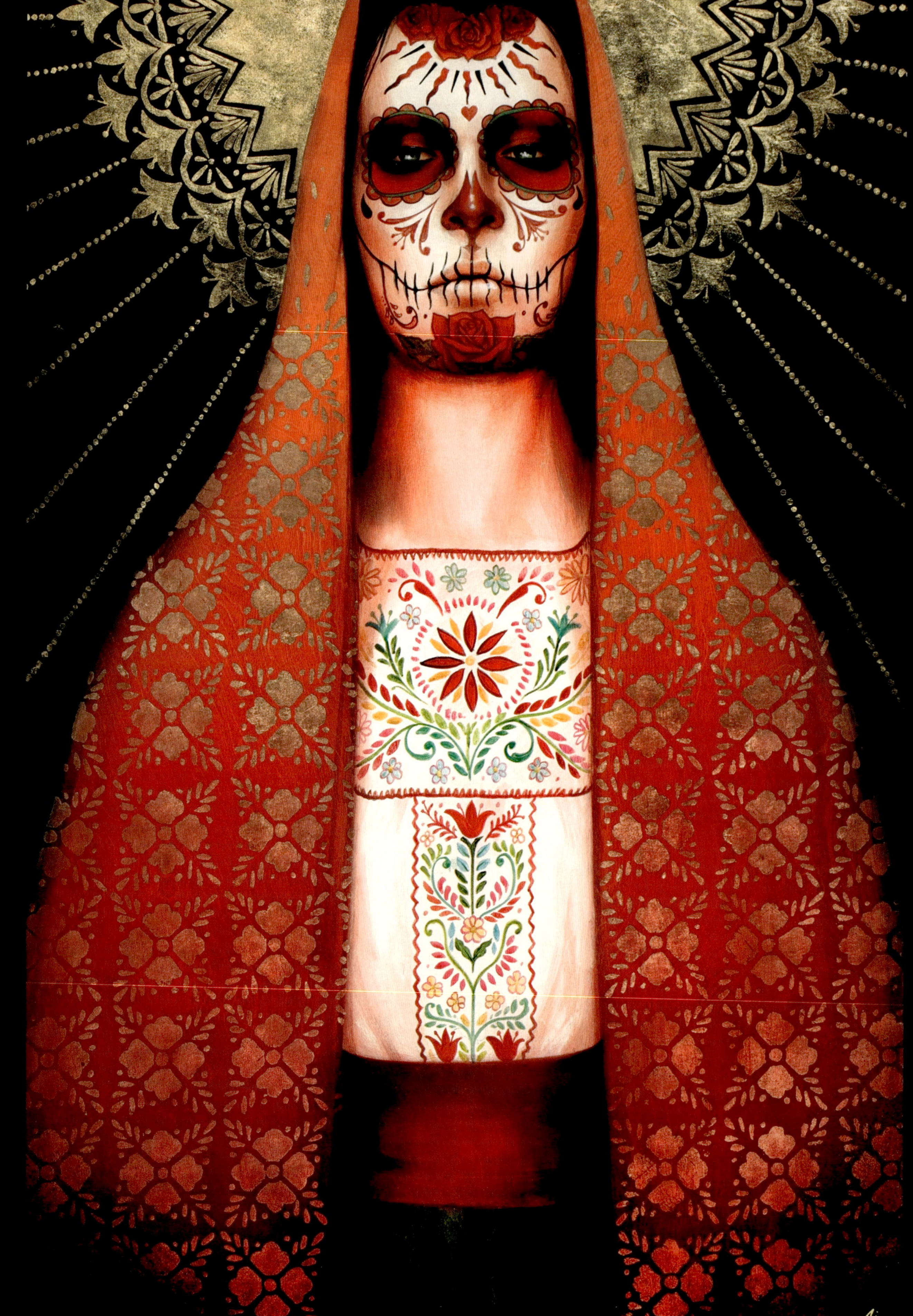

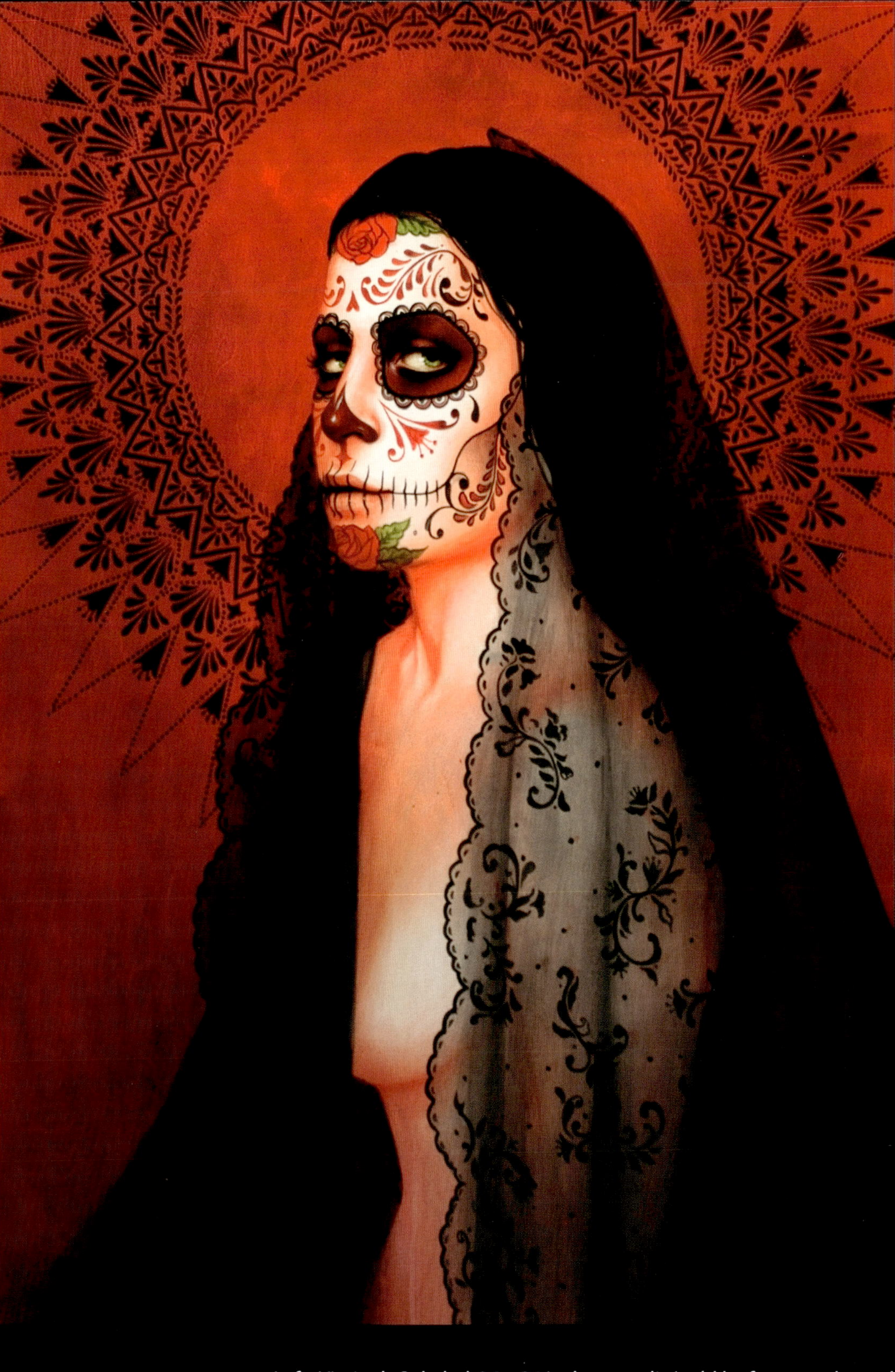

Left: *Virgin de Soledad*; 36 x 24 inches; acrylic/gold leaf on wood panel

Above: *Black Virgin*; 36 x 24 inches; acrylic on wood panel

Sylvia Ji

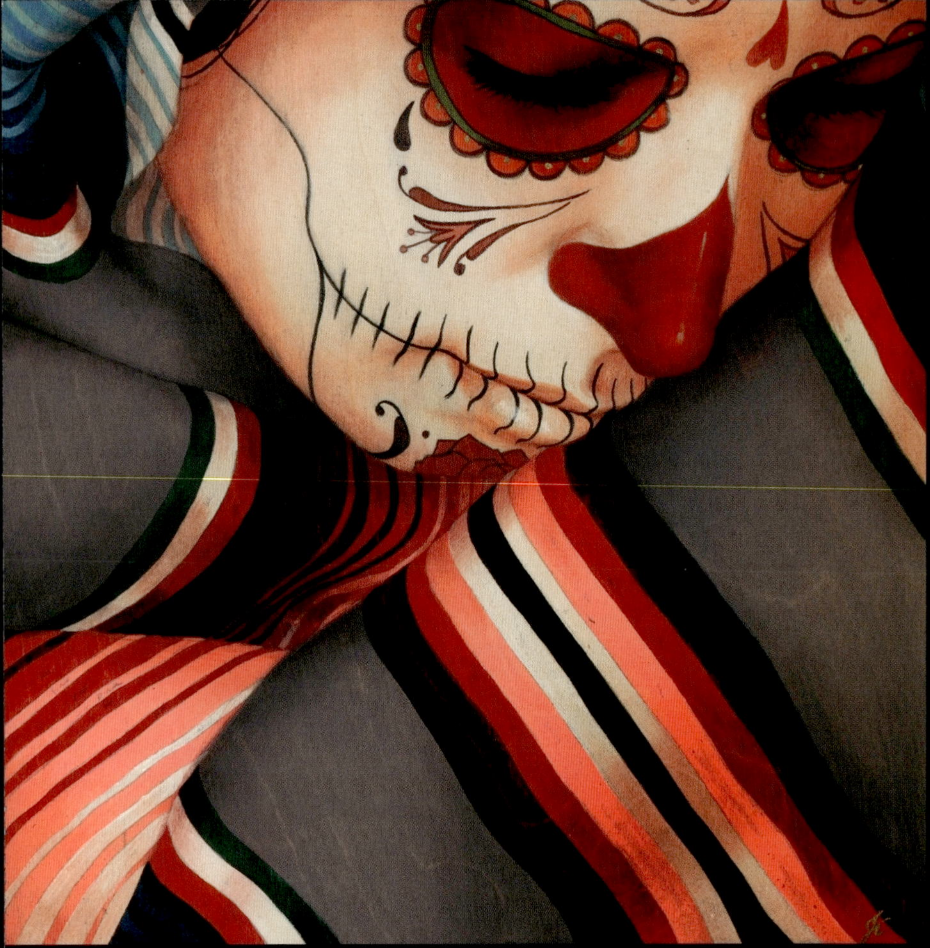

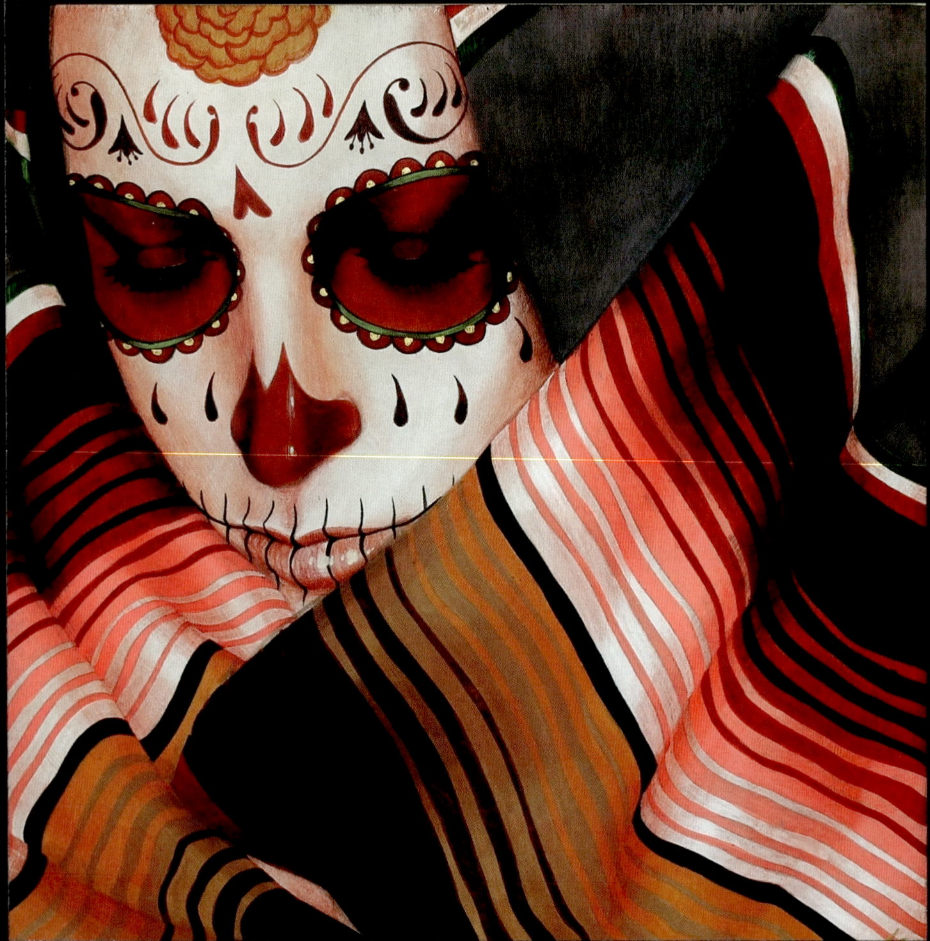

Top: *Serape, grey*; 12 x 12 inches; acrylic on wood panel

Below: *Serape, Rojo;* 12 x 12 inches; acrylic on wood panel

Right: *Sol de Oro*; 24 x 36 inches; acrylic/gold leaf on wood panel

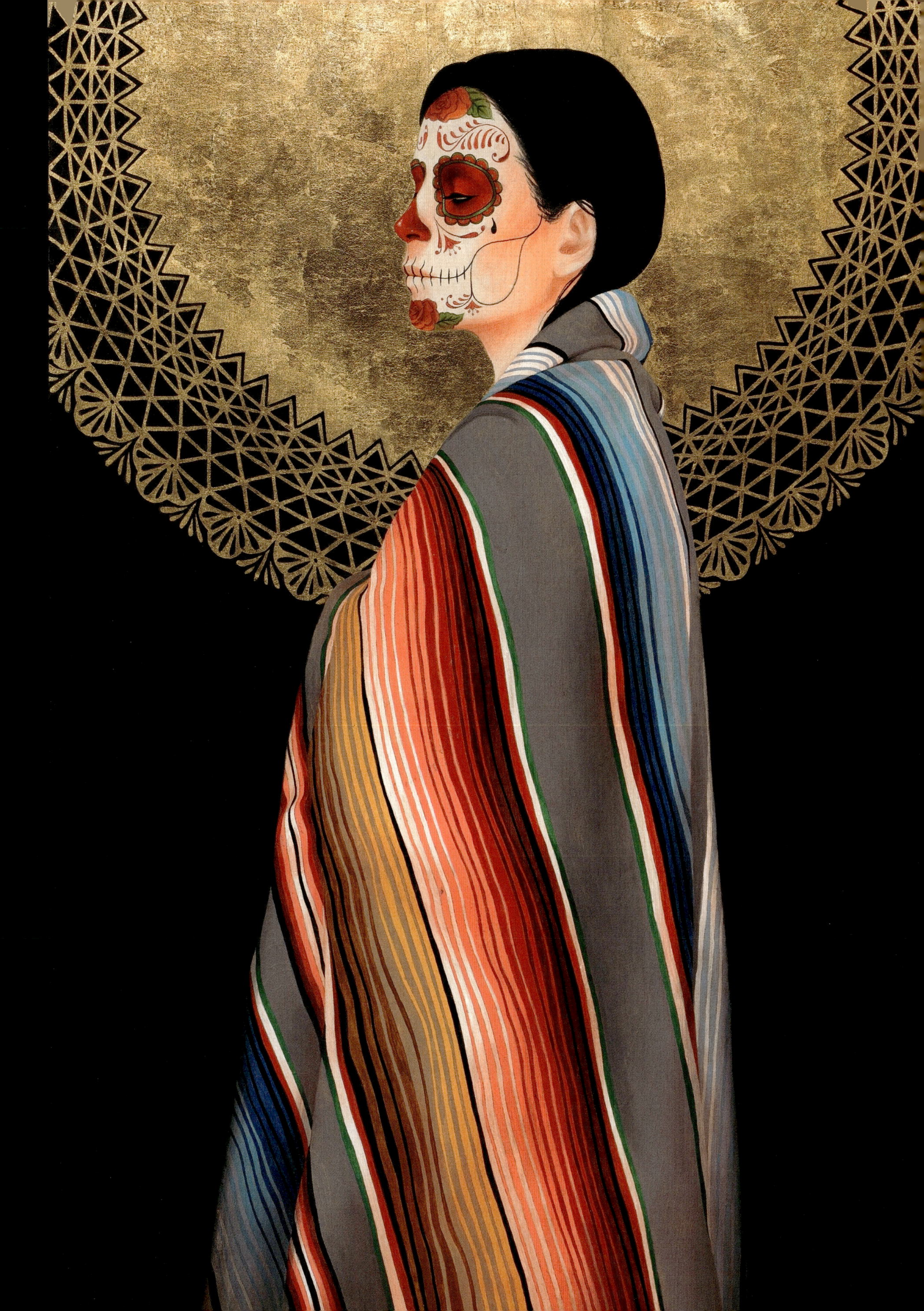

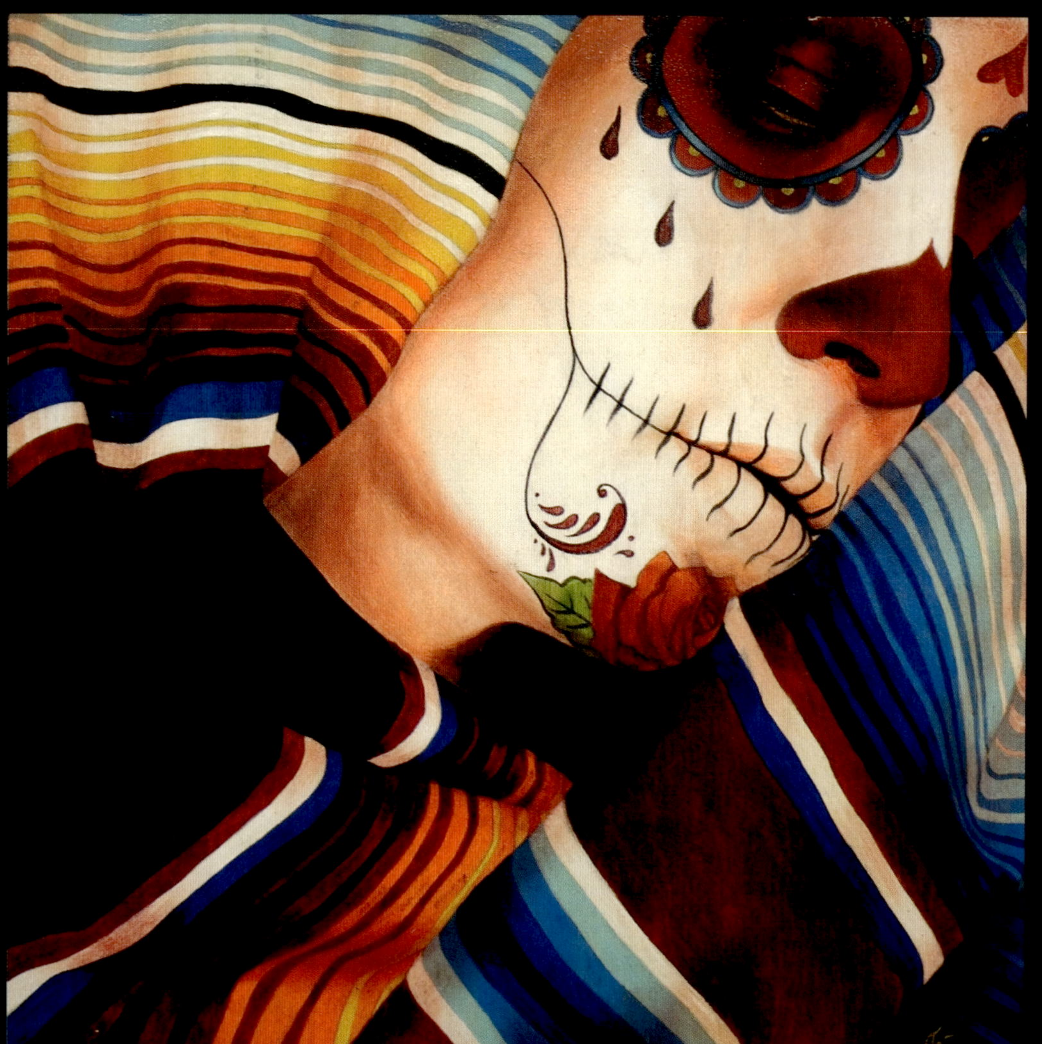

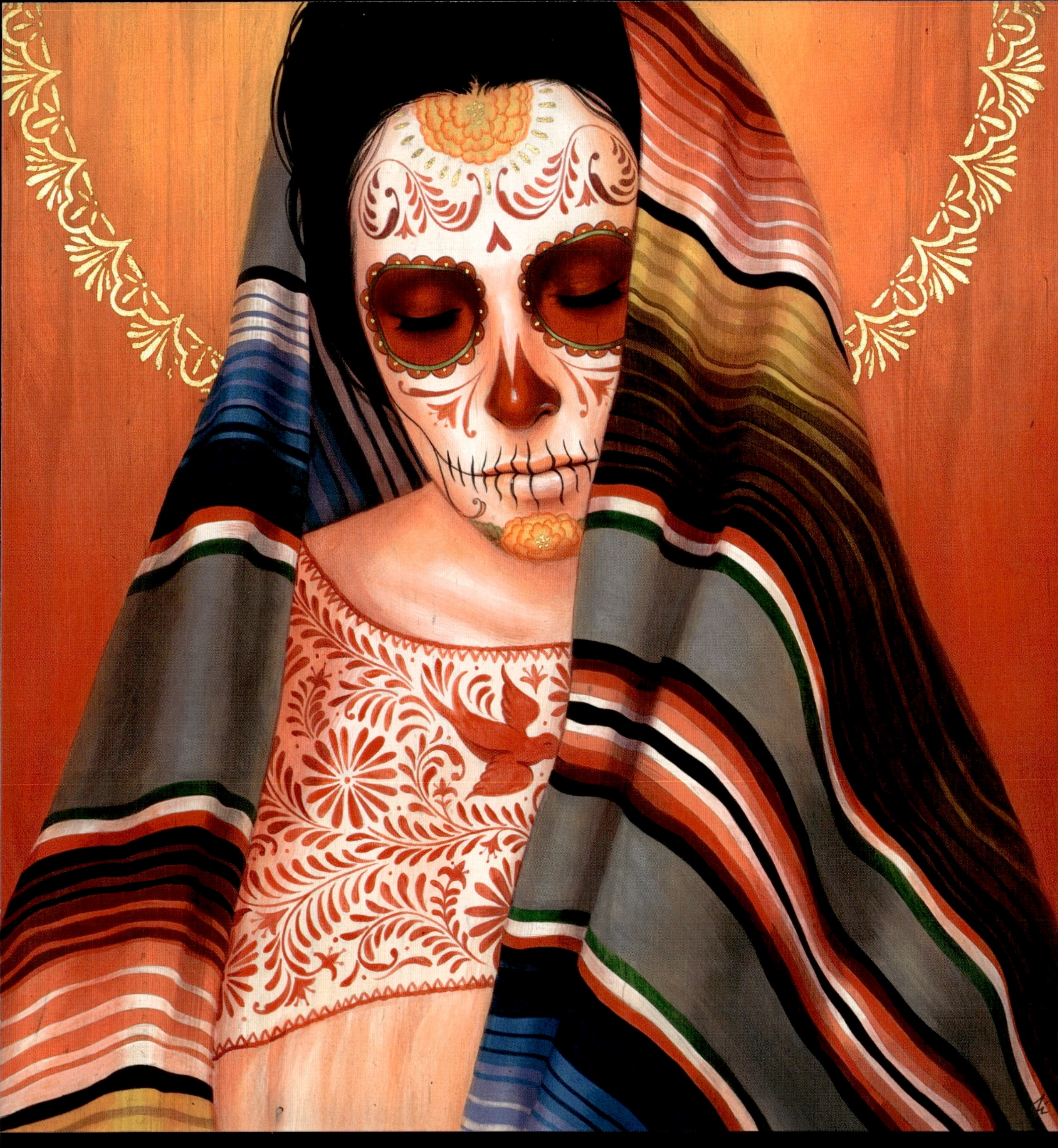

Madre; 24 x 24 inches; acrylic/gold leaf on wood panel

Sylvia Ji

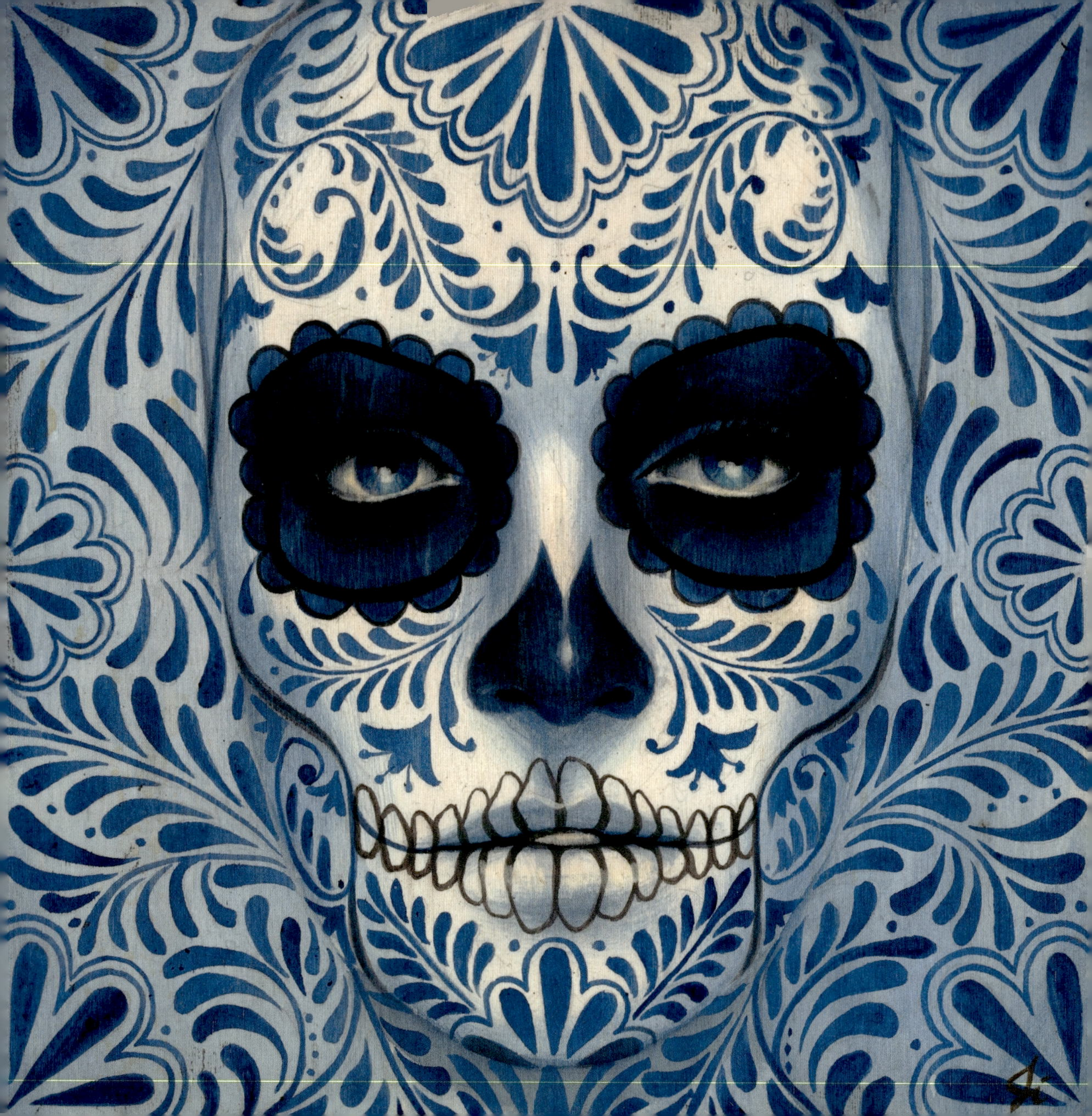

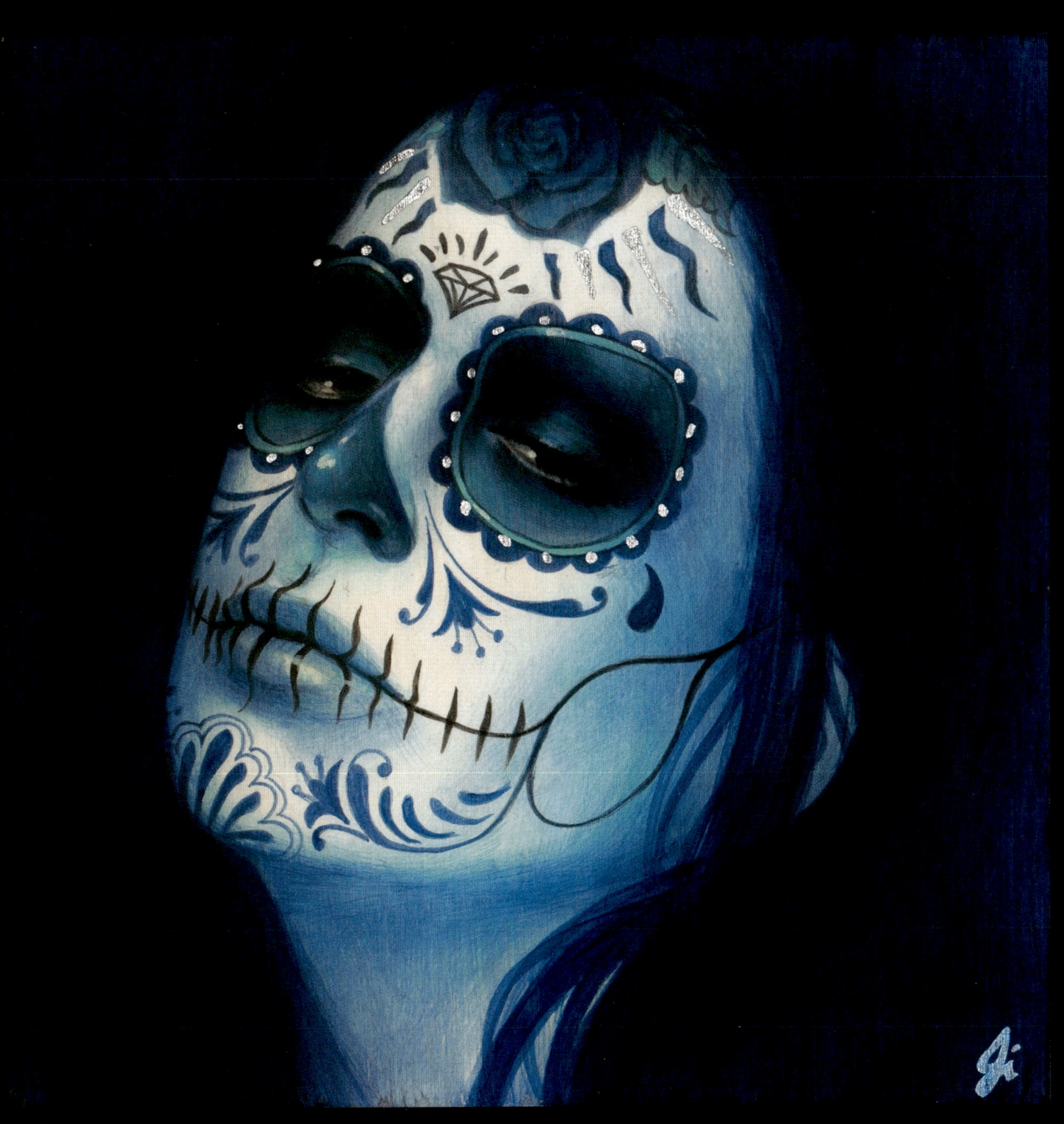

Calavera Azul Añil; 8 x 8 inches; acrylic/silver leaf on wood panel

  Sylvia Ji

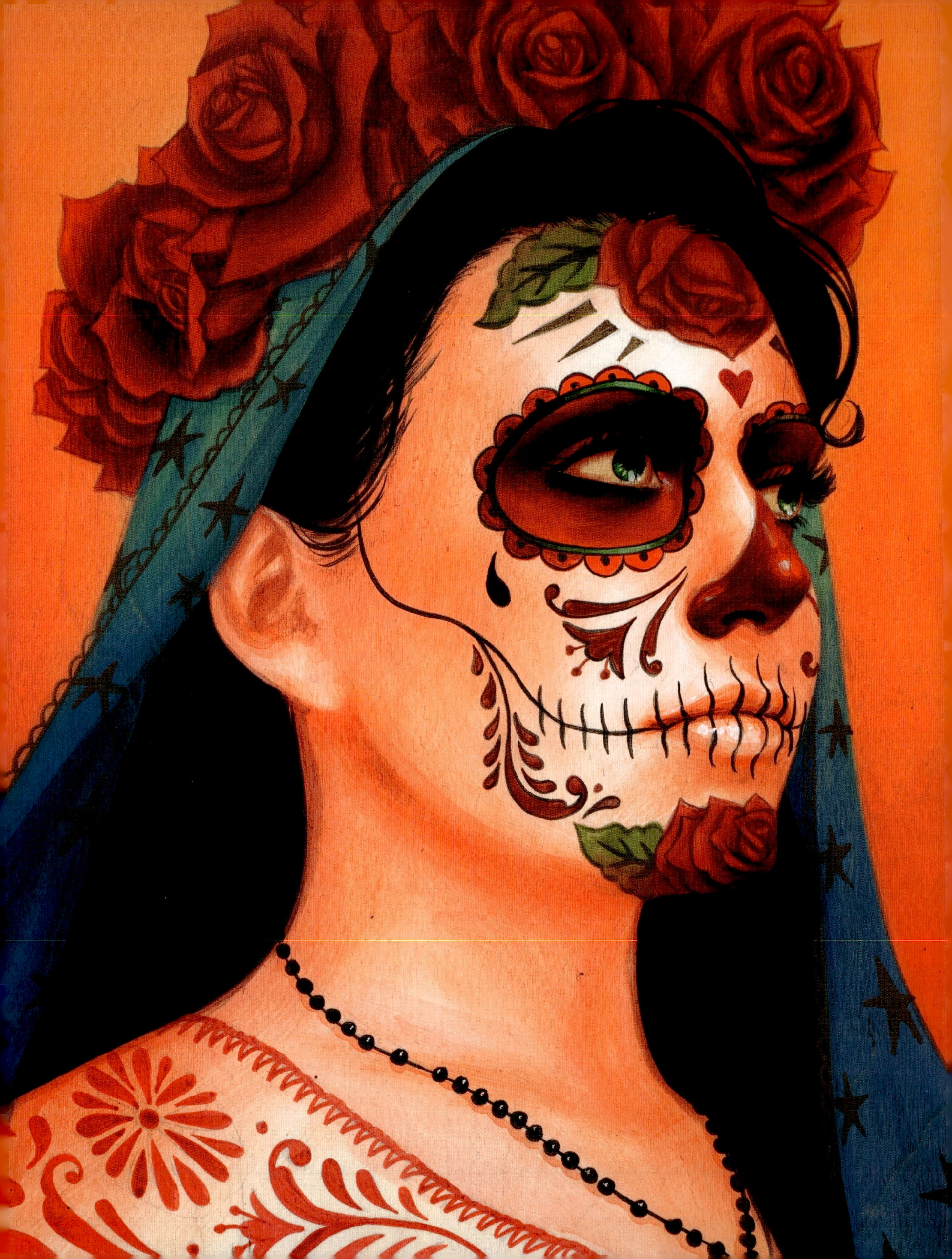

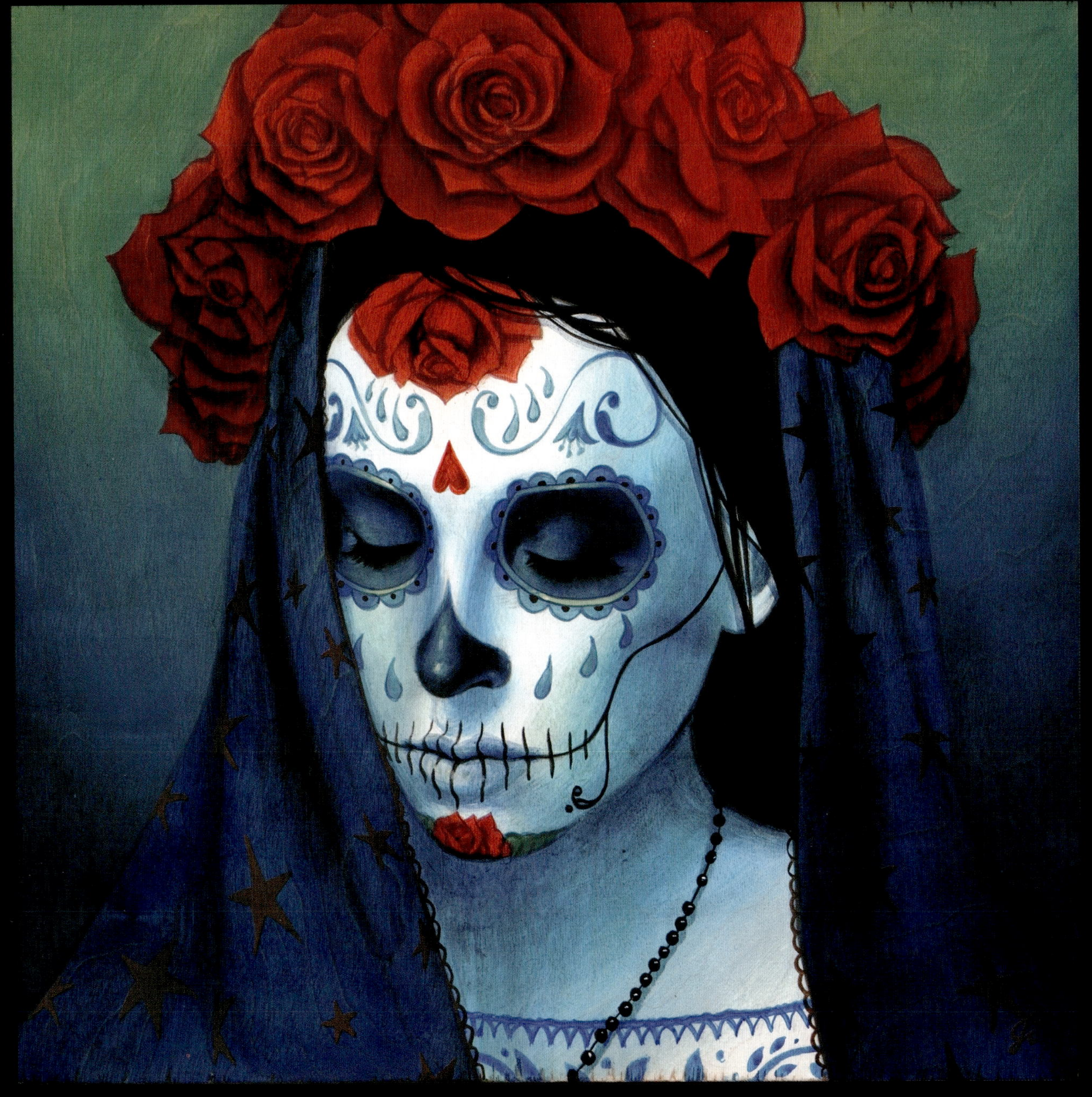

Left: *Catrina Roses;* 12 x 12 inches; acrylic on wood panel

Above: *Catrina Sueño Azul;* 12 x 12 inches; acrylic on wood panel

Sylvia Ji

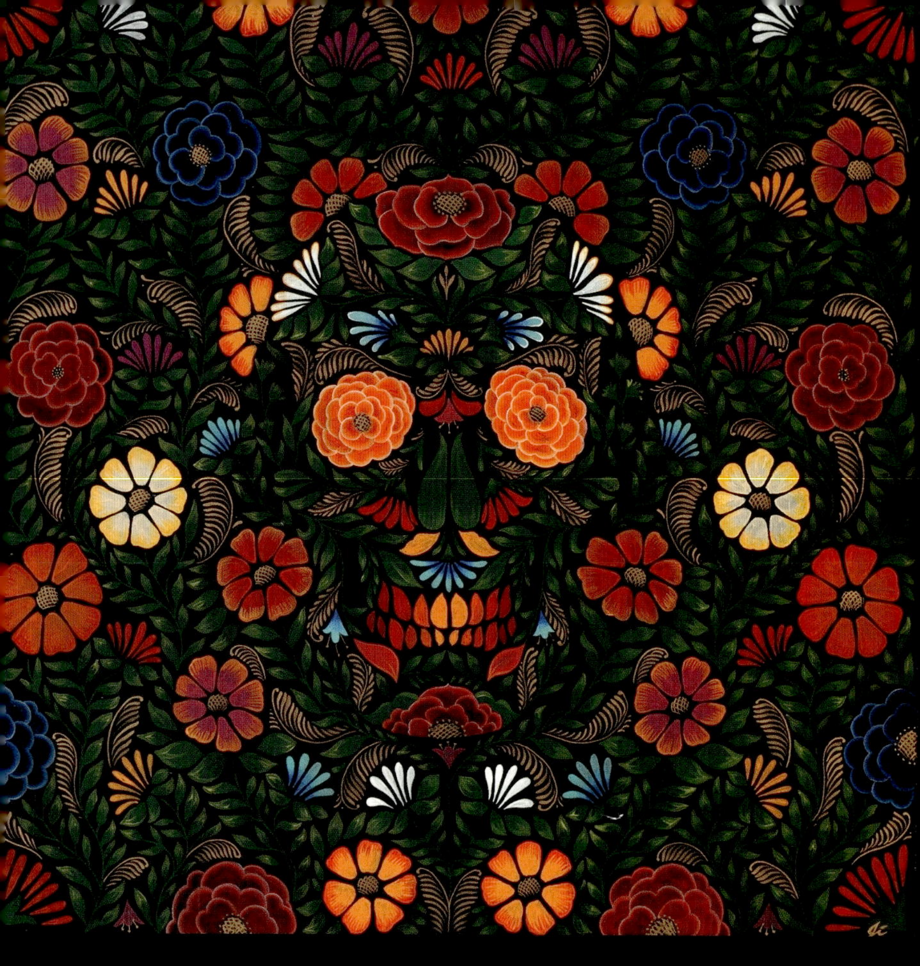

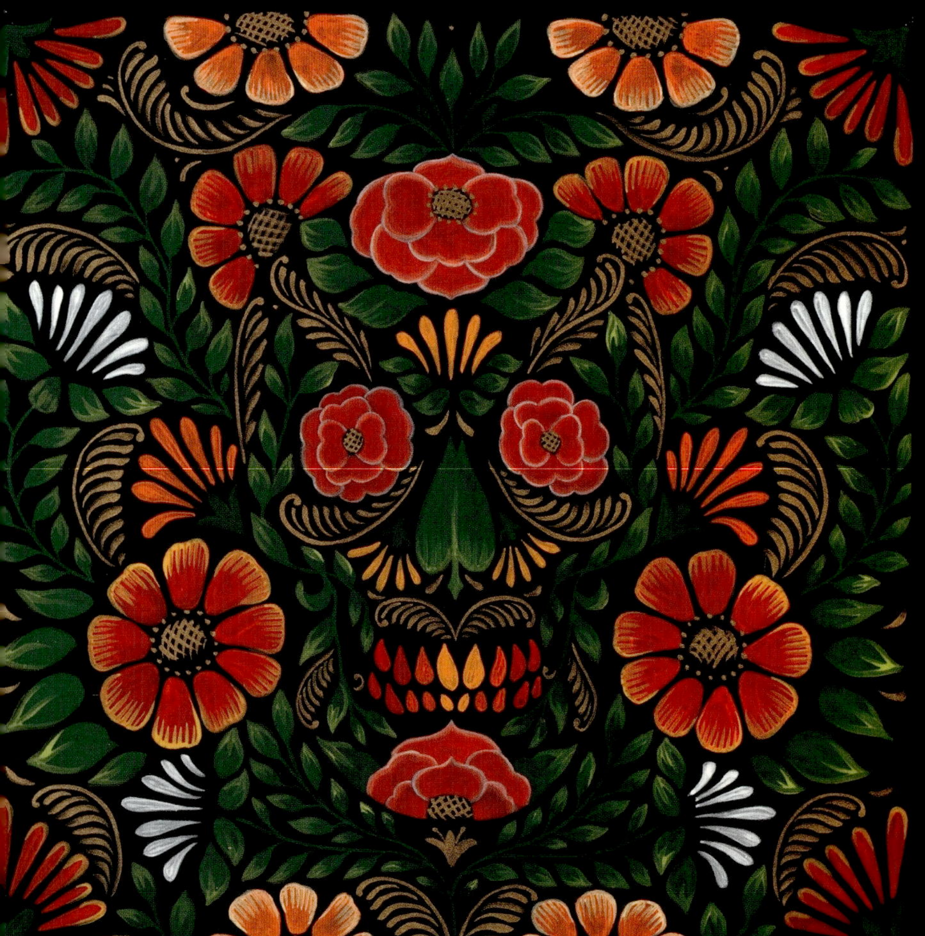

Clockwise from top left:

Calavera Batea; 30 x 30 inches; acrylic on wood panel

Flor Eterno; 18 x 16 inches; acrylic on wood panel

Womb; 12 x 12 inches; acrylic on wood panel

Calaverita; 12 x 12 inches; acrylic on wood panel

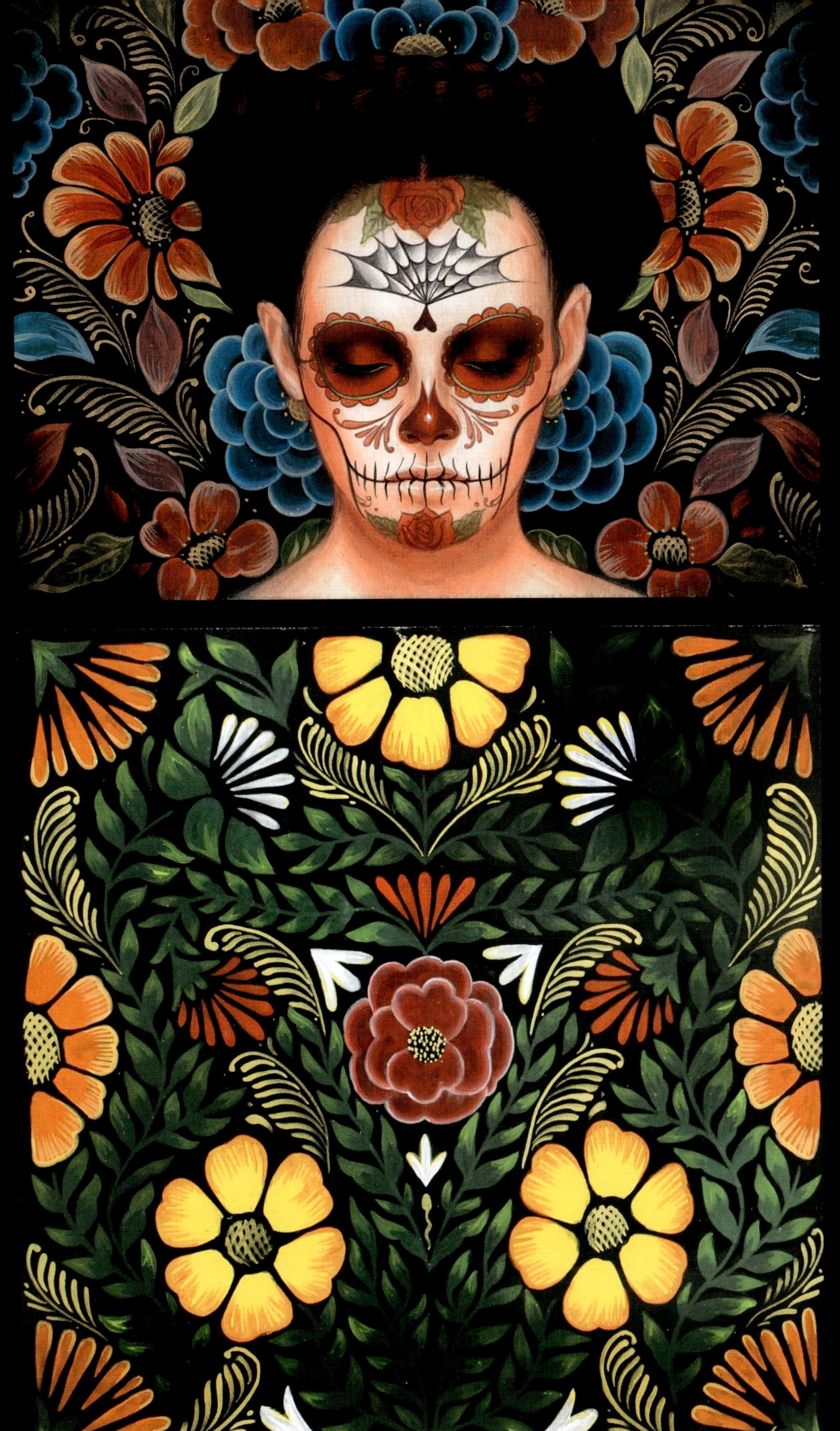

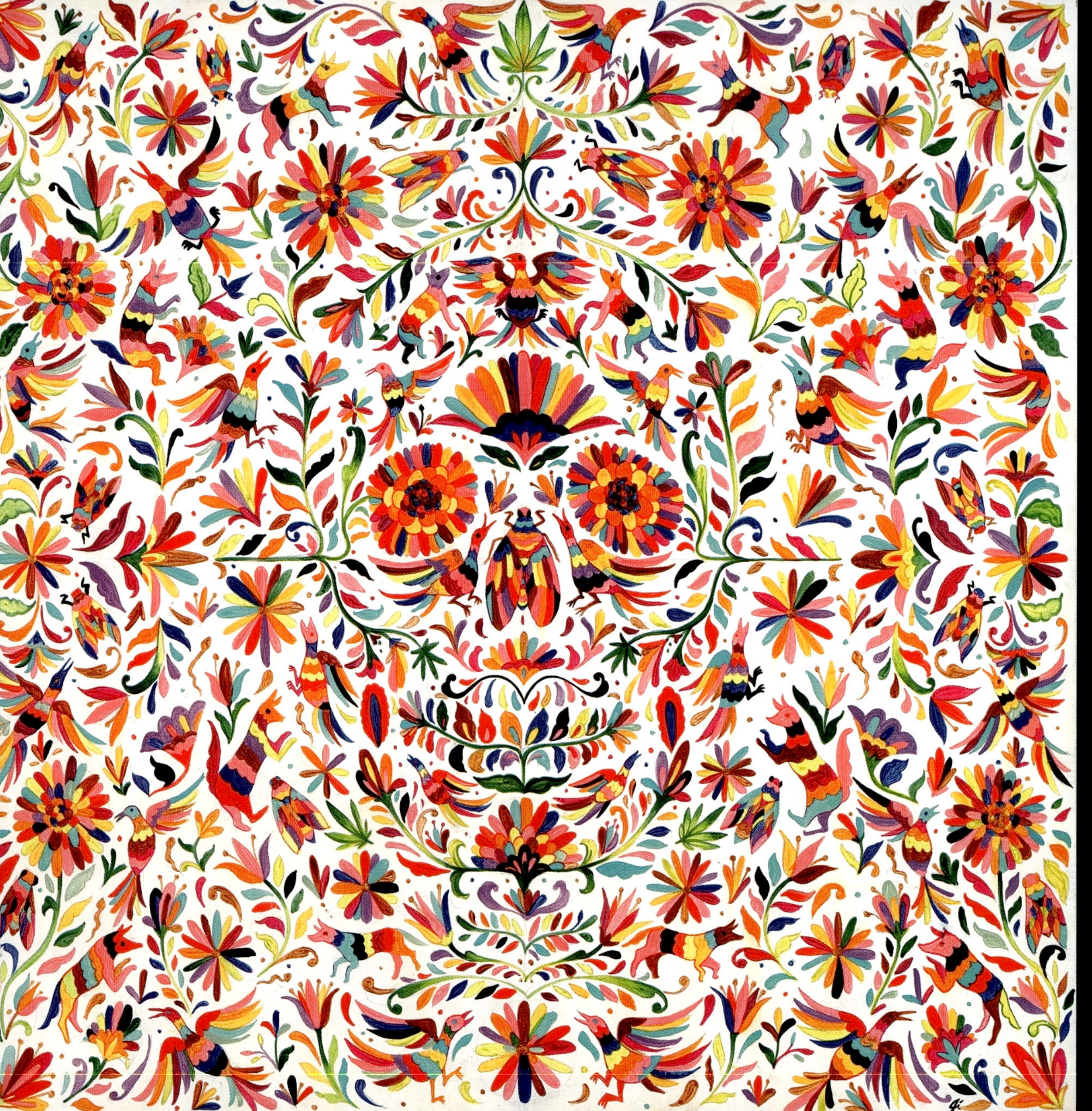

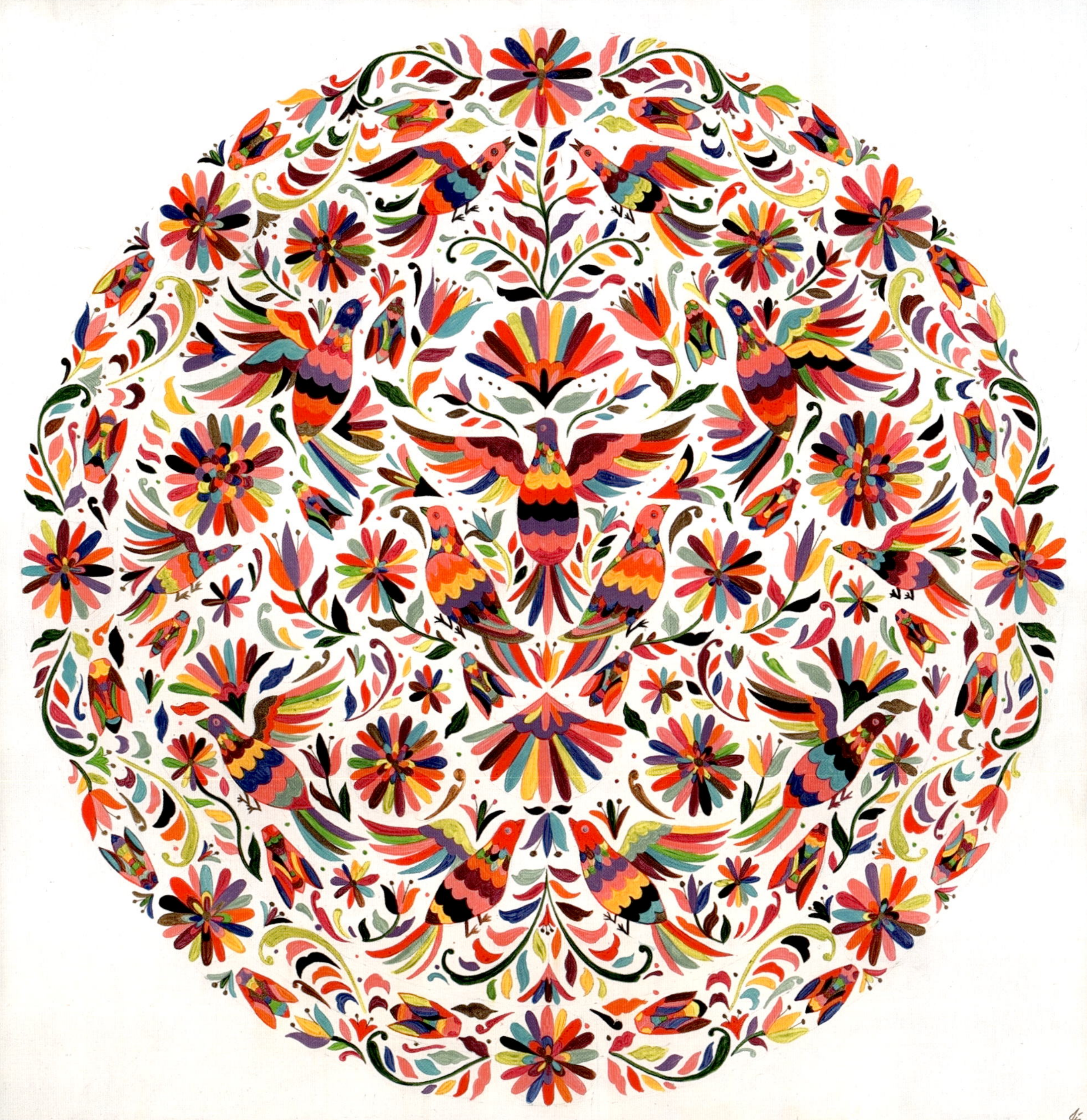

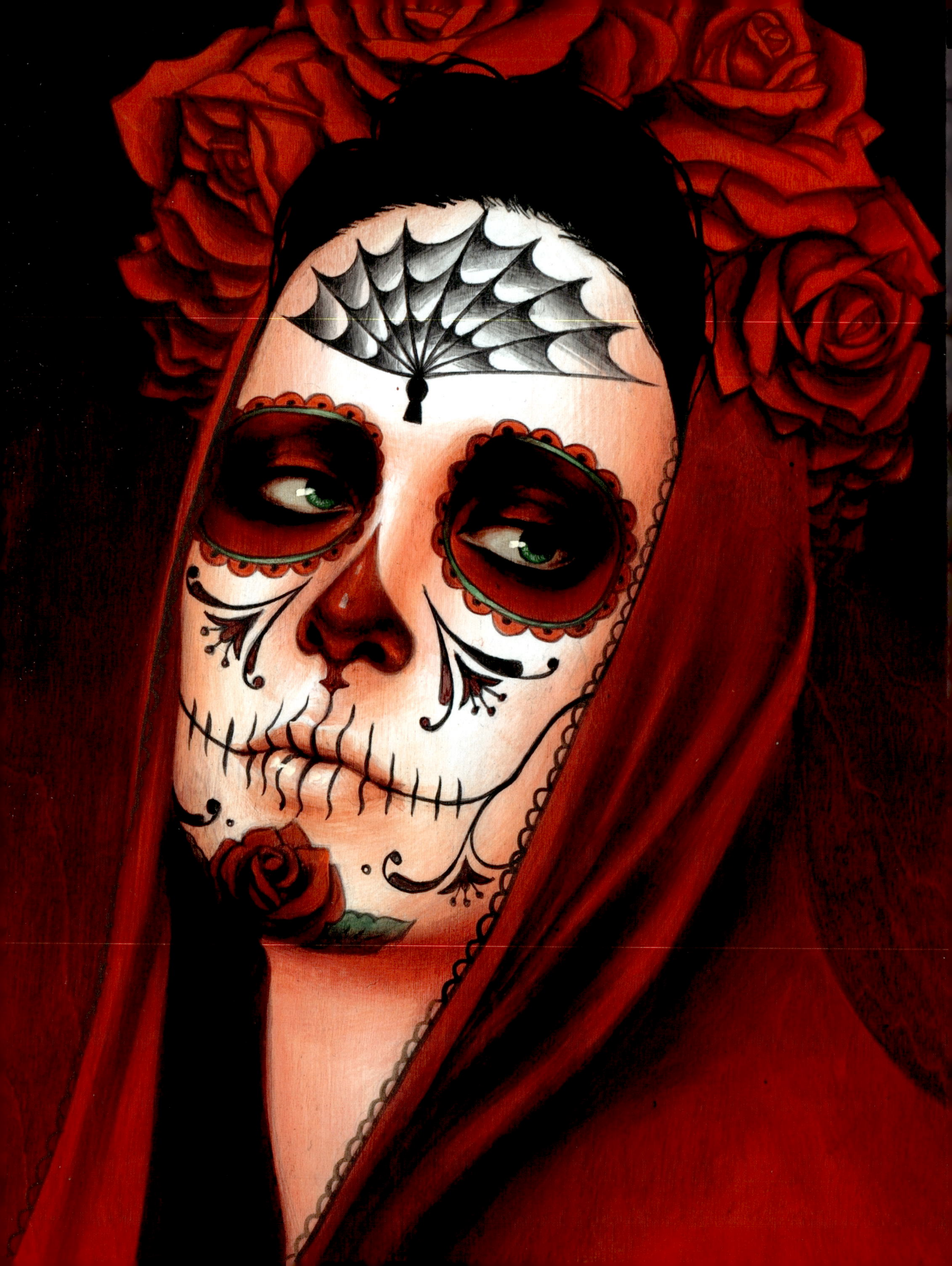

ABOUT THE ARTIST

Sylvia Ji was born in 1982, and raised by artistic parents in San Francisco, California. Her interest in art was implanted at a very young age, when she would look through her mother's sketchbooks and watch her father paint. Ji graduated with distinction in 2005 from the Academy of Art University of San Francisco with a Bachelors degree in traditional illustration, and had her first ambitious and successful solo show while still in her last year of school. After graduating, she relocated to Los Angeles in 2005, where she currently resides.

Ji's work encapsulates an alluring beauty that is both cutting-edge and a nod to time-honoured techniques. Her paintings are symbolic reflections of herself, portraits of people she knows, or nameless faces set in a landscape of fleeting and decaying beauty. Possessing an artistic voice as unique as the times we live in, Ji is at once contemplative, spiritual, enigmatic, and yet whimsically funny.

Above all else, it is perhaps beauty that emerges as Ji's defining characteristic, and her art reflects this: an extension of herself; a passionate appreciation of simple aesthetic pleasure fused with intimately complex subject matter. Ji's work has been featured in numerous gallery and museum exhibitions and art fairs worldwide. She has been profiled in many publications, too, including *Juxtapoz*, *Trace*, and *Mesh Magazine*, and her painting *Dona Dolorosa* graced the cover of the *LA Weekly* for a feature story about *Juxtapoz* magazine's Laguna Museum retrospective, "In The Land of Retinal Delights".

ACKNOWLEDGEMENTS

Sylvia Ji would like to thank the following people: Chuck Pyle, Josh Hak Song, Gill Gold, Andres Guerrero, SF/LA, Henry Lewis, Shawn Barber, Kim Cogan, Daarken, David Choong Lee, Chloe Early, Connor Harrington, Stephanie Escobar, Joshua Petker, Richard Scarry, Chippy, Adam Flores, Sarah Folkman, Sherri Trahan, Jan & Bruce Helford, Corey Helford Gallery, Korin, D*Face, StolenSpace Gallery, JV Hulle, Kirsten, Roq Le Rue, Thinkspace, Mike Giant, Joshua Liner, the Machalas, Janine Jarman, Ryan Malley, 827ink, Dana Jazayeri, Claude McIver, Aaron Rodriguez, Brian Rodriguez, Melody Tsai, Leg Avenue, Kenwood, Johnny VamPotna, Lauren Resler, Alex Stupak, Empellòn, Mary & Joe Rodriguez, Roman Cho, Maria Santinella, the Schwartz Family, Bob Self, Anna Sheffield, Chalisse Skis, Cassie Swindle, Hannah Stouffer, Sharon Tapias, John Trippe, Fecal Face, my family, Mona, Oliver, Mia and Phill Schwartz.

Left: *La Reina Rojo*; 12 x 12 inches; acrylic on wood panel

Following page: *Cruz Azul;* 8 x 10 inches; acrylic on wood panel

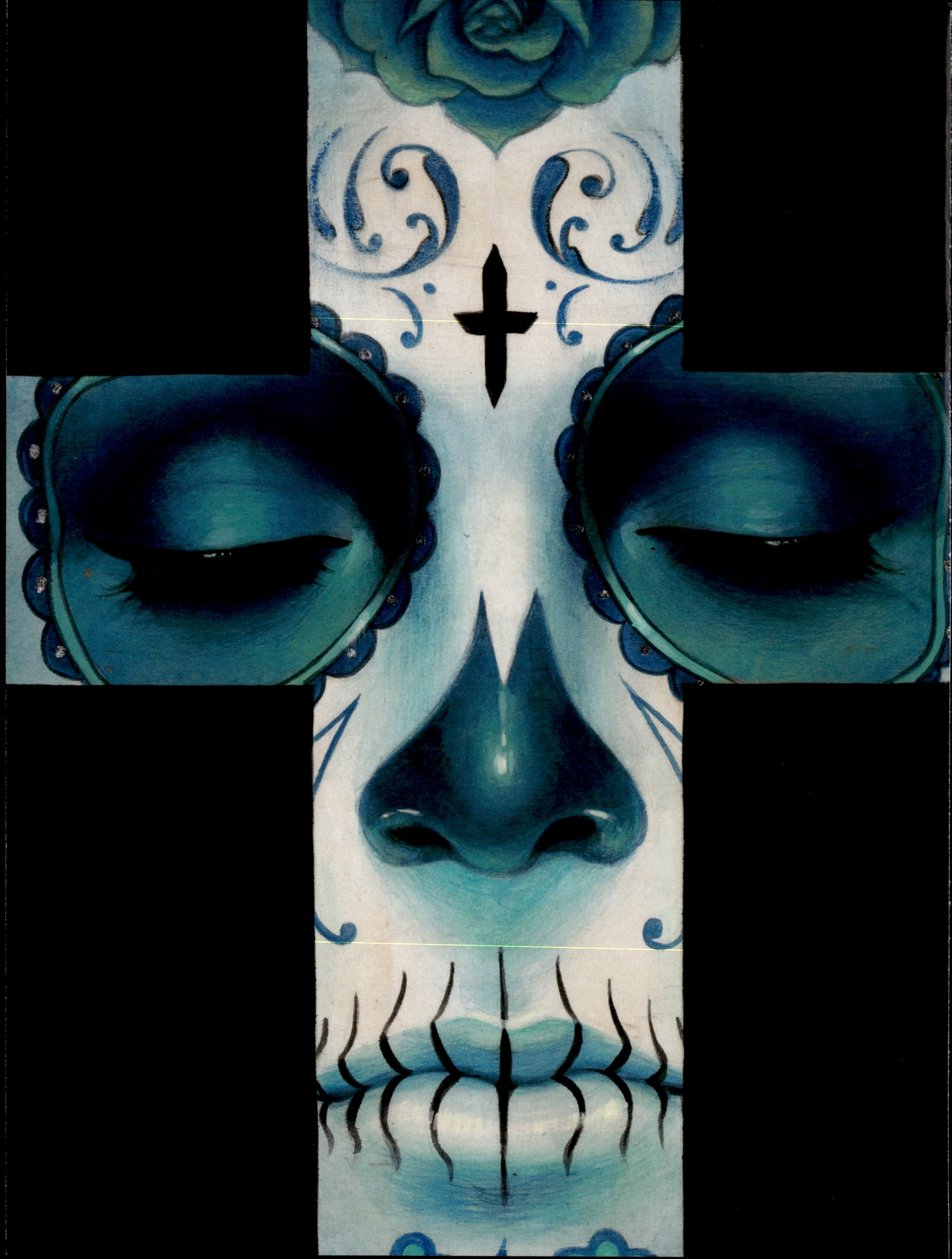

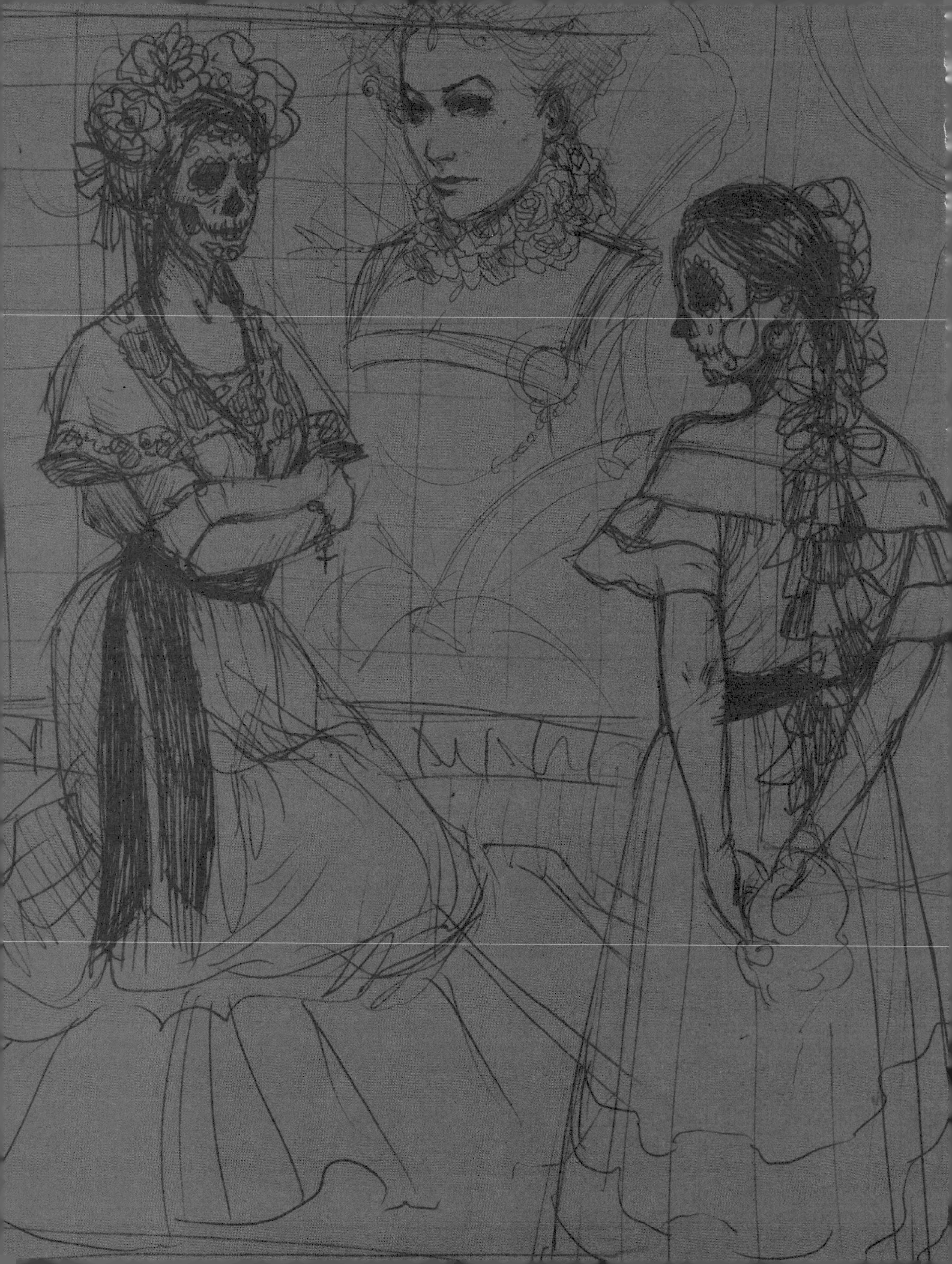